Getting Started in
401(k)
Investing

The Getting Started In Series

Getting Started in
401(k)
Investing

Paul Katzeff

John Wiley & Sons, Inc.

New York • Chichester • Weinheim • Brisbane • Singapore • Toronto

Library of Congress Cataloging-in-Publication Data:
Katzeff, Paul, 1948–
    Getting started in 401(k) investing / Paul Katzeff.
        p.   cm.—(Getting started in)
    Includes index.
    ISBN 0-471-32685-2 (pbk. : alk. paper)
    1. 401(k) plans.   I. Title.   II. Series.
HD7105.45.U6K37   1999
332.024'01—dc21   99-19898

Printed in the United States of America

10 9 8 7 6 5 4 3 2 1

Contents

Acknowledgments

I wish to thank the many people who helped make this book a reality. In particular: Wes Mann, Susan Warfel, Chris Gessel, and Paul Sperry of *Investor's Business Daily* for their collegial support; Doug Rogers of *IBD* for invaluable feedback; Carrie Coghill of D. B. Root & Company, whose significant contributions made the income work sheet possible; David Wray of the Profit Sharing/401(k) Council of America for his generosity of time and input; Lipper, Inc., CDA/Wiesenberger, Hewitt Associates LLC, The Vanguard Group, Spectrem Group, and Towers Perrin for data; Don Roberts of the IRS; Gloria Della and Sharon Morrissey of the U.S. Department of Labor; Clark M. Blackman II of Deloitte & Touche LLP for his extensive contributions regarding tax consequences of distributions; and Debra Englander of John Wiley & Sons.

I also want to thank my friends and family for their patience. And, of course, Janet for her encouragement and patience (yet again) while I invested so many of our hours into this book.

Hopping onto the 401(k) Bandwagon

Picture yourself in a perfect world. . . .

Your bank account is bigger than the sultan of Brunei's.

You love your job, and you've got a great pension plan.

You're looking forward to retirement, when you can move to your dream home in a crime-free community.

You'll spend sunny mornings on the golf course with your spouse. Afternoons, you'll go fishing aboard your cabin cruiser . . . or work on your tennis game back at the country club. Saturday mornings you'll make handsome furniture for your grandchildren in your lavishly equipped basement workshop . . . or volunteer at the local hospital. A few nights each week, perhaps you'll enroll at the nearby college in that philosophy class you've always wanted to take.

Don't forget weekend evenings. That's when the two of you will drive into the city for dinner at a fine restaurant. After coffee and dessert, you'll head to the concert hall to enjoy the local, world-famous symphony.

And did we mention that your health is fine, thank you, and you're looking forward to making Willard Scott's 100th-birthday greeting list? All those years, your living expenses will hardly make a dent in that huge bank account of yours. Besides, you'll have your pension checks and Social Security.

Ahhhh. . . . The good life.

Now imagine the real world.

Your bank account is smaller than the sultan of Brunei's butler's. *Much* smaller.

How small? Well, the average American bank account has only $8835 in it, according to the Federal Reserve Bank of Boston. That won't buy much if you try to spread it over, say, 20 years of retirement.

And chances are your checking or savings account holds a lot less. That's because the $8835 average includes the bank accounts of such deep-pocketed depositors as General Motors and AT&T. For the zillion-dollar accounts of those corporate colossi to average out below five figures, imagine how little is in most people's passbooks. A balance of $100 or $500—by itself—won't cover golfing greens fees for more than a month or so, let alone living expenses for decades of retirement.

Your pension plan? The bad news is it may be headed for extinction. Worse, it won't pay for much, anyway.

Traditional pension plans have been disappearing at the rate of about 10,000 a year since the mid-1980s, reports the Employee Benefit Research Institute.[1] Only 84,000—fewer than half—remain, according to EBRI's latest figures.

Anyway, a pension won't pay for much. Yearly pension income for men 65 or older averages merely $7800, according to EBRI. For women, it's a meager $4200.

And Social Security? Its *own* future is not very secure, let alone its ability to provide for *yours*. Even if it somehow survives until the time you retire, it won't pay for much.

According to the Social Security Administration, millions of baby boomers marching into retirement are expected to push the system into red ink in 2021, and by 2032 the system is projected to go flat broke.

If the rickety system pulls off a miracle and clings to life support, it certainly won't pay for much.

If your income now is $30,000, you'll be lucky if it covers a little more than half of your budget in retirement. If your income is, say, $80,000, it won't pay for even a quarter of your postretirement living expenses.

---

[1]"EBRI Databook on Employee Benefits," 4th ed. (Washington, D.C.: EBRI, 1997): Table 10.2, 84.

THEIR PAYOFF MAKES THEM
INCREASINGLY POPULAR

Getting the picture?

Unless you *are* the sultan of Brunei, you'll need a 401(k) plan—*now*—to provide income in retirement to buy groceries, pay your Florida condo fees, and gas up the car.

And that's even if your spending goes way down once you retire. Most people, for example, get by on about 70 percent of their preretirement income.

If you plan to take any round-the-world cruises, pay all or part of your grandchildren's college expenses, or even buy a new set of fancy golf clubs, you'll need lots more.

Your best bet for getting more is from a 401(k) plan.

In comparison, bank accounts, pension plans, and Social Security look like the proverbial 95-pound weaklings of retirement finance.

The typical 401(k) account now has been pumped up to $51,939, according to Fidelity Investments, the nation's largest manager of 401(k) plans. Better yet, about one out of every 10 plan participants has a cushy account balance of at least $100,000, according to a joint study by EBRI and the Investment Company Institute.[2]

The relative advantage of 401(k) plans is growing. Fidelity says account sizes have increased yearly. Before the most recent level, the average account size was:

- ✔ $43,750 in 1996.
- ✔ $38,877 in 1995.
- ✔ $28,509 in 1994.

One reason is that the stock market rewards long-term investors—like 401(k) plan participants—with growth.

Workers recognize a good thing like this when they see it. Recognizing that their money can't grow unless it is put to work, plan members have been boosting the amount they contribute.

---

[2]Jack VanDerhei et al., "401(k) Plan Asset Allocation, Account Balances, and Loan Activity," *Issue Brief* (EBRI), 205 (Jan. 1999): 13.

The Profit Sharing/401(k) Council of America reports that:

✔ Rank-and-file workers now kick in 5 percent of their paychecks, on average. That's up from 4.2 percent five years earlier.

✔ People high on the corporate food chain funnel an average of 6.1 percent of their pay, up from 5.4 percent.

Just a bunch of fuzzy numbers to you? If all those decimals and percentages just give you a headache and a flashback to eighth-grade algebra class, think of them this way: Rank-and-file workers voluntarily increased their contributions by roughly one-fifth. Would you voluntarily jack up your home mortgage payments by that much? Or your weekly grocery bill?

That shows commitment. People understand the payback benefit.

For that reason, more people have been hopping onto the 401(k) plan bandwagon.

Twenty-five million Americans now participate. As Figure I.1 shows, that is more than double the number of members a decade earlier, accord-

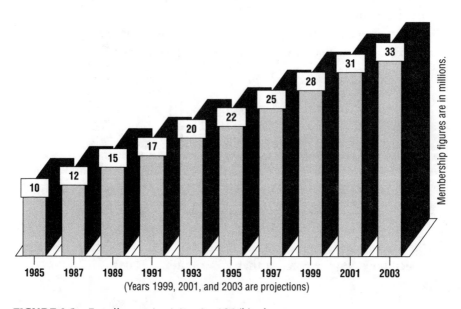

1985   1987   1989   1991   1993   1995   1997   1999   2001   2003
(Years 1999, 2001, and 2003 are projections)

FIGURE I.1   Enrollment is rising in 401(k) plans.
Source: © Spectrem Group 1998; used with permission.

ing to Spectrem Group, a financial services research organization. The ranks of 401(k) plan enrollees are expected to continue to grow.

Take a closer look. Enrollment is not increasing just because there are more plans (there are) or only because there are more Americans working (there are, but enrollment rises *even when employment drops*). Plan membership is on the rise because more people understand the merits of joining. More eligible people want a piece of the action.

As Figure I.2 shows, the percentage of qualified employees signing up for their company plan has climbed to 78 percent. The participation rate has risen by roughly one percentage point a year.

So it is not only new workers who join plans. It is people who have had the right to join a plan but have not taken advantage of the opportunity.

Once they see how easy it is to save and invest . . .

Once they hear from recently retired friends about added retirement income . . .

Once they learn how pain-free it is to contribute automatically . . .

Once they jealously ponder their coworkers' right to invest while reducing their taxes . . .

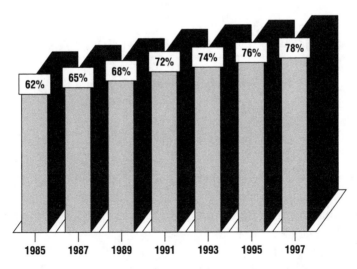

FIGURE I.2 The percentage of eligible people who join a 401(k) plan continues to climb.

Source: © Spectrem Group 1998; used with permission.

Once they realize how tough it is to depend on other sources of retirement income . . .

. . . More of them decide the time is right to sign up.

"If you want financial resources to pay for daily expenses, get into your 401(k) plan," is the blunt advice offered by Dallas Salisbury, president of EBRI, a benefits-research organization in Washington, D.C.

"Social Security is a safety net. It was not intended as a national pension plan. And do not count on your traditional pension plan, either."

If you're even lucky enough to have a conventional pension plan, remember this: Companies use their plans to encourage worker loyalty. They couldn't care less about your old-age comfort. Payment formulas commonly boost rewards only for the last few years of very long service. Many workers don't stick around—or survive—that long.

"A traditional pension will only provide meaningful supplemental income to anyone with 25 or more years of employment," says Salisbury. "Only about 15 percent of the labor force stays with one employer that long. Frankly, even if you're in that 15 percent, you probably won't get retirement medical benefits. So, if you want to protect yourself against medical disaster or just pay for health contingencies, you've got to build financial assets through an income source like a 401(k) plan."

GROWING MONEY WITH *YOUR* 401(k) PLAN

Americans are helping themselves not only by boarding the 401(k) bandwagon in greater numbers and by feeding more dollars into their accounts. They are also using their dollars more shrewdly.

Increasingly, people are investing in things that get better financial mileage.

One of Wall Street's most basic lessons is that stocks (and mutual funds that invest in stocks) pay greater rewards over time than bonds (and funds that invest in bonds). And Americans are shifting their dollars into stocks and stock mutual funds.

That's precisely the right thing to do. *Getting Started in 401(k) Investing* will explain why stocks and stock funds perform better. The book will also explain how to take advantage of that in your plan.

Bonds, bond funds, money market funds, and other related investments have a different role. *Getting Started in 401(k) Investing* will explain what that is, and how to benefit from that, too.

But relying on them for your primary investments can cost you big bucks in the long run. *Getting Started in 401(k) Investing* will describe how to avoid that expensive—but common—mistake.

And you won't need a Wall Street dictionary to understand what *Getting Started in 401(k) Investing* is saying.

MAKING IT EASY TO UNDERSTAND

Without a large enough retirement nest egg, get ready for retirement's ultimate booby prize.

"If you don't prepare yourself financially, you'll get the grand opportunity—to work forever," warns Salisbury.

The alternatives are equally upsetting: postponing retirement, lowering your expectations—or getting used to the idea of panhandling.

This book will help you avoid all such dire consequences. Instead, you can aim for a more comfortable lifestyle once you know how to get the most from your 401(k) plan.

Getting Started in 401(k) Investing will do that by explaining in plain English:

- ✔ What a 401(k) plan is and how it works.
- ✔ The best and easiest way to make your money grow.
- ✔ How to choose investments that are right for you.
- ✔ Dos and don'ts of using your account for *nonretirement* financial goals.
- ✔ Where your 401(k) plan fits into your overall retirement planning.
- ✔ How to get a handle on how much income you'll need during retirement.
- ✔ How to minimize your taxes.
- ✔ How your 401(k) plan stacks up against—and can supplement—other retirement accounts like IRAs.
- ✔ What you need to know to avoid hassles and rip-offs.

You'll find that information organized into three easy-to-understand sections:

Part One: "Understanding Your 401(k) Plan"
Part Two: "Setting Your Financial Goals"
Part Three: "Making a Game Plan—and Winning"

And don't worry.

Learning how to make the most of your 401(k) plan is simpler than you might think. You won't have to master any mysterious jargon. This book won't use Wall Street lingo. It will translate fancy terminology into down-to-earth language.

On your own, you'll learn how your plan works and how to make your money grow.

You'll learn how to do those things without having to wait for infrequent visits by representatives of your plan's mutual fund or insurance company. And you won't have to rely on your company's human resources (HR) person. Even when they are well-meaning professionals, those people may not be able to answer your most important, personalized questions.

Getting Started in 401(k) Investing will teach you to how to navigate your own way—at your own pace. Whether in the privacy of your own home or at your leisure aboard the commuter train, *Getting Started in 401(k) Investing* will teach you how to use your plan and make investment decisions that suit your needs and goals.

Plain and simple, this book will help you build your retirement nest egg bigger and faster than you ever thought possible.

PART ONE

Understanding Your 401(k) Plan

What It Is, How It Works, and Why You Need One

You've heard all about them—401(k) plans are almost everywhere. The only people who don't seem to have them are professional football players and bank robbers. And you're not so sure about the football players.

But you don't know as much as you want to about your 401(k) plan. It's for retirement money. It involves investments. And that may be about it.

Exactly how it works, what you're entitled to, the dos and don'ts—it's all a blur.

And it doesn't matter whether you actually know a lot, only a little, or nothing at all.

If you're already an avid participant in your plan, you can still use help in understanding certain features and in getting a handle on whether your investments are your best possible choices.

And most people know a lot less about their plan. After all, everyone has other time-consuming responsibilities, at work and at home. It's tough enough to pay the bills without having to worry about stealing from your own paycheck to put money away for your retirement—which may be *very* far in the future. Besides, all that jargon can give most people a headache. And Wall Street? It seems like a very private club, with its own secret rules, located far, far away from where you live and work.

Part One of *Getting Started in 401(k) Investing* will explain what your plan is, how it works, and how it can help you.

And *Getting Started in 401(k) Investing* will do this in plain English. That may be a foreign language on Wall Street. But it's what everyone speaks on Main Street, U.S.A.

1

Basics of Your
401(k) Plan

Right here, right now, let's cut to the chase.

Question: Why is your 401(k) plan important to your future?

Answer: Because it is a free pay raise.

If you don't need money, you can stop reading. Go to the movies. Watch some TV. Walk the dog. Good-bye and good luck.

The rest of you, read on.

A 401(k) plan does indeed provide you with a free pay raise. In fact, by putting more money into your pocket up to three different ways, it gives you as many as three pay raises.

1. Your contributions lower your taxes.

2. Your investments grow without being taxed year-by-year. You can plow those would-be taxes back into your investments.

3. Your company almost certainly matches your contribution with a bonus that goes into your account.

No other source of savings or income duplicates that triple play—not your savings, not your pension (if you've got one), not Social Security.

A 401(k) Plan versus an IRA

An individual retirement account (IRA) comes closer than savings, pensions, or Social Security to matching a 401(k). But even an IRA—whether it's a Roth, a regular deductible, or a nondeductible—lags behind a 401(k) plan account in two crucial ways:

First, the most you can contribute each year (even if you can double the amount with a spousal contribution) is much less than the amount you can put to work inside a 401(k) account under federal rules.

Second, an IRA provides no company match!

A CLOSER LOOK AT THOSE THREE KEY ADVANTAGES

The edge that a 401(k) plan gives you has to do with how those three pay raises work.

Cuts Your Taxes

Money you contribute is subtracted from your taxable current income. It is *tax-deductible "before-tax" money.* Not only do you get to invest it; it also reduces your taxable income that year. It may even put you into a lower tax bracket. Unless you are a monetary masochist who thinks bigger is better when it comes to taxes, this is a great deal!

Tax-Deductible   Your 401(k) contribution is what accountants call "tax-deductible." That's because you subtract your contribution from your other taxable income. The amount left over is what you figure that year's tax bill on.

Your contribution's tax-cutting power is so important that it deserves to be talked about in a little more detail.

Think about it. Your 401(k) contribution puts money back into your pocket by doing two things:

1. It reduces your taxes.

2. The money you save on taxes can be invested so it grows—along with your contribution itself. It turns a loss into a gain. This is as close as you'll ever get to the proverbial free lunch.

"Before-Tax" Money   Because your contribution is made before your taxable income is calculated, your contribution is referred to as "before-tax" money.

Lowering Your Taxes

Here's how a tax-deductible contribution helps you.

A tax deduction is taken into consideration while you are figuring out your tax bill. For instance, if you are in the 28 percent bracket, when you make a $2000 contribution to your 401(k) account, that $2000 is not taxed. You save 28 percent of that $2000, or $560.

Don't confuse a tax deduction with a tax credit.

If you are entitled to a tax credit, you subtract it from your tax bill. After you calculate your tax bill, for example, a $2000 tax credit reduces your taxes by $2000. It doesn't matter what tax bracket you're in.

Best of Both Worlds

Your contributions to your 401(k) account are tax-deductible. It's as if you did not earn the money. That lowers your current tax bill.

But your contributions are counted for purposes of calculating your Social Security and Medicare taxes. A tax payment of any kind may not exactly be cause for celebration. But it means that your 401(k) contribution is included in the calculation of how large your Social Security and Medicare benefits will be later in life.

Postpones Taxes on Your Investments

This is a humongous benefit. *Not . . . paying . . . taxes.* It used to be that the only way you could pull that off was if you were a gangster, sending deposits to a numbered account in Switzerland.

Now all you have to do is join your 401(k) plan, not your local chapter of the Cosa Nostra.

This privilege is called *tax deferral.* It means that you escape current taxes on the money you invest each year. It also means you don't have to pay yearly taxes on your 401(k) account balance or its investment earnings until you withdraw funds.

Tax Deferral   That's the name of the tax break that applies to your money so long as it's inside your 401(k) account.

Yes—eventually Uncle Sam expects to be paid. But not until you take the money out of your account. A gangster may never worry about paying taxes. But using a 401(k) plan won't get you sent to the Leavenworth federal prison.

This benefit cannot be exaggerated.

First the money you contribute is not treated like income by the Internal Revenue Service. The IRS ignores it when it comes to totting up your tax bill. Then, while the money is sitting inside your account, both that money and everything it earns are *tax-sheltered.*

Dividends you earn on your ordinary bank account don't enjoy that tax break. Nor does your regular income. Nor does any profit you make on the sale of stocks and bonds.

If you own a mutual fund that pays you dividends, you'll typically owe taxes on that income—unless that fund is sitting inside a tax-deferred account like a 401(k) plan.

Best of all, your money remains tax-sheltered as long as it remains cocooned inside your 401(k) account. You probably won't withdraw it until retirement, so it could remain tax-sheltered for decades.

That means your money and its earnings can continue to grow through compounding without being whittled down by taxes. That's why money inside a tax-deferred account like your 401(k) grows more than the same money outside a protected account. And it can enjoy that advantage for decades.

However, if you withdraw money before age $59^1/_2$, generally whatever amount you take out will be subject to income tax plus a 10 percent penalty. Only under certain circumstances can you avoid the tax and penalty. (See Chapter 9.)

Creates Matching Contributions

Would you like a pay raise? That's what this feature is.

Better yet, it is usually a pay raise that you can give to yourself. Most matches go up when your own contribution does the same.

Typically, you don't have to ask anyone's permission. You don't have to sweat through a job review. (Unless the match hinges on company profitability or your own performance.) It is commonly yours for the taking.

Technically, a matching contribution is bonus pay.

Better yet, it is a bonus that gets the same tax break as your own contribution to your account. It is not taxed as regular income. Further, this bonus—along with its earnings—remains sheltered from taxes until you withdraw it.

This tax-sheltered bonus is unique to 401(k) plans. There is nothing like it in the world of IRAs.

Its purpose is to help your employer encourage you to save and invest for retirement. The fewer retired people who end up on welfare, food stamps, and street corners selling pencils from a tin cup, the better.

A company match is usually triggered by your own investment. But sometimes it depends on your age, years of employment, or how well the company is doing.

One way or the other, 93 percent of 401(k) plans offer some matching contribution, according to benefits consultants Hewitt Associates. Figure 1.1 shows the types of company matches. Most simply give a set amount or percentage of your pay. That's known as a *fixed match*. Sometimes there's an upper limit to a fixed match. For instance, a company may kick in 50 cents for every $1 you contribute, but only up to 5 percent of your pay; you may be allowed to contribute, say, as much as 10 percent of your pay, but you won't get a match for anything above 5 percent.

A *graded match* changes (rather than ends) at some specified trigger point.

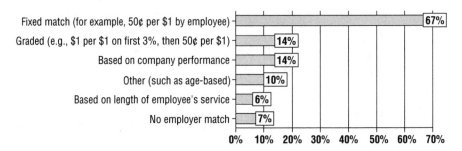

FIGURE 1.1 Types of company matches and the percentage of plans that offer each kind. By far the most common type of employer contribution is a "fixed match."
Source: Hewitt Associates LLC.

The size of the employer's match can differ from company to company. Some give more. Some throw in less.

The most common fixed match is 50 cents for every $1 contributed by the employee. Dollar-for-dollar matches are the next most common. Whatever its size, the company match is virtually a pay raise that you can award to yourself. And often you can get more of it simply by increasing your own contribution.

Sure, more is better. But this is one gift horse whose mouth you should not bother looking into. Even a small match is good. That's because it is free money. It is a pay raise. And often it is a pay raise you can give to yourself. All you have to do is contribute more of your own money and—presto!—your company must pony up more (unless and until you hit any match cap there is).

Figure 1.2 shows how common each level of employer fixed match is. The table also shows categories within each level.

Figure 1.3 shows how large the most common types of graded matches are. The most widespread graded match is one in which a company antes up $1 for every $1 you contribute up to a specified limit. Then it contributes an additional amount, usually at a lower rate.

As Figure 1.1 illustrated, graded matches account for 14 percent of all the types of company matches. Figure 1.3 lists what percentage of plans offers each type of graded match.

Fixed Matches		Percent of Plans
All matches of less than 25 cents for each employee $1		1%
All 25-cents-per-$1 matches		5%
25 cents per $1 of first 6%	*3%*	
All other 25-cents-per-$1 matches	*2%*	
All matches of more than 25 cents per $1 and less than 50 cents per $1		2%
All 50-cents-per-$1 matches		35%
50 cents per $1 of first 6%	*21%*	
50 cents per $1 of first 4%	*5%*	
50 cents per $1 of first 5%	*4%*	
50 cents per $1 of first 8%	*2%*	
50 cents per $1 of first 3%	*2%*	
All other 50-cents-per-$1 matches	*1%*	
All matches of more than 50 cents per $1 and less than 75 cents per $1		4%
All 75-cents-per-$1 matches		3%
All matches of more than 75 cents per $1 and less than $1 per $1		<1%
All $1-per-$1 matches		14%
$1 per $1 of first 6%	*4%*	
$1 per $1 of first 5%	*3%*	
$1 per $1 of first 3%	*3%*	
$1 per $1 of first 4%	*2%*	
All other $1-per-$1 matches	*2%*	
All matches of more than $1 per $1		<1%

FIGURE 1.2 Fixed company matches come in many sizes. Some are more common than others. Fifty cents for each dollar contributed by an employee is the most widespread.
Source: Hewitt Associates LLC.

Graded Matches	Percent of Plans
$1 for each employee $1 on first 3%, 50 cents per $1 on next 3%	2%
All other $1-per-$1 matches on a specified initial percent plus additional match on higher percents	6%
All 25-cent matches on a specified initial percent plus additional match on higher percents	2%
All other graded matches	4%

FIGURE 1.3 Some sizes of company graded matches are more widely provided than others.
Source: Hewitt Associates LLC.

MORE WAYS A 401(k) PLAN CAN HELP YOU

A yearly tax cut . . .

Tax-free growth of your money . . .

A company match . . .

If those were the only advantages conferred by your 401(k) plan, they would be more than good enough reasons for you to sign up and fork over.

But there are additional incentives as well:

✔ Automatic deposits.

✔ Flexibility.

✔ Control.

✔ Extra perks.

✔ Portability.

✔ Best deal.

Automatic Deposits

You don't have to write a check once a week, once a month, or once a quarter. After you choose how much you want to contribute, money is taken automatically out of your paychecks.

This has numerous advantages. First, it makes contributing pain-free. Money is diverted into your 401(k) account before it ends up in your paycheck or in your pocket. You don't miss it because you never had it.

Second, it increases the amount of money working for you. It does that by eliminating chances for you to forget to make a deposit on your own. And the more money you have invested, the bigger your nest egg.

Third, it cuts down on paperwork and administrative hassles. You only have to make arrangements once. No muss, no fuss.

Fourth, automatic investing reduces your stress while promoting better investment results. With automatic investing, you will not obsess about every contribution—especially during the stock market's inevitable rocky periods.

If you had to write a check for every contribution, you would end up playing Hamlet every time the stock market wobbles (*to pay or not to pay, that is the question*). All you would get out of that, however, is skipped contributions and more gray hairs on your head.

You'd also make the rest of your money less productive.

How? You'd play it "safe" by making more conservative investments. But those investments will lose ground to inflation and grow less than your other investments in the long run. We'll talk more about the crucial difference between short-term safety and long-term safety, starting in Chapter 13.

For now, what you should bear in mind is that automatic deposits help you stay the courts—a more productive, less anxiety-ridden course.

Flexibility

Unlike a conventional pension plan, a 401(k) plan lets you choose the size of your contributions (up to certain limits). That gives you the freedom to boost the size of your nest egg. It gives you more influence over how much money you'll receive from your account yearly.

Control

You are usually free to select investments from a menu. You can tailor your investments to suit your own financial goals and time frame.

> **Defined Contribution**   A 401(k) plan is known in benefits jargon as a *defined contribution* plan. That's because the amount you contribute is specified, or "defined." The size of your eventual benefit is not specified in advance. It depends on such things as how well your investments do and how much money you contribute over what length of time.
>
>   In contrast, a traditional pension plan is known as a *defined benefits* plan because the plan promises to pay you a set amount of money.

But . . . uh-oh. Select your own investments? If that sounds scary, don't let it frighten you off.

Chances are your choices are largely—or entirely—mutual funds, other bundled investments, and your own company's stock. Making good selections basically means choosing something in the right category. It is much easier and simpler than shopping for individual stocks out of the zillions available.

Whether your plan offers only a small number or a wide selection, we'll explain how to choose your investments in Part Three.

Extra Perks

Your plan may offer additional benefits, such as opportunities to borrow money from your account. (This particular option can come in handy, but you must beware of its long-run cost. See Chapter 4.)

Portability

Another major difference between a traditional pension plan and a 401(k) plan is that your 401(k) account belongs to you. If you leave your job for any reason (except extremely rare cases of criminal activity), you can take the portion of your money in which you are *vested.* You are always fully vested (100 percent ownership) in your own contributions, right from the first day. You gain ownership of your company's matching contributions either when you sign up or according to a timetable spelled out by your plan.

Best Deal

A 401(k) plan is routinely a better deal than other comparable retirement plans. If you take full advantage of its contribution and investment opportunities, no other plan gives you as rich a chance to reduce taxes and build up a nest egg.

Even the much-ballyhooed Roth IRA can't compare. A 401(k) plan's higher contribution ceiling lets you accumulate much more money. And, even if you contribute the *same* amount of money annually you're better off with a 401(k) plan. By the time you retire and start to withdraw funds, a 401(k) plan will put more after-tax take-home money into your pocket than a Roth IRA if, like most people, your tax bracket goes down after retirement.

Heck, if it will make you feel better, after retirement you can put your money into a *legal* Swiss bank account.

Time and Money: Your Plan's Wealth- Building Weapons

T he bedrock principle of 401(k) plans is very simple: Time is money.

But the reason so many people are puzzled by Wall Street is that time is not always worth the same amount of money. For people on Main Street, it is too hard to predict which investments will make money grow quickest.

Unsure about what to do, people often do the very worst thing: nothing.

You might as well rip up hundred-dollar bills.

In truth, time is worth a lot of money. That's why it is so important to join your plan.

"Time is probably the biggest ally that people have," says David Wray, president of the Profit Sharing/401(k) Council of America.

GIVE YOUR MONEY TIME TO GROW

One reason time matters so much is something learned in the previous chapter: your plan gives you money at least two different ways—probably three.

1. It cuts your tax bill every year you contribute to your plan. That's nice by itself. But its added benefit is that it may persuade you that you can afford to jack up your contribution to your account.

2. Your investment earnings grow more because the IRS ignores them.

3. Your company probably matches your contribution with one of its own to your account.

Time is the tool that enables you to earn more wealth with those sources of money.

Here's how it works: Your investment earnings accumulate their own earnings. This monetary snowball may start out small. But it builds on itself.

Look what happens when you put a dollar bill on the table and then place a dime next to it. It may not seem like you've added much money. Still, you only need to increase the total by 10 percent eight times before you more than double the cash.

Make that dollar bill into a $1000 investment, and with 10 percent yearly growth it is transformed into $2000 in less than eight years.

Money snowballing like this is called *compounding*. It's no accident that everyone in the financial industry refers to it as the *power of compounding*.

Figure 2.1 illustrates this financial growth process for three hypothetical investors. Each sticks to a very different strategy.

Investor #1 (whom we'll call John) starts at age 25 and socks away $2000 a year for 10 years. From age 35 through retirement at age 65 John does not invest any more money. But his money earns, say, 10 percent annually for the entire 40 years. By retirement, he has invested only $20,000 from his own pocket. But his account has grown to $611,817.

Investor #2 (whom we'll call Susan) also invests $2000 a year, earning the same 10 percent as John. But Susan doesn't start until age 35 (the same year John stops making new contributions). Also unlike John, Susan continues to invest money yearly until retirement. So by age 65 she has contributed $2000 annually for 30 years, or a total of $60,000. Yet her nest egg at retirement is only $361,887.

The outcome seems to defy common sense. But the arithmetic be-

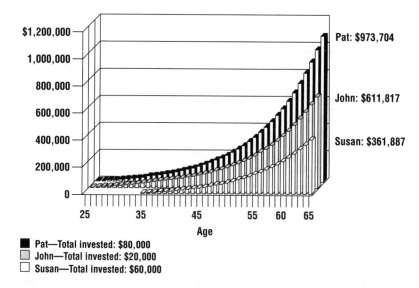

FIGURE 2.1 Time is money: the power of compounding. The amount of time you invest can influence the eventual size of your nest egg even more than the amount of money you invest.

hind it is beyond doubt. Even though Susan shells out three times more money than John, she ends up with much less—all because she started later and gave her money less time to *compound.*

Compounding Compounding is what goes on when you earn money on your initial investment as well as on the new earnings.

With a $1000 investment that earns 10 percent annually, for example, you'll have $1100 at the end of one year. During the next year, both your original $1000 and the new $100 earn another 10 percent. So by the close of year No. 2 your investment will be worth $1210.

Some investments compound (or earn more money) at set intervals. For example, a bank may pay compound interest daily, weekly, monthly, or at some other interval of time.

John's 10-year head start makes the difference. Time is indeed money.

The virtue of starting early and then sticking to an investment game plan is illustrated by a third investor, Pat, who starts at age 25, the same time as John, but diligently continues to invest $2000 annually for 40 years. Pat earns 10 percent, just like the others. But by putting the most time as well as the most money to work, Pat naturally accumulates the largest retirement account: a comfy $973,704.

A PRICEY PROBLEM TO AVOID: MAKING UP FOR LOST TIME

Time is money when you waste it, too.

Figure 2.2 shows exactly how painfully expensive Susan would find it to catch up to John. To make up for John's 10-year head start, she would have to invest much more cash than John does to build the same size nest egg by age 65.

Susan would have to invest $3381.26 every year for 30 years to accumulate the same $611,817, all other things being equal. John invested only $2000 a year, and that was only during the 10 years when John actually paid into his account.

Susan must dip into her paycheck an extra 20 years to catch up to John. Meanwhile, John contributes *zero* during those decades!

All tolled, Susan must invest more each year for 30 years. John pilfers from his wallet only 10 years.

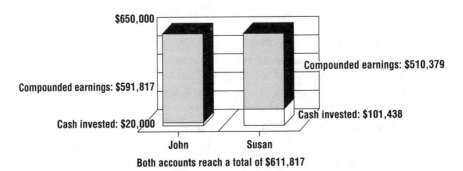

FIGURE 2.2 Making up for lost time: Because she started her 401(k) contributions a decade after her fellow worker John, Susan must invest more than five times as much money to build the same size retirement account by age 65.

So, by the time she reaches retirement, Susan would have to pay $101,438 out of pocket—more than five times John's modest $20,000—to make up for lost time.

Another way to look at this: It costs Susan more than five times what John must pay to buy the same retirement nest egg.

To compensate for her delay of a measly decade early in her work career, Susan must pay an extra $81,438. That's how much compounded earnings she lost. Now it is her penalty fee.

Think about it:

✔ Spending five times as much cash to buy the same retirement fund.

✔ Spending more money three times longer.

✔ Spending four-fifths of your cash outlay to make up for lost compound earnings—something you could have had for free.

The price for procrastination is steep.

So don't postpone enrolling just because you're afraid of making the wrong investments. Put your money to work. Enroll now if you haven't. And increase your contribution if you can. Take advantage of time.

TAX DEFERRAL: HOW IT MAKES YOUR MONEY GROW FASTER

Okay, so time is money.

Tax deferral is a process that lets you speed up time inside your account.

If you had the same investments outside a 401(k) plan, in an ordinary brokerage account, you'd have to pay taxes on earnings every year. In your 401(k) account you get to keep that money instead of paying it in taxes. And as long as it stays in your account, it can rack up more earnings.

It's like having more money—because it *is* more money. It is also like having more time to accumulate earnings. Except it *doesn't* take extra time.

Each year, you end up with more money than if you had made the same investment outside your tax-deferred 401(k)-plan account.

Figure 2.3 shows how this works. Let's say you are a single taxpayer, earning $40,000, and in the 28 percent federal tax bracket. Suppose your state tax rate is 5 percent.

	Saving in a Taxable Account	Saving in a 401(k) Plan
Salary and Taxes		
1. Gross income	$40,000	$40,000
2. 401(k) investment	0	3,000
3. Standard deduction *(1998 nonitemized)*	4,250	4,250
4. Personal exemption *(1998 nonitemized)*	2,700	2,700
5. Taxable income (Line 1 minus Lines 2, 3, and 4)	$33,050	$30,050
6. Federal income tax *(1998 rates)*	6,381	5,541
7. State income tax	1,653	1,503
8. FICA @ 7.65 percent (of Line 1)	3,060	3,060
9. After-tax pay (Line 1 minus Lines 2, 6, 7, and 8)	$28,907	$26,897
10. After-tax investment	3,000	0
11. Net take-home (Line 9 minus Line 10)	$25,907	$26,897
Savings Accumulation		
12. Investment	3,000	3,000
13. Investment return @ 10 percent *(earnings)*	300	300
14. Tax on earnings (State/Federal)	99	0
15. Net investment gain (Lines 12 plus 13 minus Line 14)	$ 3,201	$ 3,300
Total		
16. Bottom line (Line 11 plus Line 15)	$29,108	$30,197
17. Extra money you own (excess over Column 1)	–	$ 1,089

Note: Some calculations appear distorted due to rounding.

FIGURE 2.3 Tax deferral puts more money into your pocket.
Source: Towers Perrin.

In a tax-deferred 401(k) account, the amount you invest is not counted as part of your taxable income. As far as the IRS is concerned (except for calculating your Social Security payments *and benefits*), it's as if you didn't earn the money. Nice, huh?

A person saving outside a tax-deferred account does not enjoy the same tax break. As a result, this Other Guy pays more in federal and state taxes (Column 1, Lines 6 and 7).

Your investments enjoy the same edge as your contributions. Even though you and the Other Guy invest the same amount of money in the same things (where they grow at the same rate of return), the Other Guy gets hit by taxes again. You don't. This time it is his investment earnings that Uncle Sam takes a bite from.

Line 15 shows how your savings in a 401(k) plan pile up higher than the Other Guy's. Taxes grind his rate of investment growth down to 6.7 percent, while your investments balloon at the rate of 10 percent a year.

This explains how you end up owning more money at the end of the year: $1089. Part is from income tax that you escaped (on the contributions to your account). The rest is $99 from tax on investment earnings that stays in your account instead of going to the IRS.

YOUR ADVANTAGE GROWS OVER TIME

That's the edge you gain from tax deferral after just one year. Imagine how good it gets over the course of many years.

Figure 2.4 illustrates that. When you put your tax savings ($99 in our example) along with your yearly contribution ($3000 in the example) to work in your 401(k) plan for, say, 40 years, year after year they produce more earnings. Each year those earnings escape taxes. The money that doesn't go to the IRS remains on the job, working hard for you.

It's the snowball effect we talked about earlier.

The money you save in taxes, plus its earnings, grow into a retirement nest egg more than double the size of the Other Guy's nest egg. Even though both of you invest an equal $3000 a year in the same mutual funds, for instance, growing at the same 10 percent annual rate, you end up with $1,327,778 in your account. The Other Guy's account grows to a more modest $554,495.

It's as if you are investing more money than the Other Guy. In fact, that's exactly what is happening. You do have more cash to invest, in the form of salary not lost to taxes plus its earnings.

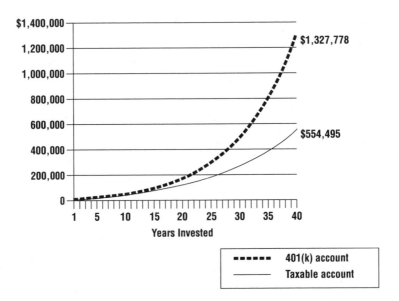

FIGURE 2.4 Tax deferral speeds up your money's growth. Instead of being handed over to Uncle Sam as taxes, more of your cash continues to work for you.

Assumptions: ▪ Each investor contributes $3000 annually ▪ Federal taxes: 28 percent; state taxes: 5 percent ▪ Each account grows 10 percent annually.

Source: Table data provided by The Vanguard Group.

A COMPANY MATCH

Tax savings . . .

Tax-sheltered annual earnings . . .

And a company match.

Those are the big three in terms of how your 401(k) plan gives you extra money.

If tax deferral turns your slowpoke family station wagon of a retirement account into a hot rod, then a company match jacks up the horsepower even more. It completes your car's transformation into a turbocharged drag racer.

The added oomph of tax deferral combined with a company match speeds up the effect of compounding inside your account. You're paying less in taxes—even though you've got more money coming in, going to work for you. It's hardly a surprise that your account mushrooms more quickly.

A company match is a free pay raise. Typically, you can award it to yourself. Ordinarily, you can increase it at will. All you have to do is increase your own contribution.

Best of all, it is a free pay raise that doesn't get mauled by taxes.

How powerful is this benefit? Figure 2.5 shows how much more your money grows by comparing your account to the Other Guy's one more time. The scenario is the same as the one in Figure 2.4. You both contribute $3000 a year, you invest in the same mutual funds, and your accounts both grow at 10 percent annually. As before, investments in your 401(k) account grow tax-deferred. The Other Guy's get mowed down by the IRS every April 15.

But we've added a new wrinkle. This time your account is pumped up with a matching contribution from your employer. Let's say it is the most common type of company match: 50 cents for every dollar you kick in.

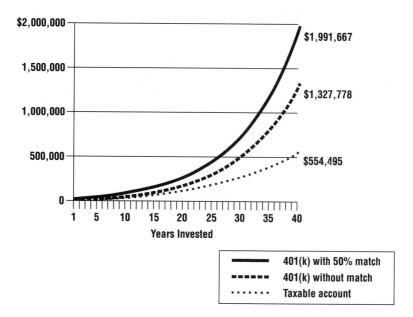

FIGURE 2.5 Twin engines of growth: tax deferral and a company match. A matching contribution from your company turbocharges your tax-deferred 401(k) account.

Source: Table data provided by The Vanguard Group.

The payoff is super. After 40 years, your account zooms to $1,991,667 in size. Inside a 401(k) plan but without a 50-cent matching contribution, you ended up with "only" $1,327,778.

Meanwhile, the Other Guy puts less money to work. And what he does have is taxed more. Lacking tax deferral and a company match, he accumulates less than one-third what you do: $554,495. Saving in his account is like trying to climb a sand dune—trying hard, but slipping with every step, slowing progress. The Other Guy can only envy your account's tax-deferred status and its infusion of free cash in the form of a company match.

In fact, a company match is a unique as well as powerful benefit from your 401(k) plan. Other retirement plans, including some IRAs, can reduce your taxes by making your contributions tax-deductible. And you can stockpile earnings inside an IRA without taxes diluting them.

But no IRA provides a company match. Only your 401(k) plan can do that. It is an extra advantage that you can't get from anything else.

PUT IT ALL TOGETHER . . .

Time is a valuable resource. You mustn't waste it.

Start saving and investing as early as possible. No matter what age you are, you can start now—making the most of every moment of your future time.

Understanding More of the Advantages

A 401(k) plan is the Swiss Army knife of personal finance. As we discussed in Chapters 1 and 2, this do-it-all retirement account:

✔ Cuts your taxes.

✔ Speeds the growth of your retirement account.

✔ Offers you the chance for a pay bonus in the form of a company match.

If those were the only benefits offered by a 401(k) plan, they would be more than enough reason to sign up. The company match alone is a special advantage that you can get only from a 401(k) plan.

But there are additional personal-finance tools tucked inside a 401(k) plan. A few are available in other retirement accounts, although several are unique to 401(k) plans. No other type of retirement account or conventional pension plan comes close to matching the 401(k)'s overall scope and flexibility.

Within rules set by your plan and the government, you're free to:

✔ Decide how much to contribute.

✔ Select your own investments from a menu offered by your plan.

✔ Choose your investment game plan: aggressive, moderate, or cautious.

✔ Decide whether to change the amount you contribute.

✔ Determine how to fine-tune your investment lineup.

In addition, you can:

✔ Contribute money through automatic payroll deductions.

✔ Take your money if you leave your job.

Further, your plan most likely allows you to:

✔ Borrow from your account.

✔ Make an emergency withdrawal.

✔ Make after-tax contributions.

We'll now discuss how those features work.

AUTOMATIC PAYROLL DEDUCTION

Once you enroll in your plan, your contributions are diverted into your account from your pay automatically.

This is as helpful as it is simple.

You don't have to sign a check every week or two. That means that you can't forget to make contributions, or use the money for something else—like buying an anniversary gift for your spouse just when you happen to be low on cash.

Over the course of decades, forgotten or hijacked contributions now and then can add up to a lot of money. As you learned in the previous chapter's discussion of compounding, it is hardly your own contributions that would be lost. You would also lose their earnings, then their earnings' earnings, and so on. A hundred bucks now becomes a thousand later. A lost thousand grows into a lost ten thousand.

And if your employer's matching contribution is triggered by your contributions, every deposit you neglect to make would cost you that free pay raise from your company. Plus *its* earnings. And so on.

Automatic payroll deduction is important for another reason.

It prevents you from chickening out of making contributions. That could happen when the market goes into a downturn. If you had to make each contribution yourself, it would only be human nature to hold back while the market slides because banks in Tokyo are coming to grips with bad real estate loans, or Wall Street's favorite blue-chip corporation unexpectedly announces lousy profits.

Again, over time each delay would cost you that one contribution, plus all of its earnings' offspring.

Worse, you could fall into one of the worst possible habits. If you start to watch the stock market and wait for what you think is the right moment to invest, you'll have fallen into the trap of thinking there *is* a best moment to invest.

There is. But nobody knows how to find it reliably. The market is too big, too unpredictable, and too vulnerable to too many uncontrollable variables.

Don't Chase a Mirage

The strategy called market timing takes place when an investor tries to buy low and sell high—more precisely, at the market's very lowest and very highest points.

Of course, the market does have low and high points. The difficulty is in trying to anticipate—or time—them.

People who try routinely lose money. Market timers guess wrong too often. Instead of buying at the lowest point or selling at the highest point, they end up spending more than they meant to and getting paid less than they hoped for.

Meanwhile, their delayed investments cost them money in the form of lost earnings. Studies have repeatedly shown the futility of trying to outguess Wall Street. It's a mirage even the pros can't catch up to.

The cost of trying? Exorbitant—as in, "Stick 'em up!"

Take a look at what would have happened if you had

(Continued)

bought shares in an index mutual fund. That's a fund which cautiously mimics its chosen segment of the market, rather than trying to outthink it. Let's say you had invested in an index fund that mirrors the Standard & Poor's Composite Index. That fund tries to duplicate the performance of 500 of the market's biggest, leading stocks (the S&P 500).

Those blue-chip companies grew 14.8 percent yearly from 1986 to 1995.[1] That means if you had plunked your money into an S&P 500 index fund, your investment would have grown 14.8 percent a year (minus fees) during that decade. That's how much you would have made if you had just let your money ride: one investment at the start, then no trades along the way.

In striking contrast, if you had tried to outsmart the market but had guessed wrong on merely the 10 days when the S&P 500 had made the most money, your annual rate of return would have plunged to 10.2 percent.[2] A bad guess on 10 days out of approximately 2500 business days—and your return would have been slashed by nearly one-third.

How tough is it to do better than that? Well, when's the last time you goofed only once a year for 10 years straight?

If you had guessed wrong on the market's 20 best days, your gains would have nose-dived to less than half what the S&P 500 achieved.[3] In other words, by investing in a simple index fund and then ignoring the stock market for the next decade, you would have done twice as well. Plus, you would have saved yourself a small fortune in transaction fees and taxes on any puny gains you lucked into.

The lesson? Forget market timing. You would have made twice as much money by investing in that index mutual fund and then going fishing, playing golf, and talking to your spouse!

[1]Charles P. Jones, *Investments: Analysis and Management*, 6th ed. (New York: John Wiley & Sons, 1998), p. 397.
[2]Ibid.
[3]Ibid.

HOW MUCH YOU CAN INVEST: GOVERNMENT LIMITS

The government's generosity has limits. (Surprise, surprise!) To make sure Congress has enough money to spend, it has rigged 401(k) plan rules so that you don't escape from *too* much in taxes.

As a result, your freedom to choose how much to contribute to your account is limited by two sets of rules: the government's and your plan's.

The government's rules impose upper limits on your yearly contributions with three potentially overlapping barriers:

1. Ceiling of $10,000 for employee contribution.
2. Cap of $30,000 or 25 percent of pay on combined employee and company contributions to all *defined contribution* plans such as 401(k) and profit-sharing plans.
3. Limits for highly paid employees.

Annual Dollar Limit of $10,000

That's the maximum tax-deductible amount you are allowed to contribute in 1999. That ceiling rises with inflation, but only when inflation increases enough to justify $500 increments by a government formula.

Your plan might permit you to make nondeductible, *after-tax* contributions in excess of the $10,000. (See Chapter 6.)

Cap of $30,000 or 25 Percent

Your contributions *and your employer's* to your 401(k) plan—in addition to any other defined contribution (DC) plans, such as a profit-sharing plan or an employee stock ownership plan (ESOP)—are not allowed to total more than $30,000 or 25 percent of your yearly pay, whichever is less.

This restriction supplements the basic $10,000 limit. It does not replace it. Your annual 401(k) contribution limit is still $10,000 regardless of whether you have another DC plan. You can decide how much you want to put into each DC benefit, within the $10,000 and $30,000/25 percent caps.

Limits for HCEs

The amount contributed by certain *highly compensated employees* (generally, those earning more than $80,000) can be limited depending on how much is contributed by lower-paid employees.

Here's How the $30,000/25 Percent Cap Works

Let's say you contribute $10,000 to your 401(k) account. Suppose your company's matching contribution is another $5000. Imagine that your company also offers you an additional $6000 in profit sharing. That totals $21,000, well within the $30,000 collective limit.

But there's a catch (big surprise, huh?). The 25-percent-of-pay ceiling is calculated on only the first $160,000 of your compensation. So if you earn, say, $80,000, the 25 percent ceiling would be $20,000. And since that's less than $30,000, the $20,000 ceiling would prevail.

You'd have to cut back $1000 from your monetary benefits. You could cut the $1000 from any one of the benefits, or in any combination you can arrange that adds up to $1000. You could keep putting the full $10,000 into your 401(k) account, for example, and reduce other benefits by a total of $1000.

Basically, HCEs (as the rules call them) as a group can contribute only a slightly higher percentage of their salary than rank-and-file workers do.

This rule is exactly what it looks like: It is the government's way of making sure that 401(k) plans are not run simply for the benefit of the boss's cronies and key employees. If you are paid more than $80,000 and find out you won't be able to contribute anywhere near the $10,000 because lower-paid people aren't enrolling in the plan or aren't coughing up enough money, you can help yourself by trying to persuade other workers to join and contribute more.

It encourages you to become part of the educational process. And that serves the government's public policy goals.

Who is an HCE? It can include a lot more people than the company president and other bigwigs. David Wray, head of the Profit Sharing/401(k) Council of America (PSCA), says that an HCE is:

✔ Anyone who owns at least 5 percent of the company, regardless of how much or how little he or she is paid.

In addition, your company must include people who fall into one of the following groups:

✔ Anyone who earns more than $80,000.

✔ Anyone who is in the top-paid 20 percent of the company, no matter what the dollar amount of his or her pay is.

Plans are required to prove to the government that HCEs and rank-and-file workers contribute about the same percent of pay. HCEs are allowed to exceed other workers by only a slight amount (very roughly 2 percentage points), which is set by a complex formula.

This is known as the *antidiscrimination rule.*

The worst-case scenario is that if non–highly paid workers lag too far behind HCEs, the brakes can be put on contributions by HCEs. Or the plan may have to refund excessive contributions—with a bite taken out for taxes!

Incredibly, nearly 16 percent of plans flunk the antidiscrimination test and must refund money, according to the PSCA's Wray.

Your benefits officer can tell you whether you are an HCE. You should also find out whether your plan is in danger of flunking the antidiscrimination test, and what the fallout from that would be.

HOW MUCH YOU CAN INVEST: YOUR PLAN'S LIMITS

As if those government restrictions weren't draconian enough, your plan can set limits too.

✔ Your company plan can restrict you to a yearly contribution of less than $10,000.

✔ Your company plan can also set a minimum annual level.

In setting a ceiling below $10,000, your plan can limit your contribution to any level. It is not allowed, however, to establish a ceiling above $10,000.

Ordinarily, a plan will let you kick in anywhere from 1 percent to 15 percent of your pay. Fifteen percent is average.[4]

That's usually moot, though, because so few workers contribute the max. Fewer than one in 12 workers deposits the most allowed.[5] HCEs contribute barely 6.1 percent of their pay, while rank-and-file workers fork over merely 5 percent of their pay on average, according to the Profit Sharing/401(k) Council of America.

Don't Penalize Your Own Retirement

Don't set your contribution level too low. You have complete freedom to fine-tune it, so up the ante periodically. See whether you can afford it.

Remember, your contributions occur through automatic payroll deductions. It is not money you have to take out of your own pocket. In fact, it is money you never see. It is easier than you think to deposit money that you don't have to write a check for.

Plus, the more you contribute, the lower your taxable income becomes. It is a self-administered tax break.

And don't forget your free pay raise. Money you contribute probably triggers a matching contribution from your company.

If making your own contribution larger truly turns out to be a hardship, you can always reverse course.

CHOOSING YOUR OWN INVESTMENTS

One of the biggest strengths of a 401(k) plan is how much control it gives you over how to invest your money. Not only can you set your own contribution level within the limits previously described in this chapter, but you have flexibility over how to invest your money.

---

[4]KPMP, LLP, "Retirement Benefits in the 1990s: 1998 Survey Data."
[5]Ibid.

Pension Plan: Predictability—Not Flexibility

A traditional pension plan gives you zero control over how your money is invested. That's because in a pension plan you don't own shares in any outside investments. What you have is a right to receive a monthly check or a lump sum after you retire.

There are fewer decisions for you to make. But you also have no chance to increase the size of your nest egg by exercising control over investments in your account.

In fact, that flexibility is increasing.

- ✔ The average number of investment choices in a plan is eight, according to Hewitt Associates.
- ✔ In 1995 the average number of options was 6.3.
- ✔ In 1993 the number of choices averaged 4.5.

A small number of plans offer as few as one investment option. But it is far more likely that your plan offers a wide choice. Approximately one out of every six plans gives you a menu with 10 or more choices.[6]

Two choices you'll find in almost every plan are company stock and mutual funds. Only a small number of plans will let you buy stocks (other than company stock) and bonds instead of or in addition to shares in mutual funds. You're more likely to find a situation like that in a workplace where plan members are independent-minded professionals like lawyers, who are willing to spend more time catering to their investments.

However, even so-called self-directed plans like that are becoming less of an oddity. Fewer than 1 percent of plans offered this self-sufficient approach in 1995. But as many as 5 percent of all 401(k) plans were letting members march to their own investment drummer by 1997.[7]

Elsewhere, mutual funds rule; stock funds of various stripes and fla-

---

[6]Profit Sharing/401(k) Council of America.
[7]Hewitt Associates LLC.

vors are offered by 95 percent of 401(k) plans.[8] More than half of all plans offer company stock.[9]

The reason for offering so many choices is to let you tailor your portfolio (the investments in your account) to your needs. After all, your circumstances differ from almost everyone else's. The more choices you have, the more exactly you can mold your mix of investments to suit your financial goals, time frame, and moxie.

For example, there are mutual funds that concentrate on large U.S. corporations. These are the funds that have dominated the record-setting *bull market* of the 1990s.

Bull Market Wall Street slang for a strong stock market. The term characterizes a rise in stock, bond, or commodities prices that lasts at least several months. During a bull market, a lot of trading (buying and selling) usually goes on, reflecting the desire of investors to gain a piece of the action.

There are also balanced funds, which invest in both stocks and bonds. The idea behind that mixed approach is to build in shock absorbers that protect the fund from suffering too much in a stock market downturn.

Not surprisingly, these hedge-your-bet mutual funds have become the single most common choice in plans. They are now in 76 percent of plans, up from 66 percent two years ago.[10]

And for people who are willing to trade the comfort of a set rate of return in exchange for losing a shot at higher growth, there are "stable value" accounts, which include things like guaranteed investment contracts (GICs). GICs promise to pay interest like a certificate of deposit, only they are issued by insurance companies rather than banks.

[8]Ibid.
[9]Ibid.
[10]Ibid.

FINE-TUNING YOUR AGENDA

Thanks to technology and the politics of shoe leather, it is increasingly easy for you to check the status of your 401(k) plan account and to fine-tune it. The role of technology is to speed up your plan's ability to tell you how much your account is worth. Once you know that, you can start to make informed decisions about:

✔ Changing the amount you contribute.

✔ How your account is split among various investments.

Companies make this information available to plan members more frequently because members want it. They want it out of curiosity. They want it because they prefer to exercise control over their financial destiny. And if they don't get it, they look for it from another employer.

Your company would rather provide this information to hold onto you and other valued employees. Your company's alternative is to have to recruit and train new workers.

As Figure 3.1 shows, the percentage of plans that provided account valuation daily nearly doubled between 1993 and 1995, according to Hewitt Associates. It rose almost another 20 percentage points during the following two years as well.

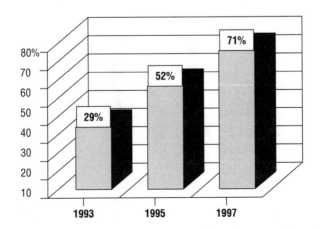

FIGURE 3.1 Daily valuation is growing more common.
Source: Hewitt Associates LLC.

A rising stock market made plan members more interested in Wall Street and the status of their accounts. The booming economy also enabled them to vote with their feet. Workers could switch jobs to be in a 401(k) plan that provided more frequent valuation information.

Not surprisingly, once armed with that information, plan members have asked for the right to use it—and their wish has been granted.

Figure 3.2 illustrates the trend toward allowing more frequent transfer of money already within plan members' accounts among various investments. Now, almost two-thirds of plans (64 percent) allow members to shift dollars among investments, according to Hewitt Associates. This lets members pull their money out of slow-growing investments and pour those dollars into faster-growing ones.

Back-office technology that currently enables members to do this was so expensive and uncommon in 1988 that virtually no plans offered daily transfers then.

In recent years it has become increasingly easy for plan members to get information and make account changes. They can use a telephone to call a plan service center or an automated response system. More companies have dedicated computer terminals or telephones with touch-sensitive computer screens in easy-to-use locations like the benefits office or cafeteria.

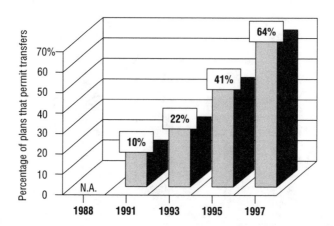

FIGURE 3.2 Trend toward allowing transfer of existing balances: It is increasingly common for plans to let members move their money among existing investments.
Source: Hewitt Associates LLC.

Most recently, plan operators like Fidelity Investments have made available Web sites where members can get account information, test-drive various combinations of investments, and execute changes in their accounts.

One way or another, 92 percent of all plans let members fine-tune their accounts daily, monthly, or quarterly, as Figure 3.3 highlights. At least four times a year, those plans allow you to add or subtract an investment from your lineup, change the amount you contribute, or shift the way your money will be divided among future investments, according to Hewitt Associates.

"Many, many years ago, you could make a change in your account only annually," says David Wray, president of the Profit Sharing/401(k) Council of America. "Then it was semiannual, then quarterly, then monthly. And each time, the window of opportunity was open to you only briefly.

"Now it's whenever you want. That's not only more convenient; it also helps people avoid making bad changes. They no longer feel pressured to do something—*anything*—during those infrequent opportunities."

Haste Makes Waste In Chapter 20 we'll discuss how often you should fine-tune your account, and how to decide what to do.

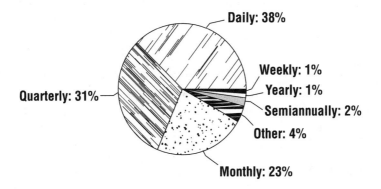

FIGURE 3.3 How often you're allowed to fine-tune your account.
Source: Hewitt Associates LLC.

MORE FEATURES OF YOUR PLAN

After-Tax Contributions

Your usual contributions to your account are with before-tax money. As you learned in Chapter 1, before-tax money is not taxed. (It is not taxed as part of that year's taxable income. Nor is it ever vulnerable to taxes as long as you keep it inside your account.) By subtracting before-tax contributions from your taxable income, you actually reduce your taxable income.

An *after-tax contribution* is counted with your taxable income in the year you earn it. Unlike before-tax contributions, it is not tax-deductible.

Pros and Cons   We'll discuss after-tax contributions more in Chapter 6.

But if your plan allows you to make contributions with after-tax dollars, the *earnings* on that money grow without being gnawed by taxes. That's the same as with regular contributions.

Portability

Unlike a traditional pension plan, you own your 401(k) plan account. If you change jobs, you can take your money with you. (More in Chapter 6.)

Loans

You can't get at your money in most other plans before retirement without suffering taxes and penalty. Your 401(k) plan probably offers you an early-bird special: the right to borrow from your own account, without penalty. (More in Chapter 4.)

Hardship Withdrawals

Sometimes you need more than a loan. Most plans will let you take emergency withdrawals. If there's no other place you can turn to, this feature

can be the personal-finance version of the cavalry riding to the rescue.
(More in Chapter 5.)

LEARNING ABOUT YOUR OPTIONS

You can find out more about what's in your own 401(k) plan by checking
the literature, videotapes, and other educational materials made available
by your plan.

Knowledge Is Power We'll also discuss in later chapters
what educational material is readily available, what material
you have to ask for, and how to understand all of it.

It is important to know as soon as possible whether your plan is
among the dwindling few perpetuating restrictive practices:

✔ Offering only one investment choice.

✔ Offering only a few choices on an all-or-nothing basis.

✔ Limiting how much money you are allowed to invest in any one
option.

✔ Dictating how it invests its matching contribution (much more
common than the other restrictions).

We'll also discuss in more detail, starting in Chapter 14, how to tell
one investment choice from another and how to decide which ones work
best for you in your account.

Chapter

4

Borrowing from Your 401(k) Account

Your daughter is going to graduate from high school next June. She has worked hard and will graduate with honors. Better yet, she's just been offered admission to the college of her choice.

To show how proud you are, you and your spouse would like to surprise her with a two-week trip to Montreal (exotic—but safe) before she has to settle in at her summer job. (She's a chip off the ol' industrious block.) The only question is how to pay for it.

"Maybe," you think, "I should use money from my 401(k) plan."

Think again.

Even if you have tens of thousands of dollars in your account, and retirement is still more than a decade away, borrowing from your account usually is not a good idea.

The heart of the problem: Borrowing from your account deprives you of living expenses for retirement. Your reason for borrowing rarely, if ever, is good enough to justify such a drastic consequence in your Golden Years.

But what if you've already made up your mind to lend yourself the money? After all, the loan feature may be why you joined your plan in the first place. It's a popular come-on, with about 75 percent of all plans permitting members to borrow from their own accounts, according to the Profit Sharing/401(k) Council of America.

But before sticking your hand into the cookie jar, look at all of the pros and cons. You may be surprised by how many disadvantages there are—obvious ones as well as hidden ones. Weigh the pluses and minuses so you know what's in store for you.

BASICS ABOUT BORROWING

Start by making sure you understand how the loan feature works.

Availability

It's up to your plan to decide whether to let members borrow from their accounts. Find out whether your plan offers this option.

If you're not sure, ask your benefits officer or the plan administrator. You can also check the summary plan description (SPD), which is the rule book for your plan.

How Does It Work?

You must repay your loan with interest. The law forbids sweetheart deals. Commonly, this means you'll pay one or two percentage points above the *prime rate*. That's the same ballpark area as a home-equity loan. But well below the rates on credit cards and personal loans.

> **Prime Rate**   The interest rate banks charge their best and most creditworthy customers.

How Much Can You Borrow?

Generally, you can borrow as much as half of the money in your account, up to a maximum of $50,000. (See rest of chapter for an explanation of all the ifs, ands, and buts.)

Length of Loan

You'll have to repay your loan within five years unless it's for buying a principal home. In that case, you'll have more like 30 years to repay.

If you quit your job to work elsewhere or are fired, you'll likely have to pay your loan off within as little as 60 days.

Minimum Size

Your plan may ban loans smaller than a specified size, but the minimum can't be higher than $1000.

ADVANTAGES OF BORROWING

Ease

Most plans let you borrow for any reason. Check to see what restrictions, if any, your plan has.

Pros of Borrowing

- Ease of obtaining a loan.
- Speedy arrangements.
- Avoidance of credit-check hassles.
- Repayment to yourself—with interest.
- Low interest rates.
- Possibility of more than one loan at a time.

Speed

You may be able to receive your loan within days. Exactly how fast may depend on how often your plan balances each account's books—daily, weekly, monthly, quarterly, whatever.

Convenience

Since you aren't borrowing from a bank, you have far fewer hoops to jump through. All that may be necessary is a call to your plan's 800 number, or a visit to your benefits office. Even if you are required to fill out paperwork, it's not nearly as bad as laboring over a bank's credit application or signing over your firstborn as collateral.

Accessibility

It's your money, so you don't have to worry about a credit check or being stretched thin by other loans—say, for the kids' education, home improvements, or a boat.

Pay Yourself

Repayments, including interest, go right back into your own account.

Low Rates

The interest rate will typically be almost 50 percent lower than what a bank would charge you for a personal loan.

Multiple Loans

Your plan may permit you to take out more than one loan at a time.

Motivation

Even if you never use your right to borrow money, if having the feature encourages you to join your plan in the first place it is a very good thing.

DISADVANTAGES OF BORROWING

Most drawbacks stem from the cost of borrowing. Let us count the ways. . . .

Lost Potential

You wipe out all of the future earnings of money you borrow. They are lost forever. You lose much more than the loan itself. You lose all of that money's compounded growth through time, which can be huge. This is the most serious reason for resisting the temptation to take out a loan.

> **Cons of Borrowing**
>
> - Lost earnings.
> - Shortfall from interest payments compared to investments.
> - Expensive fees.
> - Cost of replenishing your account.
> - Extra taxes.
> - Your financial game plan upset.
> - Better alternatives.
> - Time bomb.
> - Spousal consent.

A loan puts your future into hock. Remember the ad slogan, "Pay me now, or pay me later"? Borrowing from your account is a case of paying now *and* paying later.

Shortfall

At first glance, repaying your loan with interest sounds like a win-win situation. You get early access to your cash—*and* you replenish your account.

It even sounds as though it makes up for lost earnings. Hardly.

Interest you pay yourself is likely to be much less than what your money would earn if you had left it inside your account.

Suppose you pay yourself 9 percent or 10 percent interest. Not bad, you smile. But a simple, low-cost index mutual fund investing in large, stable, blue-chip stocks would have earned nearly double that rate on average during the past 10 years.

Fees

Sure, loans from your account are convenient. Sure, they require less paperwork than a bank loan. Sure, the interest rates are low. But you know what? You often pay through the nose, anyway.

Fifty-seven percent of plans charge you a fee for the privilege of borrowing your own money, according to benefits consultants Hewitt Associates. Twenty-nine percent hit you with a bill to keep track of your loan every year.

Fees: Same as Paying a Much Higher Interest Rate

Loan application fees range from $3 to $100. The median size is $40. Servicing fees tend to be as small as $3 and as large as $75. The middle of the pack is $15.

Those numbers may not sound so bad. But, once you add them up—*ouch!* Suppose you take a $1000 loan for five years and the application fee is $40. A yearly service fee of $15 adds another $75 over the life of the loan. That's an extra $115, equivalent to an 11.5 percent interest rate.

Now let's say your actual interest rate is 9 percent. Combined with your fees, your interest rate becomes 20.5 percent. That's what you'd pay to a loan shark . . . or a credit card.

Ironically, the smaller your loan, the worse the *relative* cost of these fees is. The larger the loan, the worse the *overall* cost is.

And remember: You get the interest. But the fees? Say bye-bye. Fees go into your company plan's own coffers.

Hidden Costs

You'll probably have to raise cash for the loan by selling shares of one or more mutual funds or stocks. If you do that when the market happens to be down, replacing the same number of shares after the market recovers will cost you more money.

Extra Taxes

You make regular contributions to your account with *before-tax* dollars— that is, with dollars before they can be taxed and before they can be counted as part of your taxable income for the year. That's the good part.

But you repay a loan with *after-tax* money—dollars left over after toting up your taxable income and writing a check to the IRS. Nevertheless, because of a catch-22 in the federal tax code you have to pay taxes on the repayment (plus its earnings) *again* after withdrawing it during retirement.

Basically, the IRS plays a game of semantics concerning what has been taxed and what hasn't. And, since it's the IRS's game, you lose.

Upsets Your Financial Plan

Count on it: At no point will this book advise you to pick investments by throwing darts at the mutual fund and stock tables in your newspaper. You will choose your investments for several reasons (unless you are stuck in one of the dwindling number of plans that require members to accept a fixed group of investments, without any alternatives, on a take-it-or-leave-it basis).

You will try to choose investments that are the ones most likely to provide the amount of money you need:

✔ For specific spending goals.

✔ When you need it.

✔ In a style that does not bounce up and down more than you can bear in the course of Wall Street's inevitable gyrations.

> **Your Game Plan** Forming an investment game plan is central to getting the most out of your 401(k) plan. We'll discuss how to form a game plan, starting in Chapter 14.

So far so good. But when you borrow from your plan, your sensible decision making gets thrown out the window.

Money for the loan must come from one or more of your investments (some plans let you choose; some make the decision for you). Whichever fund or stock the borrowed money comes from shrinks in size relative to your other investments.

That's bad if the one that is cut down is your best long-term growth-oriented mutual fund, which you chose because it would do the best job of building your nest egg for retirement.

It's like replacing your car's powerful V-8 engine with a wimpy V-4. It'll take longer to get you up the mountain of retirement planning. It may not make it on time.

Unless you beef up the horsepower with a painful injection of more cash to the funds or stocks chosen to meet your goals, your game plan won't work!

You Can Do Better

You may be able to obtain a home-equity loan at a comparable interest rate. Better yet, the interest generally will be tax-deductible. Interest on your 401(k) loan is not tax-deductible.

Time Bomb

If you fall behind in repayments, you could find yourself in default. But why sweat? After all, it's only a loan to yourself. What's the big deal? Well, it's a big deal to the IRS. They will treat the entire unpaid balance as a withdrawal, and you'll have to cough up the resulting taxes and any early-payout penalties.

Spousal Consent

Your plan may require your spouse to *sign off* on a loan before granting it. (Your spouse would not be *co-signing*—taking on joint responsibility for your repayments. Your spouse would simply be giving her or his permission for you to borrow against your retirement nest egg.)

WHAT IS THE MOST YOU CAN BORROW?

Suppose you think a loan is justified after considering all of the pros and cons. Your next step is to figure out how much you will be allowed to borrow.

As we said earlier, generally you can borrow as much as half of the money in your account, up to a maximum of $50,000. Naturally, the government adds enough fine print to that simple rule to assure that you'll need a handheld calculator to figure out how much you can actually borrow.

Here's how to do the math. First we'll explain the rule; then we'll show you how it works.

The rule: You are allowed to borrow up to whichever is smaller:

✔ $50,000, minus other money you've borrowed from your account. The exact amount you subtract from the $50,000 is the high-water mark of any previous loan(s) that you still owed at any time during the preceding 12 months. (Suppose you borrowed $20,000 10 months earlier and had paid back $10,000 by the time you sought the second loan. The $50,000 ceiling would be reduced by the full $20,000 rather than $10,000.)

Or:

✔ The larger of either $10,000 or one-half of your vested account balance.

Figure 4.1 shows how that plays out in the real world if you have no loans outstanding.

If one or more loans are currently outstanding from your account, use Figure 4.2 to calculate the maximum new loan you can take.

Your Vested Account Balance	Maximum You May Borrow
$20,000 or less	$10,000
$20,000 to $100,000	One-half of the vested amount
$100,000 or more	$50,000

FIGURE 4.1   Your loan ceiling if you have no loans outstanding.
Source: IRS.

Part 1

Divide the vested amount in your account by 2.	Line 1: (Your vested amount) ÷ 2 = $_____.
Enter whichever dollar figure is larger: The amount in Line 1, or $10,000.	Line 2: $_____.

Part 2

$50,000 minus the highest amount owed at any point during the preceding 12 months on previous loan(s).	Line 3: $50,000 – (peak amount oustanding) = $_____.
Your loan limit is whichever dollar amount is smaller, Line 2 or Line 3.	Loan limit: $_____.

FIGURE 4.2 Your loan limit with one or more loans outstanding.
Source: IRS.

WATCH OUT FOR NO. 1

The loan feature is good if it helps persuade you to join your plan in the first place. After all, the most important thing is to start to contribute money as soon as you can, so it will grow into the largest nest egg possible.

But the costs of loans—out of pocket as well as in terms of lost investment growth—almost always outweigh the short-term benefits.

For a truly urgent purpose, go ahead and consider borrowing from your account. But . . .

✔ Never borrow for everyday expenses.

✔ Never borrow for things that are not important.

Remember, the purpose of a 401(k) plan is to fund your retirement. Your paycheck is suppose to pay for living expenses, large and small. Don't shortchange your future by confusing your 401(k) account with a checking account.

A Financial Reality Check

Make sure you can afford your loan. Don't borrow unless you have enough income to:

- Keep up your regular contributions.
- Pay for your regular living expenses (including big-ticket items like your home mortgage).
- Cover your loan payments.
- Pay off your loan right away if you are laid off or change jobs.

Hardship Withdrawal

O kay. So your daughter got her vacation in Montreal. Now your attention is turning to how to pay for her education.

Borrowing from your account is one way, which we ex-
plored in the previous chapter. Taking a *hardship withdrawal* is another.

Neither tactic is the ideal use of your 401(k) plan account. In fact,
neither tactic is available unless your plan permits.

If your plan does allow them, hardship withdrawals come with more
strings attached than account loans do. Most of them are courtesy of Uncle Sam.

UNCLE SAM'S GAME PLAN

The government's game plan is to encourage you to save for retirement.
Your congressional rep prefers that you will be able to afford the retirement condo of your dreams, where you can enjoy afternoons in the sun
playing shuffleboard at poolside, instead of pestering him or her with an-
gry letters complaining about how small your Social Security checks are.

Like anything affecting his or her ability to get reelected, your repre-
sentative takes this very seriously. More important, so does the IRS. To
discourage you from taking a hardship withdrawal rather than pumping
up your retirement nest egg, the IRS requires you to have a compelling
reason. The reason doesn't quite have to rank as a financial crisis (al-

though that helps). But it must be more important than buying that motorboat you've had a hankering for.

The government defines this pressing financial situation as "an immediate and heavy financial need."

Four types of expenses qualify:

1. Paying for certain medical expenses.
2. Purchasing a principal residence.
3. Covering certain education expenses.
4. Preventing your eviction from (or foreclosure on) your home.

Not just any expenses in those categories are eligible for payment with hardship withdrawal funds.

> **Wiggle Room**   The fine print of the eligibility rules leaves you a smidgen of leeway to take a hardship withdrawal for something that is not precisely one of the four types of expenses listed. Still, your reason must pass the "immediate and heavy financial need" test. Covering family funeral costs will get the nod. Paying for a junket to Bora Bora will not.

Medical

Qualifying expenses are those that exceed 7.5 percent of your adjusted gross income. The expenses can be for you, your spouse, your kids, or other dependents.

Home

The home you purchase must be your principal home, not your vacation ski lodge in Vail. Your down payment qualifies, but your monthly mortgage does not.

Education

Only post–high school expenditures in the next 12 months meet the IRS's requirements. You must use the money for tuition, related educational fees, and room and board. The expenses can be yours, your spouse's, your kids', or other dependents'. Paying for keg parties at your frat are not what the IRS has in mind.

Eviction

When Alice ventured through the looking glass into Wonderland, she might as well have entered the realm of the IRS. While the tax-collection agency won't let you use a hardship withdrawl to pay monthly mortgage expenses so you can *buy* a home, it will let you use the money to pay your mortgage to prevent *eviction* or *foreclosure*. Go figure.

MORE RED TAPE

Make no mistake about it. The government is out to bust your chops on this one.

It wants to make sure that a hardship withdrawal is your last possible way of resolving your financial plight. Even if you need the money for one of the pressing needs prescribed, you won't be allowed to withdraw the money unless:

✔ You've exhausted your other financial resources, including insurance and a loan from your plan.

If you do qualify, you'll be boxed in by restrictions designed to limit the damage to your retirement finances.

✔ You'll only be allowed to make a hardship withdrawal for the amount needed to cover the emergency, no more.

That protects your current retirement finances. To make sure you don't hock your future retirement finances as well, the IRS slaps yet another restriction in place:

✔ You cannot withdraw more than you have in your account.

Uncle Sam doesn't want you to deplete your account, so he intentionally makes it difficult and expensive to do so. But the government has caved in to the political necessity of giving you access to your own money. That doesn't mean the feds will stand by idly while you try to make a habit of it, though.

One way to discourage you from doing that is to make sure you can't have it both ways: You can't use your account like a liberal line of credit from some pushover of a bank, withdrawing money whenever you like, *and* enjoy government tax breaks that enable you to build up a retirement nest egg.

In other words, you can't reimburse your account after taking a hardship withdrawal.

Uncle Sam Won't Let You Rob Peter to Pay Paul

If you insist on pilfering cash from your account by taking a hardship withdrawal, the government won't let you replenish it.

In essence, the government refuses to let you use its tax breaks to obtain easy loans. By shoving your face into the prospect of a bleaker retirement with a smaller nest egg, Uncle Sam reminds you he frowns upon hardship withdrawals.

This inability to refill your account is a major difference between taking a hardship withdrawal and borrowing from your account. When you take a loan, you *must* repay your account.

TAX FALLOUT

Finally, the IRS does what is customary when you remove money from the shelter of your account: It sends you a tax bill.

To make matters worse, your plan will withhold 20 percent of whatever you withdraw as a down payment against the taxes, even if you're sure you'll owe less than that at the end of the year.

Also, if you're younger than 59½ you may be hit with a 10 percent early-withdrawal penalty. (See Chapters 8 and 9 for a discussion of exemptions to the early-withdrawal penalty.)

YOUR LAST RESORT

By now you're getting the picture: The government does not want you to deplete your account. It most certainly does not want you to look at your account as if it were your old piggy bank—available for plundering to pay for any expense that strikes your fancy. A hardship withdrawal should be your very last hope for covering only life's most urgent bill.

And the way the IRS sees it, if you've got enough income to pay for contributions, you don't need a hardship withdrawal.

So the government imposes an either-or regulation: If you qualify for a hardship withdrawal, you may be frozen out of your 401(k) plan for a year or more. This is the retirement plan equivalent of being sent to your room without dinner: no contributions into your account, no tax break, no company match.

That can cost you a ton of money over the long haul. It is one more reason you should avoid taking a hardship withdrawal at all costs.

COMPARED TO BORROWING FROM YOUR ACCOUNT

A loan from your 401(k) plan account and a hardship withdrawal resemble each other, only fitting for financial-feature cousins. Both involve taking money out of your account before retirement. Both are optional plan features, which your company is free to offer or not. Both are financial safety nets, and neither should be exercised frivolously.

Do You Qualify?

To learn your plan's rules for hardship withdrawals, read your summary plan description (your plan's master rule book) or check with your benefits officer or plan administrator.

They can tell you whether your plan permits hardship withdrawals, how to qualify, and what are the various dos and don'ts.

Nevertheless, there are big differences:

✔ You can take a regular loan from your plan for almost any purpose. You can use a hardship withdrawal only for certain reasons specified by the law.

✔ You have to repay a loan. You don't have to repay a hardship withdrawal.

✔ You repay a loan with interest, which goes back into your account. For a hardship withdrawal, you pay taxes and a 10 percent penalty to the IRS (unless you qualify for an exemption). Making a hardship withdrawal even more distasteful, your plan will withhold 20 percent of whatever you withdraw as a down payment against the taxes.

✔ You may be frozen out of your 401(k) plan for a year after taking a hardship withdrawal.

BIGGEST DISADVANTAGE

You should shy away from a hardship withdrawal for the same reason the IRS discourages them. It robs your future.

You lose much more than the amount you take out. Thanks to the power of compounding, every $100 you withdraw could double into $200 in less than eight years if your account grows 10 percent yearly. If you are 40 years old, $100 you take out today would have mushroomed into $1083.50 by retirement age 65; $10,000 would have skyrocketed into a nifty $108,350.

You've got to sell a lot of pencils from a tin cup to make up that kind of dough.

So be sure that your "hardship" is worth it—and won't cause you more true hardship in retirement.

Chapter

Ease of Participation

Since the start of the 1990s, the stock market has been playing leapfrog with itself.

From less than 2650 on the first day of the decade, the Dow Jones Industrial Average (the most widely used barometer of how the stock market is doing) jumped to 3000 in April 1991.

It completed its vault to 4000 in February 1995.

Because so few people understand what the DJIA number actually means (most people have better things to do with their time), ordinary folks focus instead on something they can comprehend: each 1000-point gain. Who cares what the number actually signifies? The only thing that matters is *up*.

And so it went.

✔ The Dow finished adding another 1000 when it reached the 5000 mark in November 1995.

✔ It had hopped its next 1000—cracking 6000—by October 1996.

✔ The Dow jumped through the 7000 level shortly after Valentine's Day the following year.

✔ Rising relentlessly, by that summer it had cleared 8000.

✔ In mid-April of 1998 it had hurdled 9000 for the first time.

Whatever the Dow means to math-heads, in plain English its rise means this: If in April 1991 you had invested $5000 in a bunch of stocks that represented a cross section of Wall Street, by October 1996 it was worth $10,000.

By April 1998 your $5000 had tripled into $15,000.

All within seven years.

The best part? It will do the same thing again.

The Dow

Investors watch the Dow (Dow Jones Industrial Average) for the same reason a doctor takes a patient's temperature. It is one of the vital signs of the nation's economy.

It generally measures the average value of the stocks of certain major corporations. A rise in the Dow indicates that on average the value of those stocks has gone up. That's good. When the Dow declines, it's because those stocks have fallen in value.

The DJIA is based on the stock prices of only 30 companies, although they are leading blue-chip firms. Household names, one and all: Coke, IBM, Disney. . . .

Originally, all of the companies were involved in manufacturing and industry. Today the Dow represents a somewhat broader cross-section of the economy.

There are some technical quirks in the way the Dow is calculated. That's one reason people use other yardsticks as well to assess Wall Street.

Nevertheless, the DJIA is the stock market's celebrity benchmark.

Don't worry about understanding the algebra behind the Dow. Few people bother. The only thing most people care about is whether the number goes up or down, and by how much.

Come to think of it, the process has already begun. That's true whether the stock market is up, down, or stagnant right now. The only question is how long it will take.

Wars, assassinations, terrorism, the Great Depression, runaway inflation in the 1970s, Watergate, El Niño, and AIDS. . . . There are plenty of days when it looks as if the smart thing to do is sell your stocks and mutual fund shares, load up on gold bullion, and join the survivalists holed up in the deep woods. (See sidebar.)

Never Watch Wall Street through Rose-Colored Glasses!

Just because people are fascinated by each 1000-point advance by the Dow, that does not mean the stock market defies gravity.

It doesn't always rise quickly. The stark reality is that it doesn't always rise—period. Whether during a prolonged period of prosperity like most of the 1990s or in other, less happy times, the market suffers occasional setbacks.

Your stocks and mutual funds lose value.

On October 19, 1987, the Dow plunged a heart-pounding 508 points. That was the final, bitter sag in a two-month meltdown that saw the market wilt 36 percent.

One lesson: you should always try to use a long-term strategy. Right after the crash, if you had invested in a mutual fund mimicking another key market barometer, the Standard & Poor's 500-stock index, values would have rallied enough to reward you with a 5 percent profit within two years.

But, somehow, despite the worst historic events, Armageddon never quite arrives. Instead of reverting to a barter economy, the spread of personal wealth continues. There are only two uncertainties about economic expansion: its speed, and whether you will position yourself to benefit to the max.

ELIGIBILITY: WHEN YOU CAN JOIN

The first step in positioning yourself to ride Wall Street's next great wave requires climbing aboard your financial surfboard.

That should not take long; but, unfortunately, it may take longer than you'd like.

If your plan is loosey-goosey, it can allow you to join right away. But a plan can delay your signing up, and most do. Before letting you enroll, your company's plan can make you wait up to a year after you start work or until you celebrate your 21st birthday.

The reason is that new employees are the most likely to leave the job. Deferring eligibility enables your company plan to avoid costly, wasted paperwork and education. It also makes it easier for your plan to assure widespread participation by eligible rank-and-file workers, which the government insists on.

Here's how it works: Suppose your workplace plan has a one-year-or-age-21 policy. If you are 21 or older, the longest your plan can make you twiddle your thumbs is one year. But, let's say you start work at age 19. In that case, the waiting period can be two years, until you turn 21.

However, one recent rule improvement should spur employers to let people become members early. Starting in 1999, if a company with a one-year-or-age-21 policy lets workers join sooner, the plan can count those workers separately in determining whether it has met its rank-and-file participation obligation.

Don't Be Shy

Your company plan—especially if it's small—may not know about the liberalized eligibility rule that kicked in on January 1, 1999. Don't hesitate to point out the rule change. You may be able to enroll earlier than you expected.

It is very troublesome and expensive for a company to fall short of participation quotas, which are called antidiscrimination rules. So employers make every effort to fulfill them. Your employer will probably be glad to learn about a rule that makes it easier to do that while making young, new employees happy.

Variations on Time Eligibility

Your employer is still free to limit eligibility in other ways. The most important restriction is that not all employees in your company may be allowed to join the plan. The plan may be open only to workers in specific divisions. Or perhaps only certain categories of workers may be allowed to join. Salaried and hourly employees are the most likely to qualify. Commissioned salespeople and part-time workers are often not eligible.

If you start out in an ineligible category or a business division that does not offer participation but your status changes, the time you were not qualified for enrollment usually must be counted toward your eligibility requirement, according to Ted Benna of The 401(k) Association.

When eligibility hinges on length of service, your time on the job can be figured out using one of two methods:

- ✔ You must be credited with a full year once you have worked 1000 hours or more in a 12-month period even if it took you, for instance, only 9 months.

- ✔ Your employer must credit you for a year's service as soon as 12 months have passed since you got your job, no matter how many hours you actually have worked.

VESTING: HOW SOON IS THE MONEY YOURS?

All the happy talk about how large your company match is and how fast your account grows doesn't always count. That's because you may not actually own all the money in your account—not at first, anyway.

What you do own is every cent you contribute; 100 percent of the money you deposit and its earnings are yours from the moment you kick in your first penny. All of it is yours, all of the time. If you leave the job, you can take all of it with you.

That may not be true about your company's matching contribution (if any).

Only the most generous plans give you full ownership of the company match as soon as it shows up in your account. That's little better than one-third (35.4 percent) of all plans, according to the Profit Sharing/401(k) Council of America. The rest require you to wait before you can call your company's contribution yours.

The process of gaining ownership over the money is called *vesting*.

Vesting happens either gradually in steps or all at once after a specified length of time.

There are limits to how long either formula can take. As Figure 6.1 shows, if your plan vests you 100 percent in a single stroke, it can't take

Years on the Job	Portion of Matching Contributions That You Own
Fewer than 5	0%
5 or more	100%

FIGURE 6.1 Cliff vesting schedule. With a cliff vesting schedule, you gain 100 percent ownership of your company's matching contributions all at once. The process cannot take more than five years.
Source: IRS.

longer than five years after you're hired. In the lingo of people in your benefits and accounting departments, this sort of arrangement is called *cliff vesting.*

If vesting occurs in steps (called *step* or *graded vesting*), you are given ownership of the employer's contributions according to a schedule. Each step is a plateau, where your level of ownership rises. With each step, you get at least one-fifth more ownership, as Figure 6.2 illustrates.

You must become vested in the initial 20 percent within your first three years on the job. You get each additional fifth annually until you are 100 percent vested. That means 100 percent vesting must not take longer than seven years.

Your plan can be as big a sport as it wishes. It is perfectly free to use a faster timetable. For example, it can make you fully vested in three years rather than five. It's also allowed to give you ownership in chunks larger than 20 percent. Each step can be 25 percent, for instance, so that you become 25 percent vested after three years (or sooner, if the plan permits) and fully vested three years later.

Whatever vesting arrangement it uses, your plan must spell out all of the details in its rule book, the summary plan description.

Vesting: Sometimes Faster, Sometimes Slower

Tax laws are complex, like the laws of physics. (If physics laws were simple, we wouldn't think of Albert Einstein as a genius.)

One thing that makes tax laws complicated is all of the *whereas*es and *wherefore*s. Because the vesting rules affect how quickly plan money is yours, you should know about the important exceptions to the general

Years on the Job	Portion of Matching Contributions That You Own
Fewer than 3	0%
3 (but fewer than 4)	20%
4 (but fewer than 5)	40%
5 (but fewer than 6)	60%
6 (but fewer than 7)	80%
7	100%

FIGURE 6.2 Step or graded vesting schedule. In a step or graded vesting schedule, you gain ownership over your company's matching contributions gradually. With each step, you get at least one-fifth more ownership. The first 20 percent must become yours within three years. You're entitled to another fifth each year after that. Your plan can make the timetable faster or the steps larger.
Source: IRS.

rules. They're a pain in the neck. You may never need them. But forewarned is forearmed.

Exception #1: Beating the Buzzer. Once you work someplace three years, if the plan changes its vesting schedule so it takes longer to become vested, you must be given the choice of sticking with the old vesting timetable.

Even if you decide to go along with the new timetable, it can affect only your future vesting. The only thing that will change is how fast you gain ownership over any part of your company's matching contribution you don't already own. It cannot take away money you're already vested in.

Exception #2: Happy Birthday. You are almost always entitled to be made fully vested once you reach your plan's normal retirement age. That's true even if it takes less time than your plan's vesting timetable allows.

Suppose 65 is your company's usual retirement age. If you celebrate your 65th birthday after two years of working there—*bingo!* You're fully vested at that moment even if your plan has, say, a seven-year step vesting schedule.

Exception #3: Wave Bye-Bye. If you work in an industry like construction or trucking, you might have been saddled with a slow vesting schedule. Fortunately, that drawn-out vesting timetable has been phased out by federal law.

This slowpoke arrangement was available to companies using what's called a *multiemployer plan*. A multiemployer 401(k) plan is a single plan covering workers at several unrelated companies. Typically, a plan like that is part of a union's negotiated contract with a number of separate employers.

The old rule was that a multiemployer plan could have a slower cliff schedule than usual. Instead of a five-year cliff schedule or a seven-year graded schedule, you could have been required to work as long as 10 years before becoming vested. Federal law has ended that snail-paced 10-year cliff schedule as of January 1, 1999.

Exception #4: Leveling the Playing Field. If your plan is very generous with certain big shots in your company, the plan must give you a break when it comes to vesting.

That's because the government is serious about making sure that the corner-office crowd doesn't get more than its share of the tax breaks offered by 401(k) plans. To level the playing field, Uncle Sam orders a faster vesting routine for rank-and-file workers.

Unless you're one of the company elite, the vesting speedup means you receive ownership of your company's matching contribution sooner.

Here's what happens: If your plan's benefits for people the IRS calls *key employees* exceed a specified level, your plan is considered *top-heavy*—that is, it leans in favor of those key workers. In that case, your plan's vesting scheduling must advance at least as rapidly as one of the following two timetables (in each year it is top-heavy):

✔ Three years if your plan wants to use a cliff schedule. This would replace the usual five-year cliff schedule. You would become 100 percent vested all at once after no more than three years. This is illustrated by Figure 6.3.

✔ Six years if your plan uses a graded schedule. This would take the place of a seven-year step schedule. Figure 6.4 shows how you

Years on the Job	Portion of Matching Contributions That You Own
Fewer than 3	0%
3 or more	100%

FIGURE 6.3 Cliff vesting schedule for top-heavy plans. In a top-heavy plan with a cliff vesting schedule, you gain 100 percent ownership over your company's matching contributions in three years or less.
Source: IRS.

Years on the Job	Portion of Matching Contributions That You Own
Fewer than 2	0%
2 (but fewer than 3)	20%
3 (but fewer than 4)	40%
4 (but fewer than 5)	60%
5 (but fewer than 6)	80%
6	100%

FIGURE 6.4 Step or graded vesting schedule for top-heavy plans. Top-heavy plans must use a step or graded vesting schedule that gives you 100 percent ownership faster than the usual seven-year timetable.
Source: IRS.

would become vested in your first 20 percent after no more than two years on the job. You'd gain ownership over each additional 20 percent portion of your company's contributions yearly, or sooner, after that.

How to Tell If Your Plan Is Top-Heavy

A plan is generally top-heavy if more than 60 percent of the money in it belongs to key employees. That's measured simply by adding up all of the account balances for key employees and for everyone else.

Your plan administrator is responsible for keeping track of this. He or she can let you know if the plan is top-heavy. Feel free to ask.

Pay Plus . . .

Nothing is simple when it comes to tax rules. Some definitions of who is a key employee are based on pay. But rather than defining pay by referring to dollars earned, Congress based it on total compensation. That includes some fringe benefits—but, of course, not others.

Compensation includes wages, salary, fees, commissions, tips, bonuses, and all of your own 401(k) contributions.

It does not include any company matching contributions, payouts from your plan, or your employer's contributions to such things as any traditional pension plan, tax-exempt health plan premiums, or group life insurance premiums.

The purpose of all this isn't merely to provide employment for lawyers (although it may seem that way). It is to prevent your 401(k) plan from being used as a private tax dodge for the benefit of people high on the corporate food chain.

It takes more than merely a fat paycheck to make someone a key employee. Generally, only the following are key employees:

✔ A company officer whose yearly compensation (pay and certain bennies) exceeds 50 percent of a level that is adjusted for the cost of living. Right now, that's 50 percent of $130,000, or $65,000.

✔ Any of the 10 employees with the largest ownership stake in the company, and whose annual pay exceeds $30,000. (However, consider this scenario, which is more likely to occur in a small company. Suppose somebody is the 20th largest owner of company stock. But combined with his wife's, his kids', and his grandkids' stock, he's got clout over, say, the fifth largest block of company stock. If his pay exceeds $30,000, say hello to one of the firm's key employees.)

✔ An employee who owns more than 5 percent of the company. If the company is a corporation, this would be someone who owns more than 5 percent of its stock.

✔ An employee who owns at least 1 percent of the company and whose yearly pay and bennies are worth more than $150,000.

"A plan in a small company that has a lot of employee turnover is especially vulnerable to falling into the top-heavy category," says David Wray of the Profit Sharing/401(k) Council of America.

Another "Top-Heavy" Benefit

A faster vesting schedule is not the only payback for being in a top-heavy plan. If your plan is top-heavy, your company commonly must contribute an amount equal to at least 3 percent of your yearly compensation to your account.

But, if your company's matching contribution for key employees—plus the highest rate contributed by any key worker to his or her own account—total less than 3 percent, your company only has to kick into your account whatever that combined rate is.

This is a bigger bonus than it may seem at first.

- Because of some complex legal mumbo jumbo, whatever amount a top-heavy plan figures out that it must pay to non-key employees' accounts generally is in addition to any matching contribution it already makes to them.

PORTABILITY: YOU CAN TAKE IT WITH YOU

Dogs and cats are both popular pets. It's nice to have either (or both) in retirement. But you'd never be confused about which is which.

There's no need for confusing a 401(k) plan with a traditional pension plan, either.

Nevertheless, right about now you may be asking, "There's a difference? Heck, isn't my 401(k) a pension plan?"

You're not alone. Many people and businesses use the word "pension" to refer to both 401(k) plans and traditional pension plans. But they are as different as, well, you know what. (Hint: small furry creatures with four legs and a tail.)

One of the biggest differences between a 401(k) plan and a traditional pension plan is what happens if you leave your job.

With a traditional pension plan, you risk losing all or part of your benefits.

With a 401(k) plan, you own everything you are vested in. If you leave your job, it's still yours. Leaving your job does not change the amount or portion you own.

You do lose your shot at gaining ownership over the unvested portion of your account, of course. But the vested balance remains yours. And it stays yours whether you leave the account inside the plan (which some plans permit), roll it over into an IRA (individual retirement account), or transfer it to your new workplace (if your new plan allows that).

Pension plans are a throwback to the days of black-and-white movies; 401(k) plans don't even go as far back as the first *Star Wars* movie.

A pension plan is a retirement program funded by an employer. A 401(k) plan is funded largely by you.

That's why if you leave your job your 401(k) belongs to you but a traditional pension plan does not. Unlike your 401(k) plan account, you don't have an individual account in a pension plan. You have a right to receive a check once a month for the rest of your life after retirement. You'll be paid a predictable amount of money. That's why a pension plan is known as a *defined-benefit plan*. It's based on years of service, age at retirement, your pay, and the plan's formula.

Typically, you penalize yourself with a pension plan by leaving your job. That cuts short the years of work that will count toward your benefit. Also, it probably means your benefit will be based on lower pay if you leave before your peak earning years.

With a 401(k) plan, though, if you change jobs you can take the money with you.

Instead of the defined-benefit categorization of a pension plan, a 401(k) plan is called a *defined-contribution plan*. That's because the amount you contribute during your working years is specified (by you). How much you receive during retirement is not specified. That depends on how you invest your money along the way.

With that flexibility, a 401(k) plan gives you the opportunity to make your nest egg grow. You have no such chance with a pension plan. All you get is what the plan offers—not a penny more.

One of the biggest advantages of a 401(k) plan is that it gives you a far better shot at beating inflation. You can invest your money to grow. You can invest it so it grows faster than inflation.

In contrast, pension payments are doomed to lose value. Unless you draw a government paycheck, your pension probably does not include a cost-of-living adjustment. While you get the same dollar amount year after year, each one of those dollars is worth less year by year due to the relentless erosion of inflation.

But cheer up. Although pensions are vanishing from the small-employer landscape, if you work for a large corporation you may receive the best consolation prize available to all of us working stiffs since the day Adam and Eve got booted from the Garden of Eden: a traditional pension *and* membership in a 401(k) plan.

What a country!

AFTER-TAX CONTRIBUTIONS

Let's say you've signed up for your company's 401(k) plan. Now you've got decisions to make—like how much to contribute to your account.

Definition Flashback!

Regular contributions to your account are with before-tax money. That means you contribute money that is not taxed as part of that year's income. Better yet, its earnings also escape taxes so long as they remain inside your account.

In very stark contrast, after-tax contributions are part of your taxable income in the year you earn it and are not tax-deductible.

On the one hand, you could jack up your monthly 401(k) plan contribution by, say, $20 or $30. On the other hand, your wedding anniversary is only six months away and you promised your beloved significant other a wild weekend of blackjack at the nearest casino.

What to do . . . ?

Actually, you can have it both ways. The solution is to use *after-tax contributions.*

In Chapter 3 we briefly described how after-tax contributions work. Basically, unlike before-tax contributions they are not tax-deductible.

Because they lack that up-front tax break it's only natural to ask, "What good are they?"

The answer: plenty. For starters, their earnings grow tax-free and stay protected until you withdraw them.

Sheltering Your Money from Taxes

After-tax money is like any money in your paycheck. It's what's left over after taxes. It's the money you use to buy groceries and movie tickets, and deposit in your checking account.

You can invest after-tax money on your own outside your 401(k) plan in a mutual fund or stocks and bonds. Like an after-tax contribution inside your 401(k) plan, it won't be tax-deductible.

The difference between after-tax investments outside your plan and inside your plan is what happens to the earnings. Outside your plan, earnings are sapped vampire-like by the tax collector.

Inside your plan investment earnings grow tax-deferred. They enjoy the same protection as earnings on regular, before-tax contributions. As a result, an after-tax investment will grow much larger inside your 401(k) plan than outside.

There's a second advantage to after-tax 401(k) contributions. By forking over taxes on the money when it is first paid as part of your salary, you typically don't have to pay taxes again or a penalty if you later withdraw the money. That's true even before age 59$^1/_2$, when you're usually penalized as well as taxed for making a withdrawal.

Earnings are not so lucky. Because Uncle Sam leaves them alone while they're compounding inside your account, he demands his share once you withdraw the earnings.

Your earnings will be socked with a tax bill as regular income as soon as you take any out. To make sure of that, 20 percent of whatever you withdraw will be withheld as prepayment on those taxes.

Like any early withdrawal of regular contributions and earnings, your after-tax earnings will be slapped with a 10 percent penalty if you take the money out before age $59\frac{1}{2}$ (unless you qualify for certain exemptions).

How to Divvy Up Your Contributions

What these tax consequences boil down to is this:

- If you're sure you'll use your money for a short-term expense like hitting a casino or paying your kid's tuition bill next semester, it's probably smarter to put your money into taxable investments outside your 401(k) plan. That's because the double whammy of taxes and penalty on the earnings from after-tax money withdrawn before age $59\frac{1}{2}$ will likely more than wipe out any advantage you might have gained from tax-deferral on that money. The earnings won't be in your account long enough to rack up enough growth.

- How long is "short-term"? That depends on how fast your investments grow (their rate of return) and your tax bracket. A rough rule of thumb: If you will need your money within three years or so, don't bother making after-tax contributions to your 401(k).

- If your company makes matching contributions on your after-tax contributions, they make more sense than ordinary, taxable investments—except for the shortest periods of time.

- If you won't need the money for five to seven years, use the money to boost the size of your pretax contributions. Especially if the extra deposits will receive a company match.

If you still can't decide whether to make after-tax contributions, weigh these factors. They help clarify the differences between pretax and after-tax contributions.

✔ Not all plans allow after-tax contributions. Half of all plans permit after-tax contributions, according to Hewitt Associates.

✔ Fewer than one-third of all plans offer a company match on after-tax contributions, according to Hewitt. Paltry as that portion is, it's rising. In recent years while companies have been fighting with one another to attract and hold worthwhile employees, more and more are offering a match on after-tax contributions.

✔ You can't borrow after-tax contributions. (But you *can* withdraw the money. Just remember: You'll have to pay taxes and possibly a penalty on withdrawn earnings. It may make more sense to deposit the money into your checking account. It may also cost you less to put the money into your pretax 401(k) account, then borrow it.)

✔ The sky is not the limit. Your company will put a cap on how much you can contribute. It will probably be less than the ceiling on your regular, before-tax contributions.

Bottom Line

If you will need your money for short-term expenditures, beware of the taxes and penalties you may have to pay on withdrawals of pre- or after-tax money from a 401(k) plan. Ask your benefits office, your brother-in-law the CPA, or your financial planner to help you figure out how much money the IRS will want to get its clutches on, and whether the tax-deferred growth of your account will outweigh that.

If you're not sure whether you'll need your money before retirement or whether you can afford more contributions to your 401(k) plan, err on the side of optimism. First try what will benefit you the most: pretax contributions. Then consider after-tax contributions.

Both are better than taxable investments—and infinitely better than blowing the money on cheap thrills rather than saving for retirement—unless you hemorrhage cash by inflicting early-withdrawal taxes and penalties on yourself.

Your nest egg will thank you.

Learning Your Way around Your Plan

T he reason 401(k) plans are confusing is because they are put together like Frankenstein: a patchwork of pension parts. Come to think of it, Frankenstein was in better shape. At least he was put together all at once. The real problem for 401(k) plans is that they've been built a little at a time. Over decades. By politicians.

The outcome is a crazy quilt of rules. Some are governed by the IRS. Some are the responsibility of the Department of Labor (DOL). Others are watched over by your company in its role as sponsor of the plan.

Understandably, it is often difficult to know who is the ultimate umpire for a question. Not that it matters. Who calls Washington, D.C., for information about their plan? You'd no more do that than telephone the secretary of the U.S. Treasury to ask how to get a new passbook for your bank account.

Likewise, you expect somebody inside your company to provide answers for your 401(k) plan questions. If the explanation lies elsewhere, you assume someone in your company's benefits or payroll office can tell you who to call at your plan's mutual fund family, bank, or other outside service provider.

It's human nature. You expect the right hand to know what the left hand is doing—and what the left hand's phone number is.

If it doesn't, you're not the one who should feel like a dunce when a question comes up.

In the Beginning . . .

Ironically, although so many people now take 401(k) plans for granted, this retirement-finance program started by accident.

In 1978 Congress slipped a new provision—Section 401, paragraph (k)—into the federal tax code. The idea was to make sure that banks' profit-sharing plans provided tax benefits equally to lower-paid and higher-paid workers.

The obscure new provision attracted very little notice.

In 1981, though, Pennsylvania benefits consultant Ted Benna was revising a bank's cash-bonus system. His challenge was to devise a plan that would persuade workers to put money into a profit-sharing plan instead of taking a cash bonus and spending it rather than saving for retirement.

"I was afraid they'd blow the whole thing on Christmas," says Benna, whose advisory firm now is The 401(k) Association.

His solution was to take provisions in the 1978 tax reform one step further than anyone had thought of. Workers would get bonus pay—but only if they put their money into a tax-deferred savings plan.

To encourage workers to do that faithfully over time, the bonus would be part of their regular pay.

That was the birth of the tax-deductible company match. Benna had linked it to a tax-deductible worker contribution. All wrapped inside a tax-deferred savings plan.

Ironically, Benna's client declined to adopt the concept. It feared his novel plan would incur the wrath of the IRS. Benna used it for his own firm.

Once the IRS approved the procedure, other corporations embraced it.

Dealing with your plan doesn't have to be as maddening as dealing with your cable TV company, though. Plans are getting more user-friendly.

The first step in obtaining information is understanding who performs which tasks for your plan. Then you'll have a better idea whom to contact. It may also help you frame any question you have.

Better yet, there is actually a system for keeping you informed about your plan. Understanding where to go for information gives you a road map to your plan.

WHO'S WHO

One way to get a handle on how your plan is organized (and how you can get information) is by comparing it to a jet airliner. Both take you somewhere. And both require a lot of people performing specialized tasks. Pixie dust works only for Tinker Bell!

Here is who's who, and what they do:

Plan Participants

Those are plan members, including you. Like passengers aboard a jumbo jet, you have a destination. In your case, it is retirement.

Sponsor

The company you work for is the sponsor. Your employer is like the airline company. It decides how the plan will be run. As the owner, it's entitled to design the plan and make the rules. (In addition to following their own bylaws, both your plan and an airline must abide by rules enforced by government regulatory agencies. In your plan's case, the rules are overseen by the IRS and DOL.)

It's up to your company to decide which stocks, mutual funds, money market funds, and other investment options to offer members like you. Also, it's entirely up to your company to decide which optional features to include. For instance, if your plan lets members borrow from their accounts or take hardship withdrawals, it's because your company decided to make those perks available. Further, the plan operates like an absolute monarchy in at least one sense: All key plan personnel owe their jobs to the sponsor, which hires or approves of all of them.

Trustee

The reason you don't hand five hundred bucks to a stranger on the street and say, "Gimme an airplane ticket!" is that you'd never see your money again. Ditto for any tickets. That's why you use a travel agent. Likewise, the trustee's job is to protect your money.

But the trustee's duty goes beyond that. Like a travel agent who's supposed to find you a suitable airline, arrange for your flight, make sure your tickets reach you, and perhaps take care of details on the far end like hotel accommodations and a rental car, the trustee is responsible for overseeing the plan.

The trustee can be an individual or group. In your company, the trustee may include someone from the benefits, payroll, or human resources departments. (In plans at large corporations, it is typically a professional organization.) The trustee sees to it that money contributed by you and other plan members ends up where it belongs: in a trust, which is legally separate from your company. That separation is important. It safeguards your money from creditors if your company goes belly-up. If your company is in financial straits, it puts your money beyond the reach of a desperate business owner who might be tempted to "borrow" cash from the plan to pay bills.

The trustee's role is to keep an eye on everything, seeing to it that the plan is run for the benefit of members. That includes making sure that the investment manager's decisions are in your best interests.

Sometimes the trustee is called the *custodian*—but, no, that's not the guy with a mop and bucket. When you take money from your plan, it's the trustee who makes arrangements. That may happen behind the scenes, however. You may deal with people in your company's benefits, payroll, or human resources departments.

Plan Administrator

Meet the airplane's pilot. This is the person with hands-on control over the plan. The plan administrator is responsible for answering any of your questions. He or she may work in your company's benefits or HR office or at corporate headquarters in another part of the United States. In fact, the plan administrator may work for an outside firm rather than your own company.

Where the Buck Stops

When your HR or benefits officer can't answer a question, the plan administrator is the person to contact. Your plan's rule book, the summary plan description (more about that document later in this chapter), spells out who the plan administrator is and how to reach him or her.

Investment Manager

This is the person or organization that provides your plan's investment options. The investment manager (sometimes called the *money manager*) is typically a large mutual fund company, bank, or insurance company. Think of the investment manager as the airplane's navigator. He or she is supposed to know how to get you and other "passengers" to your destination. It's his or her job to aim the airplane in the right direction.

Speak Up If You're Not Satisfied

If you're not satisfied with your investment choices, speak with your plan administrator. If he or she and enough plan members share your view, the investment manager should be asked to provide more or different options.

If your plan is giving you a bumpy ride and it's not because of foul weather (a turbulent stock market), one course of action is to replace the investment manager.

Record Keeper

The guys and gals in the control tower keep track of whose turn it is to land, arrival and takeoff times, and which gate incoming aircraft go to. They also watch every airplane's progress on radar. Likewise, the record keeper keeps track of your account—contributions, balance, loans, and withdrawals. The record keeper maintains your records and sends out periodic reports and statements (or forwards them to your company for mailing to employees).

The record keeper is also in charge of checking up on which employees are enrolled and which are not. The government insists on knowing this, so it can make sure the plan's tax benefits aren't being made available to only the boss's friends and family.

Pros and Cons of One-Stop Shopping

Some plan sponsors hire one firm to be investment manager, another to be record keeper, yet another to be trustee, with mutual funds from various fund families. Other sponsors pay one financial-services company to perform several jobs, perhaps even operate the entire plan. That bundled approach makes it simpler to run the plan and perhaps to get answers to questions. But it may mean you're not getting the best possible selection of investment choices.

At least once a year, think about how happy you are with your plan. Talk about it with friends and coworkers.

One question to ask is whether your investment manager is providing only or mostly mutual funds in its own fund family rather than another family's better-performing funds. If so, it may be time for a change.

YOUR BEST SOURCES OF INFORMATION

Getting information about your plan and your individual account is a little like getting information from a library. What makes it more useful than a random pile of books is the fact that it's organized. But you can't find what you need until you know what's up each aisle of book stacks. It's no use looking for romance novels or car-care books in the sports section, for example.

The same goes for your 401(k) plan. It's easier to find what you want when you look in the right place.

Plan Documents

When you want to check details about your plan overall or look up certain facts and figures, official plan documents are the best place to start.

But Don't Say We Didn't Warn You . . .

Are plan documents important and useful? Yup.

Page-turners? Not! These documents certainly are not light summer reading. They will not push the latest thriller from Tom Clancy off the best-seller list. For excitement, this material ranks somewhere between an ingredients label on laundry detergent and a bank statement.

Then again, if it's excitement you want, go skydiving. But if it's information about the rules and regs of your 401(k) plan, the plan documents should top your list of required reading.

Summary Plan Description (SPD). This is the owner's manual for your 401(k) plan. The SPD spells out how your plan works, the features it offers to you, and its rules. This is where you can find out such things as:

- ✔ Your investment options.
- ✔ How soon after starting work you're eligible to enroll.
- ✔ Whether your company offers a matching contribution and, if so, its size.
- ✔ How quickly you become vested in any matching contributions.
- ✔ When and how you can take payouts.
- ✔ Whether your plan offers optional features like the right to borrow from your account or take hardship withdrawals.

✔ The name and location of the plan administrator.

✔ How to get a copy of the *plan document* (see below).

The SPD also explains important but easily overlooked fine points, like:

✔ Grievance procedures.

✔ How you can lose certain rights or benefits (which you commonly don't have to worry about unless you steal from your company or plan).

Your plan is supposed to provide you with the SPD within 90 days after you enroll.

Plan Document. If the SPD is your owner's manual, the plan document reads like a purchase-and-sale agreement. Whatever details are missing from the SPD are in the plan document. It consists of page after page of fine print, legalese, and definitions. If you enjoy legal briefs, this will be your cup of tea.

Compared to this, the SPD reads as easily as a comic book.

Summary Annual Report (SAR). The SAR summarizes the financial information that your plan files with the government. It tells you how much money the plan has, what all of the account balances add up to, and the total amount that members have contributed during the year.

The trouble is that this information is not of much use to you. It's like getting your bank's balance sheet, when what you want instead is information about your own account—which the SAR does not provide. The SAR is a snapshot of the plan's overall financial health. But who cares? You want a snapshot of your individual account's financial health.

For whatever it's worth, your plan is supposed to send you an SAR every year. Put it in your recycling bin.

Individual Benefit Statement. This is more like it. It's a summary of your account balances and vested benefits. You'll get one a year. Its shortcoming is that it doesn't provide as much detail as your periodic account statements, your plan's Web site, or your plan's telephone information system (see "Easy-to-Use Sources of Information" section, below, concerning all of those).

Summary of Material Modifications. Your SPD may not be completely up-to-date. No one is pulling a fast one on you. Any lag time is due to ordinary bureaucratic sloth and office routine. To find out what has been changed or revised in your plan, read the summary of material modifications. Your plan is supposed to make one available after the plan has been changed. The document is also available from the Department of Labor.

Whenever you get a copy of the SPD or plan document, ask for the latest summary of material modifications as well.

Mutual Fund Prospectus and Annual and Semiannual Reports. You'll get copies of these or access to them if your plan offers mutual funds as investment choices. A prospectus is a sales brochure and a legal document, wrapped into one piece of literature. Look for descriptions of the fund's investment approach, fees, and past performance in the first few pages.

The Securities and Exchange Commission (SEC), which governs mutual funds, has given funds permission to publish shorter, simpler versions of prospectuses. These so-called plain English prospectuses have less legal mumbo jumbo and are easier to understand.

If you want to understand what makes a fund different from the others offered by your plan, this is a key document to read. A prospectus will also give you a hint about a fund's future prospects. But a fund that's done well in the past may flop in the future. Chapters 14 through 21 will discuss how to make investment choices, and how to decide whether it's time to bail out of a mutual fund.

The annual and semiannual reports provide updated details about fund performance. Funds publish them each once a year.

Helpful Organizations

Many types of plan documents are available from the Department of Labor as well as from your plan. The DOL also publishes other pamphlets and brochures that explain your rights and how 401(k) plans work.

Most are available at no charge. For others, you have to pay a modest fee or copying costs.

Pension and Welfare Benefits Administration. The Pension and Welfare Benefits Administration is the part of the DOL that governs certain aspects of 401(k) plans. The regional office is listed in the U.S. government pages of your local phone book. Or phone the U.S. Department of Labor at 202-219-8233.

    ✔ The PWBA Web site address: http://www.dol.gov/dol/pwba/.

The Profit Sharing/401(k) Council of America. This is a nonprofit association of plan sponsors. It has been a longtime champion of 401(k) plans. You can purchase its pamphlet, "Take Control: How to Save Now for Retirement," for 50 cents. The PSCA's address is 10 South Riverside Plaza, Suite 1610, Chicago, Illinois 60606-3802. Or phone 312-441-8550.

    ✔ The PSCA Web site address: http://www.psca.org/.

Easy-to-Use Sources of Information

Plan documents are a good source of information about three things:

1. How your plan works and what its features are.
2. Financial summaries about your plan overall.
3. What makes your mutual funds tick.

The trouble is that they don't often enough explain those things in plain English.

As a practical matter, most plan members get information some other way. Most often, plan members rely on other people and on the battery of communication outlets operated by plan providers.

Here's what you can expect from each, with tips on how to get the most from them:

People. People fall into two categories: those with an official role in the plan, and everyone else. Neither always knows what they're talking about.

"One of the most sought-after sources of information is other people we call 'influencers,' " says Debby Mandelker, director of group-employee services for Merrill Lynch's 401(k) plan program. "They can be official influencers or unofficial influencers. Unofficial influencers are people other workers respect and trust. It might be a retail store manager. Or someone from the accounting department. Whatever the reason, these are the people everyone goes to for advice. We call it the watercooler strategy.

"Unfortunately, they're a dangerous source of information—or at least potentially dangerous—because they're not necessarily as knowledgeable as people think they are."

As a record keeper and plan provider Merrill Lynch deals with the reality of this phenomenon, rather than sticking its head ostrich-like into the sand.

"It varies by plan, but yes, where appropriate we make unofficial influencers part of training with official influencers," Debby Mandelker says. "You mainly want to make sure they thoroughly understand why the plan was implemented and what the real benefits of the plan are to themselves and others."

Take a tip from Merrill Lynch. If you seek out the office sage for advice about how your plan operates, any of its features, your eligibility for this or that, or whatever, find out how much he or she really knows.

Advice Is Only as Good as the Source

When it comes to seeking investment advice, be especially careful. Reliable guidance is built on knowing *specifics* about your individual spending goals, timetable, and stomach for risk. For anyone else to know that, you've got to be willing to spill your guts about intimate details concerning your financial life.

Rule of thumb: Do that only with a professional who knows how to analyze such information, or someone with whom you share intimate details of, say, your love life.

Otherwise, feedback you get around the watercooler is no more reliable than that other staple of watercooler conversations: gossip. That, too, is based on incomplete information, speculation, prejudice, jealousy, and hidden agendas.

In Chapters 14 through 21, this book will give you advice about how to make your own investment decisions.

How? Ask where their information comes from. Use your own common sense.

Beyond that, remember: Stick with people whose job is to provide information about your plan and your account. Bring your questions to the plan administration or someone in human resources (HR), benefits, or payroll. If they don't know the answer, they'll tell you. And they'll direct you to someone who does.

If you need to take your question to an official plan vendor like the record keeper, the trustee, or a mutual-fund family, they'll tell you whom to contact and how.

Telephone-Based Systems. Telephone systems using voice response and other technologies are becoming standard features of plans. About 65 percent of all plans use some form of interactive phone system now, according to the Profit Sharing/401(k) Council of America. Only a few years ago, 65 percent of all plans *didn't* use such systems, which are often called *interactive voice response (IVR) systems.*

The beauty of IVR systems is the wide variety of things you can do. You can initiate changes in or inquire about the status of such things as enrollment, contribution level, account balance, how your money is divided among investments, loan scenarios, and payouts.

Not all plans let you do all of those things by IVR system. Almost two-thirds of all plans let you at least check your account balances by IVR system, according to the PSCA. More than 90 percent of large-company plans have an IVR system that allows plan members to inquire about account balances.

On the other hand, only about 15 percent of plans let you enroll by phone rather than face-to-face.

IVR systems work by responding to voice instructions that you give or to numbers and letters that you punch in on a touch-tone telephone keypad.

About six out of every 10 plans have an IVR system that lets you reach a trained operator if you have a question the computerized system can't answer.

The convenience of these systems is that they provide access around-the-clock. Got insomnia? Instead of watching reruns of *Mr. Ed* on cable TV, you can check your account balances or transfer money from one investment to another at 3 o'clock in the morning.

But don't get carried away. IVR systems are not the same as 24-hour-a-day stock market trading by way of the Internet. You might not be able to buy and sell shares of stock or mutual funds instantaneously. And information you get may not be up-to-the-minute. In fact, it may be months out of date.

That's because your account balance may not be totalled every day. Your account *valuation* may be adjusted daily or weekly, or at some longer interval such as monthly, quarterly, semiannually, or even annually. That means your account balance is based on share prices at the end of that period.

Bear that in mind when checking your account balance or inquiring about how much money you can withdraw or borrow from your account (which is based in part on your balance).

Internet Access. This is the same basic idea as IVR systems, but with more computer-based features. Some features are educational, explaining the ins and outs of your plan. Other features have to do with investment decisions.

The earliest versions of these systems weren't even on the Internet. These worked with dedicated computer terminals set up in the workplace, like in the company cafeteria or in the human resources (HR) office. Many large plans still use such systems.

More up-to-date versions of such systems, which are on the Internet, give you access to account information and let you make changes in your account.

These systems operate on a World Wide Web site (most people simply call them Web sites) run by your company or someone like the plan record keeper or investment manager.

Some let you play what-if games with your account. Basically, those let you explore various ways of dividing your contributions among different investment options offered by your plan. For legal reasons, these Web site systems usually emphasize that they are providing an "educational" or "instructional" service rather than specific investment advice. A very small number also provide specific investment advice. Those are the systems that are willing to take on legal responsibility for offering specific investment advice.

Be careful! Often the line between the two is hazy.

Both systems usually let you do what is called *modeling*. That means trying test runs with your account, looking at how your account might grow over time if your money is divided among various investments.

Whether a system is educational or actually advisory, it works by having you plug in information on a computer work sheet. The information will concern things like your age, account balance, and number of years until retirement. Then, with different investments, the system will show you the likely outcome after a specified period of time. The hypothetical scenarios will vary, depending on the investments selected. That's because investments have different historical rates of growth.

Some systems will also help you figure out which investments are best for you, based on how well you put up with gyrations on the stock market, as well as your goals, time frame, and other variables.

Meanwhile, not all plans use Web site systems because of the cost, complexity, legal issues, and security concerns. (After all, you would be posting information you might consider painfully confidential in a system that still hasn't figured out how to prevent MIT freshmen from combatting late-night boredom by breaking into Pentagon computers.)

In any event, we'll help you learn to make investments decisions in Part Three of this book. And you won't have to worry about a nosy kid from MIT peeking over your shoulder.

Account Statements. Account statements summarize important information about your personal account. And you don't need a computer to use them.

Your plan's record keeper provides each member with a statement summarizing the status of his or her account. Statements are provided at intervals, usually automatically. Traditionally, they have been provided monthly, quarterly, semiannually, or annually. Plans with IVR systems and Web sites can provide much or all of the same information through those electronic media.

Don't worry, though. Even if your plan has an IVR system and a Web site full of wonderful bells and whistles, you'll still automatically receive a printed statement, according to Ken Williams, vice president and director of Merrill Lynch's benefits products. You can digest the statement at your convenience, then file it for future reference.

Printed statements are a simple way of keeping track of important information. Not all show the same things, but statements commonly show account balance, contributions, earnings on your investments, pay-outs (called *distributions*), and the names of your investments.

Some also show whether any of your money is from a rollover from another plan (for example, if you've changed jobs) or from company matching contributions.

Elementary, My Dear Watson

Sometimes it's hard to tell whether your company's matching contribution has been deposited in your account, especially since there can be a long lag time between when your contributions are deposited and when the matching contribution is. Some companies deposit their matching money only once a year.

The problem is compounded because not all statements specify how much of your account is from your company's matching contribution.

But simple arithmetic can help you keep track. Add up your own contributions plus all earnings. Subtract that amount from your balance. Add or subtract any withdrawals or loans and loan repayments. What's left should be the matching contributions and earnings, depending on exactly how your statement reads.

Always keep your statements. That way you can see how your account changes over time.

"Statements are becoming more educational," says Merrill Lynch's Williams. "They focus more on different segments of a person's life. Some statements now have information discussing allocation of your assets among different investments, how to decide whether your asset allocation is correct given your age, income, circumstances, and so on."

One innovation matches modern technology with old-fashioned statements. It's a step that recognizes how people are more comfortable with the familiar. "Some plans are getting ready to post people's account statements on the Web," says Williams. "Not just the information, but an image that looks like the old paper statement."

Pay Stubs. The stub of your paycheck is one of the handiest sources of information about your account. It shows how much is being subtracted from your pay and put into your account.

You almost always can use your pay stub to verify that the correct amount is being diverted. Simply multiply your pay by your rate of contribution. For example, if you are contributing 5 percent of your base pay, and your base pay is $770 a week, your pay stub should show that $38.50 is being diverted into your account.

That same amount should show up in your statements, where your account balance or new contributions to your account are listed.

Your stubs will probably also show a running total of your contributions for the year so far.

Other Sources. Plans use a wide variety of additional methods to keep you informed about the status of your account and to educate you about the value of participating and how to do it.

These other methods include group or one-on-one financial counseling; seminars and workshops; audiovisual presentations; videoconferences; take-home videotape instruction; and lots and lots of pamphlets, brochures, flyers, and newsletters.

Workshops and seminars, for example, will feature people from your workplace HR department, the plan record keeper, trustee, and investment manager. The helpfulness of these dog-and-pony shows will range from good to bad. Likewise, so will the quality of other instructional methods used by your plan.

IN OTHER WORDS . . .

Naturally, you'll get more out the instructional materials and methods used by your plan if you understand what the heck people are talking about.

Financial advisers who use Wall Street jargon, for example, might as well be speaking Sanskrit.

Some basic terms concern how your plan operates or the status of your account. Here are a few of them:

✔ *Prospectus.* It's important for you to read a mutual fund's prospectus. A prospectus is basically a sales brochure that explains a fund's history, managers, financial status, investment goals, and other data. Some of the most important information is on the first several pages: descriptions of the fund's investment approach, fees and expenses, and past performance.

Some funds now offer simpler versions—so-called plain English prospectuses that have less legal mumbo jumbo—in addition to full-blown renditions of prospectuses.

Your plan does not write the prospectus for any fund. Fund companies produce them and make them available to investors. Sometimes, for administrative reasons, funds offered by a plan may not deal directly with individual plan members. In cases like that, your plan will almost always provide you with a prospectus for any of your investment options or it will see to it that you can get one some other way.

✔ *Accrued Benefits.* This is the sum of your contributions to your account, your company's matching contributions, and their earnings. In the case of matching contributions, it includes everything—whether you're vested in it or not.

✔ *Elections.* This is a fancy word that means your choices or selections. Elections can refer to such things as the investments you've selected, your contribution rate, or the portions of pay you've decided to allocate to each of your investments.

✔ *Distributions.* These are withdrawals or payments from your account. This term is usually used to indicate a payout that is taxable, as opposed to a rollover or a nontaxable loan.

✔ *Transfers.* Money (or other assets) that you shift from one investment to another inside your account.

"SAFE HARBOR" AND OTHER JARGON

Whether you're attending a plan workshop or watching a videotape provided by your plan or reading some of the plan's deadly-dull official literature like the summary plan description, somewhere along the line you're liable to hear the terms *safe harbor* or *404(c) rules.*

Section 404(c) refers to a section of the Employee Retirement Income Security Act (ERISA). That's one of the key laws governing your retirement plan.

Safe Harbor Even when it is not directly responsible for providing you with a prospectus, your plan is likely to make sure you get any you need. It does that to reduce its potential future liability for lawsuits. It is seeking what is called *safe harbor* protection under government rules.

Companies don't like to talk about it, but one of their worries is that the plan they run will be sued by unhappy plan members. Companies sweat out the possibility that plan members will sue them if their plan investments turn sour, leaving members with smaller nest eggs than they expected.

Section 404(c) spells out what companies must do to reduce this danger. Your plan must give you enough power over your account so that you are not a helpless spectator, merely along for the ride. It can do that by meeting certain standards:

Control. Giving you authority over your investments.

Information. Providing you with enough information "to make informed investment decisions."

Choice. Offering you a wide selection of investments.

Maneuverability. Letting you switch investments.

In practical terms, those rules mean several things:

✔ You must be given three investment alternatives. Each should have different risk-and-reward characteristics. This is meant to reduce your chances of taking heavy losses throughout your entire account when any one part of the stock market tumbles. In other words, your plan is supposed to let you avoid putting all of your eggs into one basket. (Your plan may refer to the three alternatives as your "core" investment options.)

✔ You must be given investment instructions for your three core investment alternatives at least once every three months.

✔ You must be given an opportunity to bail out of volatile or risky investments into a safer alternative.

Many of the steps your plan takes to keep you posted about the status of your account and your opportunities for making changes in your account stem from these regulations.

Not all plans bother to comply fully with Section 404(c). But nearly all plans err on the side of caution (because their lawyers beg them to) by obeying 404(c) rules like the ones described above. That way they can still get some protection from potential future lawsuits. Taking those precautions entitles them to what the government calls "safe harbor" status or protection.

"Education" versus "Advice"

Your plan may hire an outside company to provide investment advice to plan members. Sometimes this adviser operates a Web site for plan members, where they can get information about their individual accounts and advice about how to invest their money among the plan's choices. One reason your plan hires an outside service like this is to try to provide the sort of specific advice that many plan members want. Another reason is to insulate itself from legal responsibility for what happens to those investments.

However, most mutual fund companies and other financial organizations still emphasize that they are providing only "educational" information (rather than investment "advice"). Educational information is supposed to enable plan members to make their own investment decisions. It also reduces the legal liability for the financial organizations.

INFORMATION BLIND SPOT

We started this chapter by comparing your plan to a jet airliner. It can be a marvel of modern organizational expertise—so many people doing so many things to get you to your goal: retirement with a big nest egg.

But airline travel is not perfect. Cramped seating, lousy food, and long waits at the airport are among the drawbacks. Equally, 401(k) plans have their own shortcomings.

One of the most important concerns costs that eat away at your gains.

Basically, if your plan is like most it probably does a lousy job explaining the fees and expenses that you and other plan members pay.

Typically, you and other plan members pay many of the costs directly associated with your investments. If you invest in mutual funds, you'll find their fees and expenses listed in their prospectuses.

But banks and insurance companies are not required to disclose information as explicitly as mutual funds (and even mutual fund disclosure falls short when it comes to simplicity and clarity). So, fees and expenses you pay for investments like annuities often are not spelled out.

Administrative costs are another problem area. Much of the administrative cost of running the plan is generally picked up by the plan itself. But many plans are gradually shifting such overhead bills to plan members.

For those reasons and more, the Department of Labor is considering whether to require better disclosure of fees and expenses.

Test Your Plan by Testing Yourself

Regardless of whether the government creates new disclosure rules, ask yourself whether you understand exactly how much money your account earned last year. Also ask whether you can say exactly how much you paid (as opposed to how much the plan paid) in fees and expenses. Can you describe both of those in plain English and simple arithmetic? If you can't, ask your plan administrator why your plan does not require easier-to-understand reports that show your individual bottom line in terms of costs and earnings.

BOTTOM LINE

Technology is making it easier for plans to provide you with more information, more often. Experience is teaching plans how to provide easier-to-understand information about your account and how your plan works.

The toughest part, though, is figuring out how to invest your money. That's what we'll discuss in Part Three of *Getting Started in 401(k) Investing*.

But first, the final chapter in Part One will explain the dos and don'ts of taking payouts from your plan, and Part Two will show you how to set your investment goal.

Chapter 8

How to Withdraw
Your Money

A 401(k) plan is like the neighborhood ice-cream truck. The best part is when you open it up and take out the goodies!

You have seven basic choices for ways to take money out of your plan. Earlier, we discussed two that may be used before you retire: borrowing from your account (Chapter 4) and making a hardship withdrawal (Chapter 5).

In contrast, the remaining five methods provide cash for living expenses during retirement or let you stockpile your money for future use. Generally, these are how you can handle your money:

1. *Rollover.* Roll your money over into an IRA.

2. *Lump Sum.* Take your money out in a single lump sum.

3. *Status Quo.* Leave it in your company plan.

4. *Random Withdrawals.* Take money out as you need it.

5. *Annuity.* Arrange for your money to be paid out in installments.

Unlike loans and hardship withdrawals which deplete your account before the intended time, these ways of handling your account upon retirement are rewards that you can look forward to with satisfaction.

However, not all five options may be available to you. And some may be better ideas than others, depending on your circumstances. Precisely which you choose will depend on three considerations:

Warning! Use with Caution

Borrowing from your account and a hardship withdrawal are ways to dip into your retirement cache during your working years. That's when you're still contributing to your plan and making it grow.

    But that's their drawback: They interrupt the flow of contributions and growth of earnings. That's why they should be done as infrequently as possible—if ever. If you're between a rock and a hard place, with no other money resources, you can use them as last resorts for covering a financial emergency.

---

1. Your plan's rules and restrictions.

2. How much money you need annually during retirement.

3. Your strategy for making your nest egg last as long as possible.

Your plan's rules and restrictions are the first thing to deal with in sorting out your choices. That's what we'll deal with next in this chapter.

How much money you need each year is more complicated. For one thing, what you need and what you can afford may be two very different things. But you've known that since about the age of 12.

It no doubt became (distressingly) clearer with every degree you earned, every apprenticeship you served, every job you went after, every promotion you got, and every promotion you didn't get. And then there are the grocery bills you've paid, apartment rent checks you've signed, mortgage payments you've made, vacations you've kissed off for the sake of children's expenses.

So, you may need to compromise between what you want and what you can afford. No surprise there. We'll discuss how to estimate your retirement expenses as well as income, and then form a budget, in Chapters 10, 11, and 12.

Fortunately, how much you can afford is not an open-and-shut question. You can enlarge your nest egg by following certain strategies. Likewise, there are steps you can take to make your nest egg (whatever its size) last longer.

In fact, both of those are goals that you should embrace.

How to spend your nest egg should not be the only thing on your mind as you approach retirement. If it is, you'll doom yourself to having less money.

Spending *and* conserving it should be your dual targets. Your focus should be as much on how to keep the bulk of your nest egg growing while you spend only as much as you need for immediate expenses.

We're not talking about going on some drastic frugality kick—wearing clothes from rummage sales, buying beans in 30-gallon cans, and bartering for service with your dentist. (Although scaling back *is* a normal part of retirement. And taking simple steps to economize can be practical and painless. There's no shame in downsizing your home, and cutting down from two cars to one need not be inconvenient, for example.)

What we're talking about are ways to keep your retirement account growing. Handling your account upon retirement does not—*must not*—mean stashing all of it in a checking account. It may be handy there. But it won't be working. You're the one who deserves to retire. Not your money.

Your dollars should remain hard at work, so you can afford to kick back and enjoy your Golden Years.

To do that, you've got to select the right investments. We'll explain how to do that, starting in Chapter 14.

First, let's look at the basics of what to do with your money after retirement.

IRA ROLLOVER

This is by far the most popular way to handle money from a 401(k) plan after retirement. About half of all retirees roll their money over into an IRA, according to Spectrem Group.

It's no wonder. By moving your money or investments into an IRA, those assets can continue to grow tax-free.

Further, you are free to invest your money in ways you might not be allowed to in your 401(k) account. You can choose any mutual fund you like, for example, not merely the ones offered by your plan. You can also shift money from one fund or stock to another more frequently than your plan may permit.

Meanwhile, you can withdraw money whenever you want.

You must, however, make sure you take one all-important precaution. You must arrange a direct rollover of your money. Your plan should move your money directly to the custodian of your IRA, whether it is a bank, mutual fund, or some other financial institution.

This may be called a trustee-to-trustee transfer or rollover. The concept is simple. Only your plan and the institution where your money is headed should touch the money.

You should not. Don't take personal possession of the money. And under no circumstances should you accept a check payable to yourself. Otherwise, the rollover is liable to become a taxable payout.

You'll be hit with taxes—federal and possibly state and local as well. If you're under age $59\frac{1}{2}$, you'll also risk getting slapped with a 10 percent early-withdrawal penalty. As if that's not bad enough, you won't even see the entire amount. Your plan will withhold 20 percent of it on behalf of the IRS as a down payment against taxes due.

Unless You're a Glutton for Punishment . . .

If you do take personal possession of your IRA money, you don't get hit with taxes right away. You've got 60 days to get a grip on yourself and deposit the money in an IRA. If you act within those 60 days, you'll sidestep the taxes.

Nevertheless, you'll still have to part with the 20 percent withholding portion. You'll eventually get that back. But why trigger a lot of paperwork and hassle for yourself in the meantime?

Further, if you slip up and miss the 60-day deadline, it will be a costly error.

It gets worse. Even though your plan withholds 20 percent for the IRS, the IRS nonetheless demands that the full amount of the payout must make it into the IRA. From some other source, you've got to come up with an amount equal to the 20 percent withholding and put that into the IRA along with the 80 percent you have from your plan.

No excuses allowed. If you don't put the full amount into your IRA, you can expect a tax bill from Uncle Sam on the missing amount.

That means if you move the money yourself, instead of arranging a direct rollover, you'll need to have 120 percent of your account's original balance.

If you are careful about avoiding unnecessary taxes, a rollover into an IRA can give you the investment flexibility previously mentioned. But there's another possible trade-off.

If you retire completely and don't get a paycheck, you can't contribute to your 401(k) account even if you leave it in your former workplace's plan. You won't be able to kick in anything to an IRA either. That's because the yearly contribution limit is whichever is less: $2000 or 100 percent of your pay. Result: a draw.

But what if you do work after retirement at your old company or another workplace where you can participate in a 401(k) plan? The $10,000 annual ceiling on 401(k) plan contributions enforced by Uncle Sam is obviously higher than the $2000 IRA cap. The amount you can actually contribute may depend on your pay. But the potential advantage lies with a 401(k) plan.

The best course of action may involve a combination of the two types of retirement accounts. You are allowed to contribute to any combination of traditional, Roth, and SEP-IRAs. But you can't contribute more than $2000 a year overall.

SEP-IRA   These are retirement accounts that generally work the same as a regular IRA, except more money can typically be contributed each year. Known formally as Simplified Employee Pension Plans, these are often used by small companies and self-employed people. Instead of making your own contribution, money is contributed by your business or employer. And instead of the $2000 annual contribution limit on a regular IRA, your company is allowed to contribute up to 15 percent of your pay or $24,000, whichever is less.

You can also contribute to both a 401(k) and an IRA the same year, and whatever you put into one does not count toward your annual contribution limit in the other!

If you can afford it, you can shovel the dollar bills into both types of accounts.

Because a 401(k) plan has a higher potential limit and likely offers you a company match, you should contribute to that first. If you max out your annual contribution, then you should contribute to an IRA.

You can start your IRA with new money, or roll over money from your 401(k) account.

Once you reach age $70\frac{1}{2}$, the 401(k) plan has a clear edge. That's because you aren't permitted to contribute to a traditional IRA past that age. As long as you earn a paycheck, though, you can contribute to a 401(k) plan.

Likewise, you must begin to take payouts from a regular, deductible IRA by age $70\frac{1}{2}$. That starts to deplete the account. In a 401(k) account, however, you can leave all of your money at work, growing through earnings, so long as you are a paid worker.

Advantages of a Rollover

- You have easy access to your money and more control over the timing and size of payouts.
- You get a wider choice of investments in an IRA than you'd have by keeping your money inside most 401(k) plans.
- Earnings on your money are tax-free until you withdraw them. This lets your money grow faster than it would in the same investment(s) but outside an IRA or 401(k) plan.
- You incur no taxes or penalty if your money is transferred by a direct rollover or within 60 days.
- You have the opportunity for extra tax-deferred savings in combination with 401(k) plan contributions.

Disadvantages of a Rollover

- Your payout is taxed if it is not deposited into your IRA within 60 days.
- If your money is not deposited within 60 days, you risk a 10 percent penalty if you're not at least $59\frac{1}{2}$ years old and don't qualify for an exemption.
- While you're still eligible to deposit money, the annual contribution limit is lower than in a 401(k) account.
- Mandatory withdrawals start at age $70\frac{1}{2}$.
- Contributions are barred beyond age $70\frac{1}{2}$.

TAKING YOUR MONEY IN A LUMP SUM

This is how to get your hands on all the cash in your nest egg: Take your money out all at once. A lump sum payout is the feel-good option. You can do whatever you want with the money. Spend it, invest it, put on your bikini bathing trunks and roll around in a pile of dollar bills.

Dinars, Moolah, Greenbacks . . .

In benefits lingo, money that is taken out of a 401(k) plan is called a *distribution.*

We prefer plain English. Generally, we call money you withdraw a *payout.*

When you move money or investments from your 401(k) account to an IRA, that's a *rollover.*

No wonder this is the second most common course of action by retirees, according to Spectrem Group. Some 28 percent of workers picking up the proverbial golden watch take all of their money—and run.

However, there is one humongous drawback.

When you take money out of your plan (rather than having it transferred directly into another tax-deferred account like an IRA), it becomes taxable income. You will lose a huge chunk of it to taxes.

If you take out, say, $20,000 to purchase a car, the IRS will take a bite. If your state taxes personal income, you will owe state taxes too. You may also owe local taxes.

Worse, if you are younger than $59^1/_2$ you are likely also to be hit with a 10 percent early-withdrawal penalty. (More about that later.)

All tolled, you'll be left with a lot less than $20,000. All of sudden, this option no longer feels quite so good. It's more like the "Ouch, it hurts" option.

So don't leap at this choice. Nevertheless, if you have a need for cash that justifies the tax hit, this is the alternative to use.

Advantages of a Lump Sum Payout

- You can use your money any way you wish. You can spend it, invest it, or do some of each. Whatever you eventually do, in the meantime you'll have easier access to your money.

- No matter how many investment choices your plan offers, you'll almost certainly have even more options outside your plan. You'll be able to choose any type of stock, bond, or mutual fund; any insurance product, savings account, or sophisticated investment like a stock option.

- You'll also become eligible for certain helpful tax strategies such as forward averaging.

Disadvantages of a Lump Sum Payout

- Succumbing to temptation, you might spend the whole wad or a big chunk of it. When you wake up the morning after, you'll be stuck with the worst of both worlds—a big tax bill on the lump sum, as well as long-term worries about how you're going to pay for the rest of retirement after depleting your savings.

- You must pay taxes on your payout.

- A payout prevents your money from growing inside a tax-deferred account like your 401(k) or an IRA. You not only lose part of your nest egg to current taxes, but you also lose part of its future earnings.

- You incur a 10 percent penalty if you're not at least $59\frac{1}{2}$ years old and don't qualify for an exemption.

A lump sum payout is not all doom and gloom. One potential boon is that you become eligible for a special tax-reduction maneuver called *forward averaging*. There are two versions of forward averaging: five-year and ten-year.

Five-Year Forward Averaging

Five-year forward averaging allows you to have your lump sum taxed at a lower rate than normal, as if you had received it over five years rather than in one. Only the rate is reduced. The tax is not spread out over five years. It remains payable in a single year.

What happens is that the taxable portion of your lump sum is divided by five. (Your whole lump sum is taxable unless it includes money from after-tax contributions.) Using the single taxpayer rates, a tax is computed. Then the tax is multiplied by five. That's how much you pay for the year you took the lump sum.

This tax break is limited to your lump sum. It can't be used on any other earned income you have. It also can't be used to reduce taxes on money from an IRA, 403(b), or 457 plan.

Other restrictions:

✔ To be eligible, you must be at least $59^1/_2$. Generally, you must also have been a member of your 401(k) plan for five years or more.

✔ You must be no longer employed by your company.

If this technique sounds too good to be true, that's because it is. Congress is phasing it out. You won't be allowed to use it for lump sum distributions received after December 31, 1999.

No matter how attractive a tax-cutting strategy seems, don't be seduced with your eyes closed. Remember, the important thing is the bottom line.

Inside a 401(k) plan or an IRA, your money can continue to grow without being taxed. In the long run, your money might earn more than the amount you save on taxes through forward averaging. In that case, you'd be better off leaving the money in your plan or an IRA.

Rule of thumb: If you don't need your money right away for a specific expenditure like a down payment on a retirement condo, don't expose it to taxes. It's a waste of money you worked very hard to earn.

Another Legal Tax Loophole for Your Lump Sum

The kissing cousin of five-year forward averaging is *ten-year forward averaging*. Despite the family resemblance, however, there are two key differences:

1. You are allowed to use this tax break only if you were born before 1936.

2. It is *not* scheduled for extinction on the first day of the new century.

Otherwise, it works the same as five-year forward averaging. Because it is not being phased out, it is worth describing in more detail:

✔ It can be used to reduce the tax bite only on the lump sum from your 401(k) plan. It can't be used on pay from a job if, for instance, you work part-time after retirement.

✔ If you use averaging, you must use it on the entire lump sum distribution.

✔ Likewise, you must use it on your entire account balance. You can't roll over part of it into an IRA and use forward averaging only on the lump sum distribution.

✔ Not only that, but you've got to use it on all the lump sums you receive that year from similar, tax-deferred retirement plans (like an IRA).

✔ The smaller your distribution, the more beneficial forward averaging is. Forward averaging's formula gradually tapers off its tax-rate reduction as it applies to larger distributions.

✔ Forward averaging uses 1986 tax rates, not current ones.

✔ It's a once-in-a-lifetime benefit. Once you use it, you can never use it again.

LEAVE YOUR MONEY IN YOUR COMPANY PLAN

If your plan's rules permit, you can leave your money in your 401(k) account.

The balance continues to grow without being taxed. Because you have to do little or nothing to arrange this, this way of handling your nest egg offers you no-muss, no-fuss convenience. You get other advantages as well.

With your money tucked away inside this private tax shelter, you don't have to pay taxes or penalties.

Unlike someone arranging a direct IRA rollover, you don't have to bother with paperwork and phone calls. And unlike someone scrambling to complete a rollover, you aren't staring down the barrel of a gun cocked to fire a barrage of taxes and possible penalties if you fail to beat the 60-day deadline.

The litany of advantages goes on:

You can continue to work with a familiar plan structure and rules, choosing among familiar investment options.

If you continue to work and earn money, you probably will still be eligible for a matching contribution from your company. While other retirees will have to depend on stretching their Social Security checks, you'll be enjoying extra earned income. Not only is it a paid bonus from your company, but it's also tax-free while it remains inside your account.

Unlike a traditional IRA, that applies to all the money in your account past age $70\frac{1}{2}$. You can leave your money inside your tax-sheltered account so long as you continue to work and earn money. Part-time is sufficient. This means you don't have to start depleting your nest egg. Once you finally do stop bringing home a paycheck, you'll be living off a larger retirement bundle.

Likewise, you can continue to contribute to your account past age $70\frac{1}{2}$ if you remain a paid worker. In all likelihood, this means you'll still be able to collect those wonderful company matches too.

Not least of all, you'll probably still be eligible for other goodies on your plan's menu like borrowing from your own account. Perks like this, however, could be curtailed by your plan's rules.

Explore Your Future Possibilities

If you'd like to be able to take advantage of optional features like an account loan after retirement, lobby for it before retirement if it's not already permitted. You may persuade your plan to change its rules. Then again, what if your plan withholds certain privileges from retirees to save money? Or to encourage retirees to live within a limited-income budget? Once you hear your plan's reasons, you may come around to its side.

If you take a postretirement job at some other company, you may want to roll over your 401(k) account into your new workplace's plan.

Your right to do that will depend on your new company's 401(k) rules. Not every place permits this. If it is allowed, *how* you move it may depend on your *old* plan's rules.

Also, you'll have to deal with questions like, "Does my new plan offer the same investments?"

If not, you may have to divert some or all of your investments into an IRA.

Further, you may have to wait until you're eligible to join the new plan before you can shift assets from the old one.

If there's a lag between when you leave one plan and join the other, you may have to park your money or investments in a *conduit* IRA. Keeping your old plan assets separate from other assets may be a requirement for transferring them into a new plan.

So, leaving your nest egg alone offers continued tax protection, ease and convenience, possible access to other plan features, the comfort of familiarity, and freedom from restrictions on contributions and payouts that kick in on traditional IRA accounts at age $70^{1}/_{2}$.

That's why this course of action is the third most popular way of handling an account upon retirement.

Having to work with your former employer, which may be time-consuming at best and as unpleasant as a root canal at worst, is no doubt what prevents this from moving up in the nest egg disposition sweepstakes.

Advantages of Leaving Money in Your Plan

- Your money continues to grow without being taxed.
- The investment options are familiar.
- The plan rules and personnel are familiar.
- There's a possibility of using plan features like borrowing from your account.
- There's a possibility of receiving a company match if you don't retire completely.
- You are exempt from starting payouts at age $70^{1}/_{2}$ if you continue to earn pay.
- You are free to continue contributions past age $70^{1}/_{2}$ if you continue to earn pay.

> ### Disadvantages of Leaving Money in Your Plan
>
> - You'll be restricted to the investment choices offered by your plan.
> - You'll have to deal with your former employer, which may be inconvenient or unpleasant.
> - In comparison to a traditional IRA, it will probably take more time and effort to do things with your money like make withdrawals or shift money from one investment to another.

PAYOUTS WHENEVER YOU WANT

Keeping your money in your (old or new) company plan has another potential advantage. You may be permitted to take payouts of any size, whenever you want.

Plan rules must spell out what types of payouts are allowed. But those rules can permit or prohibit any types of payouts. If random amounts at any time get the green light, you can take them.

Payouts of any size, any time are the ultimate in convenience. Unfortunately, most plans will not let you take them. Free-form payouts entail too much paperwork and expense. The convenience, it turns out, is all yours—not theirs.

In any event, once you take money out of course it becomes taxable as income. And if you're not $59\frac{1}{2}$ or don't meet other exemption requirements, you may have to pay a 10 percent early-withdrawal penalty.

INSTALLMENT PAYOUTS

Installment payments are a form of financial balancing act. You arrange for periodic payments of roughly equal size. Meanwhile, the rest of your money remains at work, growing so it can last as long as possible.

There are three basic ways to go about this. One is buying an annuity, probably from an insurance company. The insurer takes your lump sum and pays you a pension check, perhaps monthly. The insurer takes on the task of deciding how to invest the money. You get the convenience of routine payments. But the insurer also gets to keep the difference between what it pays you and what the money earns. That's its profit and incentive.

You can also take installment payments from your 401(k) account if your plan's rules permit.

Similarly, you can arrange for installment payments after a rollover to an IRA.

Whether you buy an annuity or arrange for annuity-style installment payments, the government lets you choose any of three formats for these periodic, roughly equal payments. (More details in the next chapter.) It doesn't matter if you're taking payments from your 401(k) account, from an IRA after a rollover, or by purchasing an annuity.

Advantages of Installment Payments

- You avoid suffering a large tax bite from a lump sum payout.
- For the same reason, you avoid the "lottery syndrome": blowing your lump sum on impulse spending you can't really afford. Linda Gelfand, a Goffstown, New Hampshire, financial planner, cautions: "All you end up with is a huge tax bill and long-term worries about having enough money for the rest of your retirement."
- You control the money and investments inside your 401(k) account or IRA.
- The balance inside your 401(k) account or IRA continues to grow without being taxed.
- You may be able to change the size and timing of payments.
- If you leave your job after age 55 but before $59\frac{1}{2}$, you may be able to take installment payments without having to pay the usual early-withdrawal 10 percent penalty. (See the next chapter.)

Beware of the drawbacks, if you lock yourself into a commercial annuity.

First, inflation will erode the purchasing power of your monthly payment. A fixed payment of, say, $1000 a month today will be worth less in 10 or 15 years. Few companies offer cost-of-living increases in their annuities.

Second, an annuity contract is unlikely to provide an inheritance to your loved ones. If both you and your spouse die soon after retirement, for example, the balance between what you paid for the annuity and the benefits paid to you is unlikely to go to your children or grandchildren.

Third, you lose control over the money. Once you pay all or part of your nest egg to the annuity provider, it calls all the shots. How to invest the money is up to that financial firm. Your ability to borrow from your account is severely curtailed or ended altogether. It's the annuity provider's money, not yours.

Disadvantages of Installment Payments

- You'll owe taxes on each installment payout.
- If your payments are too large, you may run out of money too soon.
- By buying an annuity, you may be sacrificing control over your money and the ability to make it grow more.
- You diminish or end your chance to leave an account balance as an inheritance for loved ones.
- Inflation erodes the purchasing power of a fixed annuity over time.

Types of Annuities

Generally, annuities are based on life expectancy of one or more recipients. Here are some of the major basic versions.

Single-Life Annuity. This form of annuity is based solely on your lifetime. Generally, it offers the largest individual, periodic payments. But the payments continue only while you're alive. They stop when you die. Your survivors are left with nothing. A married person who wants to use this method must get his or her spouse's signed agreement. These are called single-life, life-only, or straight-life annuities.

Joint and Survivor Annuity. Payments continue for as long as either you or your beneficiary (who may be your spouse) lives. Because this method provides income for a time period that is likely to be longer than the single-life annuity method, payments almost certainly are smaller than the other method's. Also, payments typically get smaller after your death.

The size of payments to your beneficiary will depend on how large the initial payments are to you. They'll also depend on the age difference between you and your beneficiary.

Life Annuity with a Term Certain. This version provides payments for an agreed-upon time (the *term certain*). If you die before that period ends, payments continue to your beneficiary.

The longer the agreed-upon time period, the smaller your payments will be. On the other hand, your beneficiary's age does not reduce the size of any payments that continue after your death. Also, with this method you can name more than one beneficiary.

These are also known as period certain or guaranteed payment annuities.

Because your spouse does not get lifetime benefits, his or her signed agreement is required.

BOTTOM LINE

You can choose among several ways of handling your money after retirement. Some involve removing it from your account, while others don't. You can expose all, part, or none of it to taxes, depending on which course of action you take.

Your decision may be influenced by tax rules that depend on your age, circumstances, and method of payouts when you start to make withdrawals. We'll discuss those in the next chapter.

In Part Three of *Getting Started in 401(k) Investing* we'll discuss how to invest your money, before and after retirement.

Part Two

Setting Your
Financial Goals

How Much Money Will You Need?
Where Will Your Retirement
Income Come From?

There are three steps in 401(k) plan investing. The first is to understand how your plan works. Next, you need to measure how much money you'll need at retirement. Third is to achieve this goal.

How much you *need* is different, of course, from how much you *want*. How much you need depends on how much you're used to having. It also depends on your resources. The nest egg you can build up hinges not only on how you invest. It also stems largely from how much money you can put to work. So your income, savings, bingo-night winnings, and inheritance will go a long ways toward setting an upper limit on how much you can realistically aim for.

Only once you know how much you need and the size of your financial resources can you form a realistic game plan for investing.

In Part One of *Getting Started in 401(k) Investing* you learned how to understand your company plan.

In Part Two, you'll learn how to measure:

✔ How much money you'll need during retirement.

✔ Where your retirement income will come from.

✔ The size of the financial resources you can put to work for you, building that nest egg.

119

Together, those tell you where you want to go—your retirement-finance destination.

Finally, in Part Three you'll learn how to reach your destination. That will involve choosing and using an investment game plan. You'll learn how to pick investments that are right for you.

Let's turn to the issues in Part Two—measuring your financial goals and resources.

How Taxes Can Take a Bite from Your Payouts

ost people would rather do anything than think about taxes. Like take out the garbage. Or pluck their eyebrows. Or scrub shower-stall grout with a toothbrush.

Small wonder. The tax code is long and notoriously complex. The specific provisions concerning 401(k) plans alone take up volumes. But how the tax code affects payouts from your retirement accounts is unexpectedly simple to describe.

And it's important not to skip over this explanation. Understanding how to play by the tax rules can save you big bucks.

Basically, this is a game of dodgeball. The two potential stingers you're trying to avoid are taxes and penalties.

You get hit with taxes when you take your money out of a tax-deferred plan like your 401(k) account or a rollover IRA. When you take a payout, it becomes taxable income. You pay at whatever your ordinary income-tax rate is.

You get hit with a penalty when you do either of two things:

✔ You take your money or investments out *too soon*.

✔ You leave your money or investments in *too long*.

Like bothersome insects that appear only during certain seasons, these penalties are a nuisance only during two seasons of life: before age $59\frac{1}{2}$ and after age $70\frac{1}{2}$.

Between $59\frac{1}{2}$ and $70\frac{1}{2}$, penalties are pretty much irrelevant. Taxes are the only issue.

Uncle Sam's Carrot and Stick

Congress has given you a legal tax shelter: your 401(k) plan. Money you and your company put into it is tax-deductible (except for any extra, after-tax contributions you and your employer may make). And your money gets to grow without taxes whittling down its earnings.

Uncle Sam didn't give you those tax breaks on a whim. It's a trade. In exchange for letting you keep all of your money, Uncle Sam expects you to put it to work building a retirement cushion. You're not supposed to escape taxes only to blow it all on movie tickets, caviar, and new kitchen counters.

It's not that Congress has anything against Hollywood, sturgeon fishermen, or the makers of laminated plastic or polished granite. (Sure, some Congressmen scold Hollywood for its sex, violence, and generous contributions to Democrats—but that's not why Congress has created certain 401(k) plan penalties.)

The real idea is to keep you from begging on street corners in your old age. Your fellow taxpayers resent having to walk around you and your tin cup on their way into a restaurant. And their resentment can spell electoral defeat for those lawmakers.

So, to motivate you to save and invest for retirement, Congress holds out the carrot of tax favors. To keep you from wasting the opportunity, Congress wields a punitive stick.

BEFORE $59\frac{1}{2}$: EARLY-WITHDRAWAL PENALTIES

The punishment for withdrawing your money from your 401(k) account before age $59\frac{1}{2}$ is a 10 percent penalty on the amount withdrawn.

There are, however, five legal loopholes. You can escape that early-withdrawal penalty under any of the following circumstances:

1. You die or become totally and permanently disabled.

2. The payments are part of a series of substantially equal, periodic payments over the course of your life (or life expectancy) or the joint lives (or joint life expectancies) of you and your spouse or designated beneficiary.

3. The early withdrawals are used for medical expenses exceeding 7.5 percent of your adjusted gross income.

4. You were at least 55 years old any time during the year when you quit your job or were fired, laid off, or retired.

5. The early payment is to a so-called "alternate payee" designated by a court-ordered "qualified domestic relations order" (QDRO).

Take a look at each of those in a little more detail.

Death or Disability. Obviously, *death* is hardly a convenient tactic. If you do move on to that big retirement community in the sky, your death payments go to your beneficiary or estate.

Disability is according to the IRS's definition, which may differ from yours. Your gimpy knee from high school football almost certainly won't cut it. Generally, it's got to be something that keeps you from working, now and for the foreseeable future—maybe forever. As a result, you need your 401(k) account for living expenses.

Substantially Equal, Periodic Payments. This refers to annuity-type payments. By *periodic*, the law means the payments must be at intervals, such as weekly, monthly, or yearly. The payments must continue for more than one year.

You are permitted to start receiving such payments at any age but, with rare exceptions, if they are from a 401(k) plan (or another "company-sponsored" plan) you must no longer be working for that employer. (If the payments are from a non–company-sponsored plan like an IRA, where you work does not matter.)

Medical Expenses. The only medical expenses that count are those not covered by your medical insurance or some other reimbursement.

The allowable expenses include an air conditioner for allergy relief, guide dog for the visually impaired, and health-club dues when prescribed by a doctor for a medical condition. The IRS and the courts have even held that the cost of an Indian medicine man counts.

Expenses that aren't allowed include baby-sitter costs while you see a doctor, deprogramming services for a family member who joins a cult, a hair transplant, or legal expenses for a divorce even if it's on your doctor's advice.

Separation from Service. Quitting your job, retirement, or being fired or laid off are called being *separated from service* in benefits jargon. You qualify for this exemption if you go through any of those in the same calendar year you turn 55. You could be only 54 when separation occurs so long as you turn 55 later that same calendar year.

QDRO. We're talkin' divorce court here, folks. At least, that's the most common scenario. If your former spouse gets a share of your 401(k) account as part of a divorce decree, he or she is designated an "alternate payee." Your ex won't be hit with an early-withdrawal penalty if he or she gets that court-ordered payout before age $59^1/_2$.

Periodic Payments: A Closer Look

You've got room to maneuver with the second exemption just listed: substantially equal, periodic payments method. That's because there are several ways you can figure the size of your periodic payouts.

Having that control is important because each method will probably produce a different size payment. Which one you choose determines how quickly you deplete your retirement account.

You have your pick of three techniques. Each one uses life expectancy somewhat differently to calculate payments.

Here are your choices:

✔ Minimum distribution method.

✔ Amortization.

✔ Annuity.

The method you use will depend on your goals. If you don't need a lot of income from your account, you should use the method that produces the smallest annual payouts. That will help your nest egg last as long as possible. It will also reduce the taxes you pay on income from your account.

That's what the minimum distribution method does. It's especially useful for anyone who expects other sources of retirement income, or who can cut way back on spending. If you've won the state lottery, received a sizable inheritance, or can count on hefty monthly paychecks from a traditional pension plan, this may be your cup of tea.

On the other hand, if you need as much income as possible, you should choose the amortization or annuitization methods.

Minimum Distribution. This method not only lets you stretch out your nest egg the longest time, it is also the simplest to figure. It uses little more than life expectancy. All it requires is basic arithmetic.

You simply divide the amount in your retirement account by either the number of years you can expect to live or by the number of years you or your beneficiary (who may be your spouse) are expected to live. The life expectancy predictions are based on the IRS's own longevity tables or comparable tables used by insurers.

There are two techniques you can use to calculate your minimum distributions.

The *fixed-life* or *term certain* method is slightly simpler than the *recalculation* method. The latter method, as its name implies, requires you to recompute the amount of payout each year. (Both of these are explained in more detail later in this chapter, in the section discussing "Payouts after Age 70¹/₂.")

Amortization. This is the sort of calculation that banks use to figure out the size of monthly mortgage and interest payments for a given number of years. It determines equal payouts, factoring in your life expectancy (or the joint life expectancy of you and your beneficiary—whoever lives longer) at the time payouts begin and a "reasonable rate of return" on your money. The payouts are bigger—often much bigger—than minimum-distribution payouts.

However, the calculations are relatively complicated. If you think you want to use this method, consider consulting a financial planner or tax adviser.

Annuitization. This calculation is made by dividing your account balance by a monthly or annual number called an annuity factor. The annuity factor is based on life expectancy and interest rates acceptable to the IRS.

Like amortization, this will produce a larger payout than the minimum distribution method. That means it will reduce your nest egg to zero faster. Also like amortization, this is a calculation you might want to leave to a pro.

Escape Hatch

The drawback to using the substantially equal periodic payments method to start early payouts is that it begins to deplete your account.

Fortunately, there's an escape hatch. You are allowed to stop the payments after five years or when you reach age $59\frac{1}{2}$, whichever takes longer. Then you can let your money grow again, undiminished by payouts.

Whenever you start taking payouts again, you are free to use an entirely different method.

PAYOUTS AFTER AGE 70½

When you turn $70\frac{1}{2}$ Uncle Sam can lick his lips. That's because he may finally get his hands on some of your money, if you've kept all of it in your account this long.

The reason: You must start to take income from your 401(k) account by April 1 of the year after you reach age $70\frac{1}{2}$. If your 70th birthday is January 1, 1999, you must begin to take payouts by April 1, 2000. If, however, you turn 70 on, say, July 1, 1999, six months later would be January 1, 2000. You would not have to begin taking payouts until April 1 of the following year—2001.

What Happens If You Don't Begin Withdrawals

To prod you into obedience, Uncle holds the Sword of Damocles over your head: You'll be hit by a whopping tax penalty, relieving you of *50 per-*

cent of the amount you were supposed to withdraw but didn't! (In addition, any money you *do* withdraw on schedule will be taxed at the regular rate as ordinary income.)

Not only must you start to take payouts; you must also cease contributions. (Uncle Sam doesn't want to continue the tax giveaway on that money, either.)

Uncle Sam has patiently given you a get-out-of-jail-free card when it comes to income taxes on contributions to your account and their earnings. Now, at last, like the Godfather calling in a favor, Uncle wants his pound of flesh in taxes.

Uncle, however, is far more lenient than any Godfather. He provides two final tax breaks:

1. If you're still a paid employee (part-time will do) of the company where your account is, you are allowed to postpone payouts until you actually retire. This lets your money continue to grow without being drained by payouts. And the balance can grow without being eroded by taxes.

   You must not own 5 percent or more of the company. (This is to avoid turning your 401(k) plan into a private tax shelter for a fat cat, who Congress says should fend for him- or herself.)

2. You can also continue to make contributions, so long as you are a paid employee.

Both legal loopholes apply only to company plans where you continue to work. They don't apply to plans with a previous employer or to IRAs.

These are major advantages of a 401(k) account over an IRA. If you are healthy, enjoy your work, and have the opportunity to work after retirement, you should bear this feature of 401(k) plans in mind when deciding whether to roll your account over into an IRA or leave it in your company plan. Remember, you may also have a shot at a matching contribution and participation in other plan features, such as borrowing from your account.

Size of Your Payouts

Okay, suppose you don't want to postpone payouts and taxes. Suppose you're ready to enjoy income from your account. After all, you worked your butt off all those decades to build up your account so you could in fact spend it someday.

Once you turn 70$^1/_2$ and start to take money out of your account, the law requires you to withdraw at least a certain minimum amount yearly. The amount is called your *minimum required distribution (MRD)*. The idea isn't to make sure you have enough to live on. The idea is to assure Uncle Sam adequate tax revenue.

(With your Uncle's blessing you are perfectly free to take out more than the minimum. After all, the IRS will be right there, counting your taxable income.)

To calculate the minimum allowable withdrawal, you've got to make two decisions:

1. Which of two methods you'll use to forecast how long you expect to live.

2. Which of two formulas you'll use for crunching the longevity-prediction numbers you select.

Picking a Longevity Table

Which method you use to forecast life expectancy depends simply on whether you have designated someone as your *beneficiary.*

Beneficiary   Your beneficiary is the person who has been named as the recipient of your account in the event you die.

If you have not designated a beneficiary, you will have to use a single-life forecasting table (Figure 9.1). If you have designated someone as your beneficiary, you must use the joint-life expectancy timetable (Figure 9.2).

"The decision has nothing to do with whether or not you are married," says retirement planner Clark M. Blackman II, regional director of

At This Age . . .	. . . You Are Expected to Live This Many Years More	At This Age . . .	. . . You Are Expected to Live This Many Years More
59	25.0	73	13.9
60	24.2	74	13.2
61	23.3	75	12.5
62	22.5	76	11.9
63	21.6	77	11.2
64	20.8	78	10.6
65	20.0	79	10.0
66	19.2	80	9.5
67	18.4	81	8.9
68	17.6	82	8.4
69	16.8	83	7.9
70	16.0	84	7.4
71	15.3	85	6.9
72	14.6	86	6.5

FIGURE 9.1 Single-life expectancy table. Based on how long Americans typically live, this shows how many more years of life the Internal Revenue Service expects you to have at any given age.
Source: Internal Revenue Service Publication 939.

Deloitte & Touche LLP's investment consulting group services. "You may be married and both you and your spouse may depend on the income. But if your spouse or other individual is not *designated* as your beneficiary, you must use the single-life table.

"Also, if your beneficiary is not a living person—such as a charity or nonqualifying trust—you must use the single-life table."

So, what's the difference? The difference is the consequences.

With a joint-life expectancy table, you can spread out your income payments over more years. Each payout will be smaller. As a result, your money will last longer.

You

Age	70	71	72	73	74	75	76	77	78	79	80	81	82	83	84	85
59	26.9	26.7	26.5	26.4	26.2	26.1	26.0	25.9	25.8	25.7	25.6	25.5	25.5	25.4	25.4	25.3
60	26.2	26.0	25.8	25.6	25.5	25.3	25.2	25.1	25.0	24.9	24.8	24.7	24.6	24.6	24.5	24.5
61	25.6	25.3	25.1	24.9	24.7	24.6	24.4	24.3	24.2	24.1	24.0	23.9	23.8	23.8	23.7	23.7
62	24.9	24.7	24.4	24.2	24.0	23.8	23.7	23.6	23.4	23.3	23.2	23.1	23.0	23.0	22.9	22.8
63	24.3	24.0	23.8	23.5	23.3	23.1	23.0	22.8	22.7	22.6	22.4	22.3	22.3	22.2	22.1	22.0
64	23.7	23.4	23.1	22.9	22.7	22.4	22.3	22.1	21.9	21.8	21.7	21.6	21.5	21.4	21.3	21.3
65	23.1	22.8	22.5	22.2	22.0	21.8	21.6	21.4	21.2	21.1	21.0	20.8	20.7	20.6	20.5	20.5
66	22.5	22.2	21.9	21.6	21.4	21.1	20.9	20.7	20.5	20.4	20.2	20.1	20.0	19.9	19.8	19.7
67	22.0	21.7	21.3	21.0	20.8	20.5	20.3	20.1	19.9	19.7	19.5	19.4	19.3	19.2	19.1	19.0
68	21.5	21.2	20.8	20.5	20.2	19.9	19.7	19.4	19.2	19.0	18.9	18.7	18.6	18.5	18.4	18.3
69	21.1	20.7	20.3	20.0	19.6	19.3	19.1	18.8	18.6	18.4	18.2	18.1	17.9	17.8	17.7	17.6
70	20.6	20.2	19.8	19.4	19.1	18.8	18.5	18.3	18.0	17.8	17.6	17.4	17.3	17.0	17.0	16.9

Your Beneficiary

130

Age																
71	20.2	19.8	19.4	19.0	18.6	18.3	18.0	17.7	17.5	17.2	17.0	16.8	16.6	16.5	16.3	16.2
72	19.8	19.4	18.9	18.5	18.2	17.8	17.5	17.2	16.9	16.7	16.4	16.2	16.0	15.9	15.7	15.6
73	19.4	19.0	18.5	18.1	17.7	17.3	17.0	16.7	16.4	16.1	15.9	15.7	15.5	15.3	15.1	15.0
74	19.1	18.6	18.2	17.7	17.3	16.9	16.5	16.2	15.9	15.6	15.4	15.1	14.9	14.7	14.5	14.4
75	18.8	18.3	17.8	17.3	16.9	16.5	16.1	15.8	15.4	15.1	14.9	14.6	14.4	14.2	14.0	13.8
76	18.5	18.0	17.5	17.0	16.5	16.1	15.7	15.4	15.0	14.7	14.4	14.1	13.9	13.7	13.5	13.3
77	18.3	17.7	17.2	16.7	16.2	15.8	15.4	15.0	14.6	14.3	14.0	13.7	13.4	13.2	13.0	12.8
78	18.0	17.5	16.9	16.4	15.9	15.4	15.0	14.6	14.2	13.9	13.5	13.2	13.0	12.7	12.5	12.3
79	17.8	17.2	16.7	16.1	15.6	15.1	14.7	14.3	13.9	13.5	13.2	12.8	12.5	12.3	12.0	11.8
80	17.6	17.0	16.4	15.9	15.4	14.9	14.4	14.0	13.5	13.2	12.8	12.5	12.2	11.9	11.6	11.4

FIGURE 9.2 Joint-life (or last survivor) life expectancy table. This table shows how much longer any two people are expected to live, starting at any given age combination. The couple can consist of you and your spouse (or whomever you've named as your beneficiary). In the case of a married couple, the table shows how long the surviving spouse is expected to live after his or her loved one's death. For example, when one spouse is 71 and the other 63, the odds are that one of you will live another 24 years. You'll find that longevity prediction where the column showing age 71 intersects with the row showing age 63.

Source: Internal Revenue Service Publication 939.

Choosing Your MRD Formula

Your annual MRD usually is calculated by one of two methods: the fixed-life method or the recalculation method.

The IRS's Crystal Ball

Like a thoroughbred race track tote board listing odds, the IRS posts its predictions of how long you'll live. (Hey, have sympathy for the agency! They can collect taxes longer from the living than from the dead.)

You can find their predictions in Publication 939. Table V lists the single-life forecast, which this book's Figure 9.1 is drawn from. Table VI shows you the joint-life forecast, which is the basis for Figure 9.2.

Fixed-Life. This is sometimes referred to as the term certain method. You divide the amount in your retirement account by your life expectancy—the number of additional years you expect to live.

Remember, your previous decision was whether you would use a single-life or joint-life expectancy prediction. That depended on whether your spouse or someone else is your designated beneficiary.

Well, once you get to this second decision—whether to use the fixed-life or recalculation method of number crunching—your "life expectancy" means either yours alone or yours jointly with your beneficiary. Joint-life expectancy is the forecast of how much longer either you or your beneficiary will live. Odds are that one of you will outlive the other—unless the two of you pull a Romeo and Juliet. So, joint-life expectancy is a longer period of time than single-life expectancy.

When you divide the amount in your nest egg by your life expectancy (alone or jointly), the number that results is the least amount of money you are allowed to take out each year.

With this fixed-life method of calculation, the number you divide into your retirement account is reduced by one each year. Suppose you're married and your spouse is your beneficiary. Take a look at Figure 9.2, the joint-life expectancy table. Let's say you begin to withdraw money at age 71 when your spouse is 63. As the table shows, the odds are that at least one of you will live another 24 years. So, you take out one-24th of your nest egg the first year. The second year, you take out one-23d of the remaining balance. The third year you withdraw one-22d. And so on.

Recalculation. This method is similar to the fixed-life method. It makes one important change, though. As with the fixed-life method, you divide the balance in your retirement account by your life expectancy (alone or jointly). But with this method you don't simply reduce your life expectancy by one each year. Instead, you do the arithmetic over each year, using the new life expectancy that the IRS recalculates for each year of age.

Look at Figure 9.2 again. In your second year of taking payouts, when you are 72 and your spouse is 64, you would divide your remaining nest egg by your life expectancy, 23.1 years, rather than the 23 years called for by the fixed-life method. In the third year you would divide the balance of your nest egg by 22.2 years, not 22. Those small differences mean you'd take out slightly less in your early years of retirement. But your retirement account could last longer. That's a benefit you'd certainly relish if you live longer!

Mixed Breed

You have another choice. There is a third technique you can utilize. It uses the fixed-life method for one spouse and the recalculation for the other spouse in a couple. This is a complicated process, though. You should consider letting your financial adviser put his or her calculator through its paces on your behalf.

One Calculation Is Generally Enough

Once you have determined the smallest amount the IRS will let you take out of your retirement account, it generally doesn't matter where your money is. Whether all of it is still inside your 401(k), an IRA, or a combination of the two, the minimum required distribution (MRD) is a total amount you must take out. You can take it out from one or several. The government doesn't care how you spread the "damage." The government cares only whether you ante up the correct amount.

Ain't Love Grand?

If you use a joint-life expectancy table, the bigger the age gap between you and your beneficiary, the more advantageous it can be. This is especially true if your beneficiary is younger than you.

That's because the younger your beneficiary is, the longer your joint life expectancy. Your payouts will be stretched out over a longer period of time. As a result, your nest egg will last longer.

That's good for the two of you.

But it means less tax revenue for the government.

The government does nothing about it if your beneficiary is your spouse.

However, if your beneficiary is not your spouse—suppose it is a grandchild—the government limits the size of the age gap you're allowed to use. You can't use an age difference wider than 10 years.

But in any matter involving the IRS, you can expect complications. After all, it was the IRS that tried to turn Mark McGwire's historic pursuit of the single-season home run record during major league baseball's 1998 season into a business transaction. The federal agency had threatened to slap a huge gift tax on whoever caught McGwire's 62d home run. (Common sense prevailed. McGwire did surpass Roger Maris and Babe Ruth. But the agency backed off following a torrent of political criticism.)

Sure enough, there is a potential complication to the MRD.

If you have designated different beneficiaries or selected different life expectancy calculations for various retirement accounts—whether they are 401(k)s, IRAs, or any other type of qualified plan—then different calculation rules may apply to each of them.

Either keep track and use whichever life expectancy table is called for by each account's designated beneficiary. Or call in the cavalry: Ask a financial planner or tax adviser to sort everything out.

Chapter 10

Living on Less

For the vast majority of people, retirement means living on less.

It shouldn't have to mean living less well.

Usually, retired people do have less income than they did before retirement. Your main question in tackling retirement planning isn't, "How do I get my hands on a lot of money?"

The real question to ask yourself is, "How much money will be enough?"

> "I don't want to be a millionaire, I just want to live like one."
>
> —Toots Shor[1]

The answer will depend on your circumstances. The day-to-day details of how you will live in retirement are different from everyone else's. You may prefer to walk to the store. Your neighbor drives a high-octane car. You may drink expensive, fresh-squeezed orange juice. Your neighbor enjoys tap water. You've got family to visit on the other side of the country. Your neighbor's family lives right here in the same town.

---

[1]John Gordon Burke, Ned Kehde, and Dawson Moorer, eds., *Dictionary of Contemporary Quotations*, rev. ed. (Evanston, IL: John Gordon Burke Publisher, 1987), p. 295.

"Everyone is different. A person's expenditures will rise or fall, depending on their needs and income," says Bruce A. Palmer, a Georgia State University (GSU) business school professor who studies retirement-spending patterns. "A person who worked at General Motors might have generous medical benefits after retirement, so they don't have to pay for that out of their own pocket. A person who retired from a small business might have to pay for their own medical coverage. Everyone's situation is different."

Many financial planners estimate 70 percent to 80 percent of your preretirement income will do the trick. Generally, three things will make up that 70 percent kitty: your 401(k) account; savings and other sources of retirement income, like a traditional pension plan; and Social Security.

Let's see how easy it'll be for you to reach that 70 percent level. Suppose your pay plus your spouse's amounts to $50,000. Seventy percent of that is $35,000.

Subtract from that the amount you expect to receive annually from your pension. If you don't know offhand, ask your employer's personnel or human resources director.

Then subtract the amount you expect to receive from Social Security. (For now, put aside your doubts about Social Security's prospects for survival. For planning purposes, let's work with what exists currently. Let Congress worry about what 76 million baby-boomer voters will do if it doesn't sustain Social Security.) To find out your likely monthly Social Security benefits, telephone the Social Security Administration (800-772-1213) and ask for a Request for Earnings and Benefit Estimate Statement.

The amount left over is how much you need yearly from your 401(k) account and all other sources of income. That, plus Social Security benefits and pension checks, must add up to 70 percent of your preretirement income.

PIECES OF THE PUZZLE

Let's say you're getting ready to retire soon. You're still working full-time and your household income (yours plus your spouse's) is $50,000. Figure 10.1 shows how the pieces to your retirement finance jigsaw puzzle must fit together, according to the latest study of retirement income needs by Palmer's Center for Risk Management and Insurance Research at GSU.

Preretirement Income	Percent Needed during Retirement	Percent Provided by Social Security	Percent Needed from Other Sources
$30,000	77%	54%	23%
40,000	72	48	24
50,000	69	41	28
60,000	67	36	32
70,000	67	31	36
80,000	68	27	41

FIGURE 10.1 Where your retirement income will come from. Most retirees need about 70 percent to 80 percent of their preretirement income. How much *you* need will depend on your own circumstances and lifestyle. This table shows how much retirement income typically comes from Social Security and how much is needed from a 401(k) plan and other sources for a married couple with one 65-year-old wage earner and a 62-year-old spouse. When both spouses are the same age, more of their retirement income comes from Social Security. A single worker depends more on his or her pension and savings income.
Source: Dr. Bruce A. Palmer, Center for Risk Management and Insurance Research, Georgia State University, Atlanta, GA 30302-4036.

To keep up your current lifestyle, you'll need 69 percent of your pre-retirement income. Right now you could expect $20,444 a year from Social Security. Those 12 monthly checks are the easiest parts of the puzzle to figure out. To reach that 69 percent goal, you'll need another $14,039 a year from your 401(k) plan, other savings, and any traditional pension benefits you may have coming.

Finding the non–Social Security pieces of the puzzle is tougher.

If half of that $14,039 is from a traditional pension plan, then the other half—$7020—must be from your 401(k) account and other resources.

"You'll need a portfolio with $99,000 in it to generate $7020 a year if your portfolio is earning 8 percent a year," says financial planner Dave England, of Waddell & Reed in Brookline, Massachusetts.

But hold on. You'll need more to clear real-world hurdles like inflation and taxes, year after year.

And how long do you want the nest egg to last? Twenty years? What if you live 30 years after retirement? What if inflation is higher than you expect? Or you haven't got a conventional pension? Missing pieces can spoil your retirement jigsaw puzzle.

To be safe, give yourself a cushy margin for error. That's like a jigsaw puzzle with extra, spare pieces.

"Shoot for a higher return on your investments and savings even after you retire," England advises, "or cut back on spending even more. It's no fun to wake up penniless on your 76th birthday."

Your options in that event? "Rob a bank," quips England, "or get a job."

Many do. Get a job, that is.

GETTING BY ON LESS

Getting a job is indeed one of your options. You also may do that for reasons other than income. You may enjoy your work. You may want to continue contributing to and participating in your 401(k) plan. You may take pride in keeping yourself busy and productive.

But your spending will surely decline once you retire. Getting used to that is the first step in coming to grips with how much money you'll need.

In fact, spending commonly begins to decline before retirement. People's expenses typically peak between their mid-40s and mid-50s, and then they fall. Figure 10.2 shows how householders whose income is $58,000 need less money beyond their mid-50s.

Through their peak spending decade, this typical couple needs more income for everything from their kids' orthodontic braces to the monthly rent or mortgage.

But look how spending slides downward after that. Life becomes less hectic, less expensive.

Spending on entertainment falls about 25 percent as those wild nights at the disco become a distant memory of youth and it becomes difficult to muster enough energy for a quiet night at the movies. Likewise, spending on clothes plummets. That's largely because the kids have fled the nest.

Typically, you're also finished paying college tuition bills for your children. Even your own housing costs start to ease as you and your friends become empty-nesters, trading large family homes for cozier quarters.

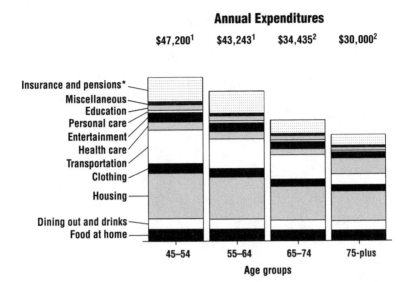

Annual Expenditures

$47,200[1] $43,243[1] $34,435[2] $30,000[2]

Insurance and pensions*
Miscellaneous
Education
Personal care
Entertainment
Health care
Transportation
Clothing
Housing
Dining out and drinks
Food at home

45–54   55–64   65–74   75-plus
Age groups

*Excludes investment income that is reinvested into
principal and is counted as income, not spending.

FIGURE 10.2 Spending declines as people age, even when their yearly income holds steady. Here's how a household with yearly income of $58,000 typically spends its money on major categories of goods and services at different age levels.
Source: [1]Bureau of Labor Statistics; [2]BLS and author's estimate.

Meanwhile, if your living expenses do decline while your income remains steady or rises, consider plowing that extra cash burning a hole in your pocket into your 401(k) account. After retirement, clothing costs tumble further. You don't need all those expensive business suits and outfits or factory uniforms. Your commuting costs evaporate. Expensive lunches with coworkers become a thing of the past. Your household's needs for a second car may end. Instead of paying taxes into Social Security, you start receiving checks from Social Security.

PLAN AHEAD

The most difficult thing about retirement may prove to be figuring out what to do with your time. You and your spouse will have to find ways to avoid tripping over each other. You'll have to make decisions about hobbies and part-time work.

As for finances, the first step is to get used to the idea of needing less income.

The second step is to figure out exactly how much income you'll need. That's what we'll tackle in the next chapter.

Measuring How Much Income You Will Need: Making Your Retirement Budget

Time for a pop quiz.

Question #1: Have you married the boss's daughter (or son)?
Answer: Yes ( ) No ( )

Question #2: Have you shamelessly brownnosed your way to the top?
Answer: Yes ( ) No ( )

Question #3: Have you succeeded the old-fashioned way—by ruthlessly scheming and backstabbing?
Answer: Yes ( ) No ( )

If any of your answers are yes, you may be able to skip to the next chapter.

Everyone else: Keep reading. This chapter is about coping with limitations.

You may want everything, but you know you can't afford it. Retirement will be the same. You'll live within your means.

Your ability to pay for things depends as much on the sum of your bills as it does on the contents of your billfold.

Your spending will decline during retirement; everyone's does. You'll need at least 60 percent to 80 percent of your present income after retirement. You may need close to 100 percent if, like more and more people, you are healthy when you retire and lead an active lifestyle.

Now it's time to figure out more precisely how much you will need.

You do that by calculating a budget for your first year of retirement.

FOLLOW THIS BLUEPRINT

To help you do that, divide the process into three parts. In the first, get a handle on your expectations in general. Take our lifestyle quiz to gauge how expensive your tastes really are.

In the second part, get more specific. Use one of our work sheets to list things you can spend less money on after retirement. Add up your projected savings. Use our other work sheet to list special spending goals, like contributing to a grandchild's tuition. See what your total expenditures could be.

Third, fill in the retirement budget. Remember, your retirement budget will change during retirement. Your spending will decline. You may take only one retirement cruise, for example. You'll probably buy only one boat.

But this will let you see how much money you're likely to need during your first year of retirement. Once you know that, in the next chapter we'll explain how to figure out how much money you need to put into your 401(k) account each year now, while you're still working and earning a paycheck.

MEASURING YOUR EXPECTATIONS

The budget process starts by figuring out *how* you want to spend money. Figuring out how *much* comes after that.

Generally, what type of lifestyle do you expect? Something fancy? Or something blissfully simple?

Have you positioned yourself for a country-club lifestyle? Or have you been looking forward to the day when you can unclutter your life, cut back on the complications as well as the bills, and enjoy life's common pleasures?

Maybe it's somewhere in between. You've never had a key to the executive washroom or a foreman's badge, and you don't expect either before you retire. You've been a team player and you've done okay. More money would be nice, but you'll do all right. You've got your self-respect and your friends. If you must economize in retirement, no problem. You'll eat out less or do without a second car.

You can get a handle on where you're heading by asking yourself those questions and by taking the quick quiz in Figure 11.1. Take it with your spouse, or take it separately if that will allow each of you to answer more candidly.

Your answers are self-explanatory. If "Expensive Goals" best describes what you want for your retirement, then obviously you are aiming for a similar standard of living to what you enjoy now, without cutbacks after retirement. You'll need more money than the two other quiz scenarios.

You can use this lifestyle exercise to get a feel for how much money you'll need. The quiz helps you estimate whether you'll need only 70 percent to 80 percent of your preretirement income, or more.

CUTTING BACK, SPENDING MORE . . . LET'S COUNT THE WAYS

Now let's get more specific by filling in the two work sheets.

In Figure 11.2, list five to ten things you expect to spend much less money on in retirement (such as work clothes, commuting costs, two cars, mortgage payments, union dues, and professional society memberships). Write down your estimated savings.

Use a pencil rather than a pen. As you make your what-if decisions, you may change your mind several times.

Then, in Figure 11.3, list five to ten big-ticket expenditures you want or expect to make.

Check your spending list again. Have you included everything you should?

✔ Will you take up new hobbies? Learn new skills? Either may require you to spend money for instruction, supplies, or memberships.

Do you want a retirement that's expensive, frugal, or something in between?

By clarifying whether your preferences lean toward filet mignon, London broil, or hamburger, you'll have a better idea how expensive your retirement will be.

Read the questions about retirement expectations and finances in each lifestyle summary, and then put a check mark in whichever one of the three columns describes you most accurately.

"Expensive Goals"

In retirement: Do you expect to fulfill fantasies and buy things you've always wanted? Take up hobbies? Attend adult education classes for the fun of it? Go to more ball games? Visit museums? Carry a mortgage the same size or bigger than the one you've got now? Visit foreign countries? Spoil the grandkids? Would you say your retirement savings, investments, and pensions are as plump as a piggy bank?

	Not at All	*Somewhat*	*A Lot*
That's you . . .			
That's your spouse . . .			

Next:

"Middle of the Road"

In retirement: Do you plan to live more or less the way you did before retirement? Do you plan to pay off your mortgage and live in the same home? Avoid major new financial responsibilities? Would you describe the balance in your 401(k) account as insufficient to put you on Easy Street?

	Not at All	*Somewhat*	*A Lot*
That's you . . .			
That's your spouse . . .			

Finally:

"Economizing"

In retirement: Will you seek a simpler lifestyle, with fewer financial obligations and a smaller house? Is it always a struggle to save for retirement, what with raising a family and keeping up with bills? Are you counting heavily on Social Security?

	Not at All	*Somewhat*	*A Lot*
That's you . . .			
That's your spouse . . .			

FIGURE 11.1   Great expectations? Your lifestyle quiz.

Things You'll Spend Less on after Retirement	Annual Cost before Retirement	Annual Cost after Retirement	Annual Savings
1.	$	$	$
2.			
3.			
4.			
5.			
6.			
7.			
8.			
9.			
10.			
Total savings	$	$	$

FIGURE 11.2 Economizing checklist.

Expensive Things You'll Spend More on after Retirement	Annual Cost before Retirement	Annual Cost after Retirement	Annual Added Spending
1.			
2.			
3.			
4.			
5.			
6.			
7.			
8.			
9.			
10.			
Total new expenses	$	$	$

FIGURE 11.3 Spending checklist.

✔ What about golf or a country club or a community center, where you can exercise and socialize? Perhaps you want to swim, do aerobics, play cards, or become a table tennis demon. Each of those may require you to pay membership or user fees.

✔ Do you plan to travel regularly or often once you're retired? How often? Where?

✔ Similarly, will you visit your family on a regular basis? Are they far across the country?

✔ Will you purchase a new home or second home to be near them? In a resort location?

✔ Will you relocate? Whether it's for a seasonal or permanent migration, a moving company will charge $5,000 to $15,000 to pack and relocate a typical household. A small truckload may cost you as little as $1,000; moving a large household, with many breakable valuables and art, can run $40,000 or higher. Don't forget to include any such expenses in your spending checklist.

Home Sweet Home

For now, assume your housing expenses will be the same or somewhat less if your mortgage is about to be paid off.

But empty-nesters taking off for a retirement community can reduce their housing expenses even more.

Most Sunbelt retirement communities have lower real estate taxes, energy costs, and utility bills than cities and suburbs in the North. Retirees can save 20 percent to 30 percent on their housing costs by moving there.

And don't forget to consider possible wish-list items like these:

✔ A new boat.

✔ A new car.

✔ A new home.

✔ Home electronics (big-screen TV, fancy audio-video home entertainment center).

✔ Recreation equipment (bicycle, stationary exercise bicycle, set of golf clubs).

✔ Gift of money for children or grandchildren (educational or home needs).

YOUR RETIREMENT BUDGET: FILLING IN THE BLANKS

Now you're ready to construct your budget for your first year of retirement (Figure 11.4).

Here are some helpful hints:

✔ Keep using a pencil instead of a pen. You may change your mind about some details as you go along.

✔ Fill in annual numbers for such things as gas for your car by figuring out how much you buy every week or two, then multiplying by the number of weeks or two-week periods in the year. Likewise, simply multiply your monthly rent or home mortgage payment by 12.

Expense	Now	After Retirement
Home		
Rent		
Mortgage principal (principal home)		
Mortgage interest (principal home)		
Mortgage principal (second home)		
Mortgage interest (second home)		
Homeowner's insurance		
Condominium fee		
Utilities:		
Electricity		
Natural gas and/or propane		
		(Continued)

FIGURE 11.4   Retirement budget.

Expense	Now	After Retirement
Utilities (*Continued*):		
Water		
Sewer		
Trash		
Phone		
Security		
Other		
Furnishings		
Appliances		
Maintenance		
Improvements		
Subtotal for this category		
Car and Other Vehicles		
Loan payments		
Lease payments		
Insurance		
Fuel		
Repairs and maintenance		
Registration		
Excise tax (if any)		
License		
Boat:		
Payments		
Insurance		
Fuel		
Upkeep		
Mooring		
Marina		
Other		
Subtotal for this category		
Health		
Medical insurance		
Life insurance		
Disability insurance		
Other insurance		

FIGURE 11.4   (*Continued*)

Expense	Now	After Retirement
Medicines		
Other medical		
Adult care (including nurse)		
Subtotal for this category		

Finance and Retirement

Contributions to your 401(k) plan

Spouse's contributions to a 401(k) plan (or another defined contribution plan like a 403(b) or 457)

Your additional contributions to an IRA (regular, SEP-IRA, Roth, etc.) or any other retirement plan

Spouse's IRA, Keogh, etc.

Social Security

Charge card #1 (total annual payments not in some other category)

Charge card #2 (total annual payments not in some other category)

Charge card #3 (total annual payments not in some other category)

Spouse's charge card (total annual payments not in some other category)

Savings deposits

Additional investments:
  Stocks
  Bonds
  Mutual funds
  Other

Bank and other financial services

Loans

Other

Subtotal for this category　　　　　　　　　　　　　*(Continued)*

FIGURE 11.4 *(Continued)*

Expense	Now	After Retirement
Lifestyle		
Food and drink (at home)		
Food and drink (dining out)		
Entertainment		
Clothing		
Cleaning and laundry		
Personal care		
Pet care		
Vacations		
Travel to visit family		
Recreation and hobbies		
Reading material		
Computer and software		
Education		
Allowances		
Gifts		
Other		
Subtotal for this category		
Other		
Alimony		
Child support		
Care for dependents		
Day care and/or nanny		
Domestic help and/or housecleaning		
Interest payments (nonhouse)		
Charity		
Union dues		
Moving		
Miscellaneous		
Subtotal for this category		

FIGURE 11.4   (*Continued*)

Expense	Now	After Retirement
Taxes		
Federal		
State		
Local		
Property		
Excise		
Subtotal for this category		
Total annual expenses		

FIGURE 11.4 *(Continued)*

TAKING THE NEXT STEP

After filling in this budget, you've got a good picture of how much you'll spend in your first year of retirement.

In the next chapter, you can fill in the Retirement Savings Work Sheet, which will show how large your nest egg must be to provide that much money. From that, you'll also know whether your savings and investments are up to the task.

If your savings and investments fall short, the Retirement Savings Work Sheet will show how much more money you need in your nest egg to generate enough income.

Chapter

How Much Money Do You Need to Save?

Use the Retirement Savings Work Sheet in This Chapter to Find Out

S ure, you look *mah-vel-ous* in a starched uniform. But trust us: At age 65 you won't enjoy learning how to smile while you say, "Would you like fries with that order, sir?"

It's far better to build your nest egg up to the right size than to be forced to explore the alternatives: a lower standard of living in your Golden Years . . . postponing retirement . . . part-time work.

And right now is the time to determine if you need to deposit an additional $10, $25, or $100 (ouch!) more a week to reach your savings goal.

After completing the budget in Chapter 11, you know how much money you'll need in your first year of retirement. That's probably about 70 percent of your current income.

Now the question is whether your 401(k) account will provide that much money. Will it be large enough?

One way to try to find out is by shelling out 50 bucks to your local tarot card reader. A less exotic but more reliable approach is to complete the work sheet in this chapter.

Don't worry. This work sheet demands no more math skill than opening a can of spaghetti requires you to be an Italian chef.

You don't need to be a certified public accountant or a Ph.D. in math to fill in the blanks. You don't need a computer or a slide rule to do its simple addition, subtraction, and multiplication. We'll lead you through everything step-by-step.

If it turns out that you do need to divert more from your salary into your investments, the work sheet will explain how much. If you can fix your shortfall by continuing to earn a paycheck, this will show you how much you need to earn.

Once you figure out whether you're contributing the right amount, you'll know whether you have to kick in more, work (part-time or whatever) after "retirement," or postpone retirement.

Basically, here's what the work sheet does:

- ✔ It starts with your first-year income requirement. (That's the bottom line from the previous chapter's budget in Figure 11.4.)
- ✔ From that amount, you'll subtract the Social Security benefit you expect.
- ✔ Then you'll subtract any income you expect to receive from a traditional pension plan.
- ✔ Also, you'll subtract any income you expect to receive from regular savings or investments.
- ✔ Next, deduct the estimated income from your 401(k) account.

If the result is zero, you've got enough. If it's a negative number, you're on track to have more money than you expect to need. If the amount left over is a regular, positive number, that shows you how much more income you need yearly. That's it.

HOW MUCH YOU NEED TO CONTRIBUTE

When it comes to your retirement nest egg, size does matter.

Our work sheet will show you how large your 401(k) account is on track to grow in any given period of time.

Then, subtracting any other sources of income you expect will illustrate whether your account will be large enough to cover the annual budget you created in the previous chapter.

You can fine-tune your calculation by plugging in the number of years until your retirement. That's important because your investments grow in value. They do that two ways: by providing income, and by rising in price. This growth is called the *rate of return*.

Rate of Return   Rate of return (or total return) describes an investment's growth. It's like interest paid on a bank account. But it also measures how much a stock, bond, or mutual fund's shares change in price up or down. That price increase or decrease, plus the investment's interest, dividends, or other income, is its return. The change is stated as a percentage rate, usually on an annual basis.

For example, suppose a mutual fund in your 401(k) account pays you dividends at the rate of 1 percent a year. Also, let's say the value of the fund grows 9 percent during the year. The fund's overall rate of return is 10 percent.

Also, the work sheet lets you play what-if scenarios by adjusting the rates of return on your investment. This way, you can see the potential impact of investing more aggressively. (We'll discuss why various types of investments perform differently, starting in Chapter 14.)

For starters, use whatever rate of return is earned by your existing investments. If you're not sure offhand how well they've done, use the following estimates. For the sake of caution, they are based conservatively on how some categories of investments have performed in recent decades.

✔ Mutual funds that invest in large U.S. corporations: 11 percent.

✔ Mutual funds that invest in small U.S. corporations: 10 percent.

✔ Mutual funds that invest in bonds: 8 percent.

✔ U.S. Treasury bills: 5 percent.

The work sheet lets you calculate the total amount or rate of money that must go into your retirement account. If the work sheet shows that you must invest $1500 a year and your employer contributes 50 cents for every $1 you contribute, then you personally need to invest $1000 of your own money.

Also, the work sheet makes the assumption that you'll use up your savings during retirement.

Don't paint yourself into a corner with an overly rosy forecast. Make conservative calculations, and assume you will live 10 years longer than you expect (or than the longevity tables in Chapter 9 predict). On your 83rd birthday, you'll be glad you still have extra money instead of not enough.

RETIREMENT SAVINGS WORK SHEET

Are you contributing enough to your 401(k) plan account? Complete this work sheet to find out.[1]

Line 1: How Much Annual Income Will You Need in Retirement?

Many financial planners estimate you'll need 70 percent to 80 percent of your current income after you retire. You can multiply your yearly income by whatever rate you think will be enough. Or use the bottom line from your retirement budget (Figure 11.4) in Chapter 11—your after-retirement total expenses figure. Fill in the appropriate amounts in Work Sheet Step 1.

$_____	(Current yearly income)
× _____	(70%–80%—or budget estimate in Chapter 11)
= $_____	(**Line 1:** Annual retirement income goal)

Work Sheet Step 1

[1]*Sources:* Carrie Coghill, D. B. Root & Company; author.

Line 2: What Other Retirement Income Are You Expecting?

How much of your retirement income can you count on receiving from other sources?

You can get a ballpark estimate of your Social Security benefit from Figure 12.1. In Work Sheet Step 2, fill in the yearly amount you expect from Social Security and any other income that will be adjusted annually for inflation. (That inflation fix is called a cost-of-living adjustment, or COLA.)

For a more precise estimate of your yearly Social Security benefit, either:

✔ Telephone 800-772-1213 and ask for a Request for Earnings and Benefit Estimate Statement.

✔ Complete and submit a copy of that request form at the Social Security Web site at www.ssa.gov/online. The Social Security Administration (SSA) will return your benefits estimate to your postal mail address.

✔ Submit a request form at a local SSA office. It takes the SSA up to six weeks to send your benefits estimate to you.

Social Security Eligibility, Penalties, and Credits

If you were born in 1938 or later, you won't be able to get full Social Security benefits until after age 65. The younger you are, the longer you'll have to wait to be eligible for full benefits. Basically, Congress is trying to save the system from going broke.

The Appendix at the back of the book has a simple but more detailed discussion (with charts) of Social Security. Turn to the Appendix to see:

- At what age you'll become eligible for your full monthly benefit.

- How the early-retirement penalty can impact your benefits.

- How much you'd gain by delaying retirement and earning bonus credits.

		Your Earnings in 1997				
Your Age in 1998	Your Family	$20,000	$30,000	$40,000	$50,000	$61,200 or More
65	You	$784	$1,043	$1,197	$1,269	$1,342
65	You and your spouse	$1,176	$1,564	$1,795	$1,903	$2,013

FIGURE 12.1 Examples of Social Security benefits. Approximate monthly benefits if you retire at full retirement age and had steady lifetime earnings similar to your 1997 earnings.

Source: Social Security Administration.

$_____ (Social Security)

+ $_____ (Any other income with a COLA)

= $_____ (**Line 2:** Total income from other sources)

Work Sheet Step 2

What Work Sheet Step 2 shows is how much of your total first-year retirement income will be provided by sources such as Social Security, which will increase yearly to keep up with inflation.

Line 3: How Close to—or Far from—Your Retirement Income Goal Are You?

In Work Sheet Step 3 subtract Line 2 from Line 1. This shows how much of your yearly retirement income goal won't be provided by Social Security and other inflation-adjusted sources. In other words, this is the amount of yearly retirement income you've got to provide yourself.

$_____ (Line 1)

– $_____ (Line 2)

= $_____ (**Line 3:** Retirement income needed)

Work Sheet Step 3

Line 4: Closing the Gap—First Step, Adjust for Inflation

Line 3 shows how far you are from the income (in today's dollars) you'll need in your first year of retirement.

Unfortunately, your income shortfall will be even larger than that. That's because inflation will reduce the purchasing power of your dollars. You'll need more money, depending on how high the rate of inflation is rising.

For example, as Figure 12.2 shows, if inflation is 3 percent a year and you are 14 years from retirement, everything you want to buy—from bread to a car—will cost more than 1.5 times what it does now.

To find out how much income you'll really need to cope with inflation, multiply your retirement-income gap (Line 3) by the inflation multiplier that fits your situation.

Here's how to find your multiplier in Figure 12.2. Look in the col-

Years until Retirement	Inflation Rate		Years until Retirement	Inflation Rate	
	3 Percent	4 Percent		3 Percent	4 Percent
1	1.030	1.040	16	1.605	1.873
2	1.061	1.082	17	1.653	1.948
3	1.093	1.125	18	1.702	2.026
4	1.126	1.170	19	1.754	2.107
5	1.159	1.217	20	1.806	2.191
6	1.194	1.265	21	1.860	2.279
7	1.230	1.316	22	1.916	2.370
8	1.267	1.369	23	1.974	2.465
9	1.305	1.423	24	2.033	2.563
10	1.344	1.480	25	2.094	2.666
11	1.384	1.539	30	2.427	3.243
12	1.426	1.601	35	2.814	3.946
13	1.469	1.665	40	3.262	4.801
14	1.513	1.732	45	3.782	5.841
15	1.558	1.801	50	4.384	7.107

FIGURE 12.2 Inflation multiplier.

umn that shows the rate of inflation. (These days, 3 percent or 4 percent is a safe guess.) Then go to the row that shows the number of years until you retire. Use the multiplier where that row and column meet. (For example, at 3 percent inflation and 14 years from retirement, your multiplier is 1.513.)

In Work Sheet Step 4, multiply your retirement income gap by that inflation multiplier. That shows how much income you'll really need, after you've adjusted for inflationary erosion of your money's buying power.

$\$$_____ (Line 3)

$\times$ _____ (Inflation multiplier)

$=\$$_____ **(Line 4:** Inflation-adjusted income needed)

Work Sheet Step 4

Lines 5 and 6: Closing the Gap—Second Step, Adjust for Any Pension Benefits You'll Receive

You've forecast most of the income you expect in your first year of retirement. If you expect to receive any checks from a traditional pension plan (which, incidentally, are unlikely to be adjusted yearly for inflation unless you work for a government agency), enter the total amount you're due to be paid in your first year of retirement on Line 5 of Work Sheet Step 5. Then subtract Line 5 from Line 4.

The result, Line 6, shows your remaining income shortfall in the first year of retirement.

$\$$_____ (Line 4)

$-\$$_____ **(Line 5:** Annual pension benefits)

$=\$$_____ **(Line 6:** First-year income needed)

Work Sheet Step 5

Line 7: Closing the Gap—Third Step, Adjust for How Long You'll Be Retired

Your calculations so far show how much more income you'll need for your first year in retirement.

But what about the rest of your retirement?

Your nest egg must be big enough to pay your living expenses for years, probably decades.

To figure out how much money you'll need, consider two things:

✔ How long will your money have to last? (In other words, how many years will you live in retirement?)

✔ How much will your investments grow while you're retired? This depends on how conservatively or aggressively you invest.

Conservative investments like bond mutual funds may provide a return of, say, 5 percent or 6 percent a year. Aggressive growth stock funds may reward you with 12 percent.

We'll discuss investment strategy in much more detail, starting in Chapter 14. For the sake of this calculation, let's assume an 8 percent rate of return. As for inflation, give yourself a margin of safety by figuring inflation will run 4 percent annually, higher than it has been in recent years. (If you're only a few years away from retirement, you can use 3 percent. But beware: That one percentage point difference will produce a dramatically different bottom line in this work sheet.)

Now let's suppose you'll live for, say, 20 years after you retire.

Look at Figure 12.3 (or Figure 12.4 if you want to assume a 3 percent rate of inflation), which shows how much your nest egg needs to grow to last while you're retired. See where the row for 20 years intersects with the column for an 8 percent annual return on your investment? The number there, 13.590, is your retirement growth multiplier.

In Work Sheet Step 6 multiply Line 4, the inflation-adjusted total income you'll need, by 14.31 or whatever your retirement growth multiplier is.

The result is the amount of money you'll need in your nest egg to buy groceries, pay the mortgage, gas up the car, buy movie tickets, and cover 1001 other living expenses in retirement.

Years in Retirement	Expected Return on Savings during Retirement at 4 Percent Inflation			
	6 Percent	8 Percent	10 Percent	12 Percent
1	0.980	0.962	0.943	0.926
2	1.942	1.886	1.833	1.783
3	2.884	2.775	2.673	2.577
4	3.808	3.630	3.465	3.312
5	4.713	4.452	4.212	3.993
6	5.601	5.242	4.917	4.623
7	6.472	6.002	5.582	5.206
8	7.325	6.733	6.210	5.747
9	8.162	7.435	6.802	6.247
10	8.983	8.111	7.360	6.710
11	9.787	8.760	7.887	7.139
12	10.575	9.385	8.384	7.536
13	11.348	9.986	8.853	7.904
14	12.106	10.563	9.295	8.244
15	12.849	11.118	9.712	8.559
16	13.578	11.652	10.106	8.851
17	14.292	12.166	10.477	9.122
18	14.992	12.659	10.828	9.372
19	15.678	13.134	11.158	9.604
20	16.351	13.590	11.470	9.818
21	17.011	14.029	11.764	10.017
22	17.658	14.451	12.046	10.201
23	18.292	14.857	12.303	10.371
24	18.914	15.247	12.550	10.529
25	19.523	15.622	12.783	10.675
30	22.396	17.292	13.765	11.258
35	24.999	18.665	14.498	11.655
40	27.355	19.793	15.046	11.925
45	29.490	20.720	15.456	12.108

FIGURE 12.3 Retirement growth multiplier at 4 percent inflation.

Years in Retirement	Expected Return on Savings during Retirement at Three Percent Inflation			
	6 Percent	8 Percent	10 Percent	12 Percent
1	0.971	0.952	0.935	0.917
2	1.913	1.859	1.808	1.759
3	2.829	2.723	2.624	2.531
4	3.717	3.546	3.387	3.240
5	4.580	4.329	4.100	3.890
6	5.417	5.076	4.767	4.486
7	6.230	5.786	5.389	5.033
8	7.020	6.463	5.971	5.535
9	7.786	7.108	6.515	5.995
10	8.530	7.722	7.024	6.418
11	9.253	8.306	7.499	6.805
12	9.954	8.863	7.943	7.161
13	10.635	9.394	8.358	7.487
14	11.296	9.899	8.745	7.786
15	11.938	10.380	9.108	8.061
16	12.561	10.838	9.447	8.313
17	13.166	11.274	9.763	8.544
18	13.754	11.690	10.059	8.756
19	14.324	12.085	10.336	8.950
20	14.877	12.462	10.594	9.129
21	15.415	12.821	10.836	9.292
22	15.937	13.163	11.061	9.442
23	16.444	13.489	11.272	9.580
24	16.936	13.799	11.469	9.707
25	17.413	14.094	11.654	9.823
30	19.600	15.372	12.409	10.274
35	21.487	16.374	12.948	10.567
40	23.115	17.159	13.332	10.757
45	24.519	17.774	13.606	10.881

FIGURE 12.4 Retirement growth multiplier at 3 percent inflation.

$_____ (Line 4)

× _____ (Your retirement growth multiplier)

= $_____ (**Line 7:** Nest egg you'll need)

Work Sheet Step 6

Building Your Nest Egg

In the work sheet, Line 7 is your bottom line. That's how large your 401(k) account must be to generate the income you want each year, whether it is 60 percent, 70 percent, or some other portion of your preretirement income. It is the money you'll need in addition to income from Social Security and any other sources you may have.

Now let's figure out how much you need to set aside annually to build your nest egg that big.

Line 8: Begin by Taking Stock of Your Current Tax-Deferred Savings and Investments

Find out how your existing 401(k) account (and any other tax-deferred retirement accounts, like an IRA) will grow between now and when you retire.

Start by taking stock of what you've got. Add up the amounts you have in each such account (Work Sheet Step 7).

$_____ (Your 401(k) account)

$_____ (IRA #1, if any)

+ $_____ (IRA #2 or any other tax-deferred account)

= $_____ (**Line 8:** Current tax-deferred savings and investments)

Work Sheet Step 7

Line 9: Then, Figure How Much Your Savings Will Grow

To find out how much your 401(k) account (and other tax-deferred accounts) will probably grow, look at Figure 12.5. In the first column, find the number of years until you will retire. Go across that row until you reach the column headed by the annual rate of return you expect on your tax-deferred investments before you retire. The number where that row and column meet is your savings growth multiplier.

In Work Sheet Step 8, multiply your current tax-deferred savings and investments amount (Line 8) by your savings growth multiplier.

The amount you get by doing that shows how large your savings accounts will become by the time you retire. (The arithmetic assumes you make no additional deposits or contributions to your accounts.)

$\quad$ \$_____ (Line 8)

$\times$ _____ (Savings growth multiplier)

$=$ \$_____ (**Line 9:** Growth of nest egg)

Work Sheet Step 8

Lines 10 and 11: Determine How Much Your Taxable Savings and Investments Will Grow

If you have savings and investments that are taxable—because they're not in your 401(k) or any other tax-deferred account—repeat the calculations in Lines 8 and 9 for them.

Do that in Work Sheet Step 9, by adding up the money you have in each such account. Then, multiply the total by your savings growth multiplier. It might be the same savings growth multiplier number you used in Work Sheet Step 8. (You originally found it in Figure 12.5. It is in the box where the row for the number of years until you retire intersects the column for the annual rate of return you expect on your investments before you retire.) Then again, it might not be the same. We explain why in the box, "The Proverbial Fine Print . . .".

	Expected Annual Return on Savings until Retirement						
Years until Retirement	6 Percent	7 Percent	8 Percent	9 Percent	10 Percent	11 Percent	12 Percent
1	1.060	1.070	1.080	1.090	1.100	1.110	1.120
2	1.124	1.145	1.166	1.188	1.210	1.232	1.254
3	1.191	1.225	1.260	1.295	1.331	1.368	1.405
4	1.262	1.311	1.360	1.412	1.464	1.518	1.574
5	1.338	1.403	1.469	1.539	1.611	1.685	1.762
6	1.419	1.501	1.587	1.677	1.772	1.870	1.974
7	1.504	1.606	1.714	1.828	1.949	2.076	2.211
8	1.594	1.718	1.851	1.993	2.144	2.305	2.476
9	1.689	1.838	1.999	2.172	2.358	2.558	2.773
10	1.791	1.967	2.159	2.367	2.594	2.839	3.106
11	1.898	2.105	2.332	2.580	2.853	3.152	3.479
12	2.012	2.252	2.518	2.813	3.138	3.498	3.896
13	2.133	2.410	2.720	3.066	3.452	3.883	4.363
14	2.261	2.579	2.937	3.342	3.797	4.310	4.887
15	2.397	2.759	3.172	3.642	4.177	4.785	5.474
16	2.540	2.952	3.426	3.970	4.595	5.311	6.130
17	2.693	3.159	3.700	4.328	5.054	5.895	6.866
18	2.854	3.380	3.996	4.717	5.560	6.544	7.690
19	3.026	3.617	4.316	5.142	6.116	7.263	8.613
20	3.207	3.870	4.661	5.604	6.727	8.062	9.646
21	3.400	4.141	5.034	6.109	7.400	8.949	10.804
22	3.604	4.430	5.437	6.659	8.140	9.934	12.100
23	3.820	4.741	5.871	7.258	8.954	10.026	13.552
24	4.049	5.072	6.341	7.911	9.850	12.239	15.179
25	4.292	5.427	6.848	8.623	10.835	13.585	17.000
30	5.743	7.612	10.063	13.268	17.449	22.892	29.960
35	7.686	10.677	14.785	20.414	28.102	38.575	52.800
40	10.286	14.974	21.725	31.409	45.259	65.001	93.051
45	13.765	21.002	31.920	48.327	72.890	109.530	163.980

FIGURE 12.5 Savings growth multiplier.

The Proverbial Fine Print . . .

The reason your savings growth multiplier might be different in Work Sheet Step 9 than it was in Work Sheet Step 8 is this:

Because Work Sheet Step 9 involves *taxable* investments, you have to reduce the rate of return by the amount of taxes you pay. This is easier than it sounds. You don't need to consult your brother-in-law, the CPA who prepares your tax returns.

All you need to do is lower your return estimate by one or maybe two percentage points.

If in Work Sheet Step 8 you estimated that your rate of return on nontaxable investments would be, say, 10 percent, all you do now is reduce that estimate to 9 percent or 8 percent.

Are you the curious sort? Do you watch over the repairman's shoulder while he fixes your clothes dryer? You can take our word about cutting back your investment return estimate by a point or two.

But if you've just *got* to know why you should scale back your return that much, dig into the following explanation by tax expert Carrie Coghill, of the Pittsburgh investment advisory firm D. B. Root & Company.

Suppose you buy 200 shares of Mutual Fund A at $50 per share. Your total investment: $10,000. Over the course of a year, the investment grows by 12 percent. Your gain is $1200. Your account now has $11,200 in it.

Not bad. But during the year the fund paid a dividend of 30 cents a share. (The fund must relay to you dividends paid to it by stocks it owned, plus interest received from its bonds, minus expenses.) It also paid out $2 per share from its profitable sale of stocks it held. (That's called a *capital gains distribution.*)

So you got $60 in dividends, and $400 in capital gains.

But Uncle Sam taxes them. "Assuming a 28 percent tax bracket for dividends and a 20 percent tax bracket for capital gains, you would pay approximately $17 on the dividends and $80 on the capital gains," says Coghill. Your total tax bill: $97.

(Continued)

By subtracting $97 from your $1200, you're left with $1103. That reduces the year's rate of return on your $10,000 down to 11 percent from 12 percent gross gain.

12% on $10,000 investment	$1200
Tax on $60 dividend at 28%	$17
Tax on $400 capital gain at 20%	$80
Net gain	$1103
Net return ($1103 ÷ $10,000)	11%

The exact size of your tax burden depends on which type of investment income you receive, how much, and your income. Dividend income is taxed at ordinary income rates. Capital gains are taxed at a maximum of 20 percent.

A larger tax bill would reduce your rate of return more.

But a one percentage point reduction is a useful, ballpark adjustment.

Look at the bright side, though. Whether you subtract one or two percentage points, you've still got more than enough left over to pay for a candlelight dinner for two at Chez Swank.

So, in Work Sheet Step 9 you may adjust downward your estimate of your annual rate of return. Then complete the calculation by multiplying Line 10 by your revised savings growth multiplier.

(If you don't have taxable savings or investments, simply enter "0" on Lines 10 and 11 and proceed with the rest of the work sheet. Naturally, you don't need to multiply "0" by your savings growth multiplier.)

$_____ **(Line 10:** Total current savings and investments in taxable accounts, if any)

× _____ (Savings growth multiplier)

= $_____ **(Line 11:** Growth of taxable savings and investments)

Work Sheet Step 9

Lines 12 and 13: Find the Remaining Savings and Investments Shortfall

Unless you're very close to retirement or you've been saving a terrific amount of money each year, the size of your 401(k) (and other savings, both taxable and tax-deferred) will probably fall short of the amount you need (Line 7).

To figure out how much you should save (invest) between now and retirement to close that shortfall, you need to do two things.

First, add Lines 9 and 11 in Work Sheet Step 10. That tells you how much your total savings and investments, taxable and tax-deferred, will grow.

```
        $_____   (Line 9)
  +  $_____   (Line 11)
  =  $_____   (Line 12: Total savings growth)
```

Work Sheet Step 10

Next, subtract Line 12 from Line 7 in Work Sheet Step 11 to find the shortfall amount.

```
        $_____   (Line 7)
  −  $_____   (Line 12)
  =  $_____   (Line 13: Amount needed to close gap)
```

Work Sheet Step 11

Line 14: Bottom Line—How Much You Need to Save Annually

To figure out how much you need to save yearly to make up that shortfall, you need to take into consideration two things:

Years until Retirement	Expected Annual Return on Savings until Retirement			
	6 Percent	8 Percent	10 Percent	12 Percent
1	1.000	1.000	1.000	1.000
2	2.060	2.080	2.100	2.120
3	3.184	3.246	3.310	3.374
4	4.375	4.506	4.641	4.779
5	5.637	5.867	6.105	6.353
6	6.975	7.336	7.716	8.115
7	8.394	8.923	9.487	10.089
8	10.897	10.637	11.436	12.300
9	11.491	12.488	13.579	14.776
10	13.181	14.487	15.937	17.549
11	14.972	16.645	18.531	20.655
12	16.870	18.977	21.384	24.133
13	18.882	21.495	24.523	28.029
14	21.015	24.215	27.975	32.393
15	23.276	27.152	31.772	37.280
16	25.673	30.324	35.950	42.753
17	28.213	33.750	40.545	48.884
18	30.906	37.450	45.599	55.750
19	33.760	41.446	51.159	63.440
20	36.786	45.762	57.275	72.052
21	39.993	50.423	64.002	81.699
22	43.392	55.457	71.403	92.503
23	46.996	60.893	79.543	104.600
24	50.816	66.765	88.497	118.150
25	54.865	73.106	98.347	133.330
30	79.058	113.280	164.490	241.330
35	111.430	172.310	271.020	431.660
40	154.760	259.050	442.590	767.090
45	212.740	386.500	718.900	1,358.200

FIGURE 12.6 Annual payment divisor.

✔ How long it will be before you retire.

✔ How much your investments will grow each year.

To do that, in Figure 12.6 look at the row that shows how far away from retirement you are. Go across to the column that shows the return you expect your investments to earn. (This should be the same rate that you used in the savings growth multiplier table.)

The number where they meet is your annual payment divisor.

In Work Sheet Step 12 divide Line 13 by your annual payment divisor. That shows how much you need to sock away in your 401(k) each year between now and retirement to meet your goal.

  $ _____ (Line 13)

÷ _____ (Your annual payment divisor)

= $ _____ (**Line 14:** Amount you need to put into your 401(k) plan account each year)

Work Sheet Step 12

That's it. Line 14 is your bottom line.

If these numbers give you a hernia, start over with new assumptions. If you can't sock away in your 401(k) as much as the work sheet says you should, you have four choices:

1. Try to squeeze out a higher rate of return by investing more aggressively.

2. Invest more of your money.

3. Postpone retirement or consider working at least part-time after "retirement."

4. Consider realistic ways you can economize.

PART THREE

Making a Game Plan—and Winning

Understanding the Biggest Threat against Your Retirement Finances, and Knowing How to Select Your Investments

You've taken the first two steps in 401(k) plan investing. The first was learning what a 401(k) is and how it works. The second was measuring how much money you'll need at retirement.

Now we'll take the third step: making a financial game plan and putting it into action.

Inflation: What It Is, How It Erodes Your Money, and Ways to Cope with It

Inflation in the 1970s was as unstoppable as the bulls on their annual rampage through Pamplona.

Prices of everything from apples to zipper repairs raced upward relentlessly. Meanwhile, if you were a working adult the company that employed you bellyached about how expensive it was to do business. A pay raise was out of the question.

Today, whether you're close to retirement or decades away, the last thing you want is a recurrence of 1970s-style inflation.

Inflation erodes savings and paychecks. It reduces the value of money. It makes your 401(k) account worth less. It's as if a thief were stealing from your account. And there isn't a thing you can do about it.

> "Inflation is as violent as a mugger, as frightening as an armed robber, and as deadly as a hit man."
> —President Ronald Reagan, at a 1978 Republican fund-raising event

For retirees living on a fixed income, inflation starts them on a treadmill that offers nothing but financial exhaustion. Even though rising inflation drives up the interest paid by money-market funds and short-term certificates of deposit, retirees' nest eggs become worth less and less.

It's a double whammy. The prices of things retirees buy rise, while the value of their money and investments plummet.

That's why it's important to discuss inflation. It affects how much you can buy with your money.

In fact, the first step in learning how to make an investment game plan is understanding inflation. That's because one of the major goals of your game plan will be to stay ahead of inflation.

Rate versus Price

Retirees are often told they should invest in things like bonds that pay interest.

But retirees and other investors are often puzzled by what happens to bonds when interest rates rise. The value (or price) of older bonds often falls. Why?

What happens is that the value of older bonds falls if they pay less interest than newer bonds. That's because those older bonds are worth less on the open, resale market for bonds—the "used-car lot" of Wall Street.

After all, wouldn't you rather own a bond paying 7 percent than one paying 6 percent? When new bonds pay higher interest than your older bonds, your bonds attract fewer buyers. Their resale price drops.

The opposite is also true. When interest rates fall, buyers will flock to your bonds on the resale market if they are paying more interest than new bonds.

Of course, the face value of your bond does not change. Instead of selling it, if you keep a bond until its *maturity* (the date at which the business or organization that issued it is due to pay you its full face value), you should receive back the original amount you paid for it.

UNDERSTANDING INFLATION

Do your eyes glaze over when you read the words "bond" or "stock"?

Don't feel guilty. Wall Street jargon is as easy to understand as San-skrit. Business news is often as much fun to read as a high school physics textbook.

So let's change the way we talk about inflation. Think about it in terms of everyday goods and services. Inflation makes them more expen-sive. The flip side of the coin: Inflation reduces how much you can buy with each dollar. Whether it happens slowly (penny by penny) or faster (quarter by quarter), inflation decreases your purchasing power.

Sizing Up the Enemy Inflation pushes up the cost of living. The best-known measurement is the consumer price index (CPI), which is compiled by the government, based on prices of goods in a theoretical market basket.

The raging inflation of the 1970s was bad. Even mild inflation, though, is destructive.

Consider these examples:

- ✔ If you have an investment that pays 8 percent a year while infla-tion is 3 percent yearly, you are actually gaining only 5 percent from your investment.
- ✔ If annual inflation is 5 percent, something that costs $1 today will cost you $1.05 a year from now.

MELTING MONEY

How bad can this get? Inflation vaporizes your money the way sunshine melts a snowman.

If the cost of living climbs 3 percent a year, the purchasing power of $1 shrinks to less than 50 cents in 24 years.

That erodes the value of your 401(k) account. It chips away at the buying power of a pension benefit. If your income doesn't rise, it means your standard of living is cut in half over those 24 years.

If inflation is higher than 3 percent, the value of your dollar is diluted even quicker. As Figure 13.1 shows, at 5 percent annual inflation your dollar shrivels to 50 cents in fewer than 15 years.

The way to defend yourself is by investing your money so it grows. One of your key goals will be to make sure your investments grow at least as fast as inflation. Since inflation makes your money worth less, you need more money. You need enough additional money to make up for the decline in its purchasing power. It's that simple.

Starting in Chapter 14, we'll discuss how to select investments that make your money grow.

But we can discuss how *fast* your investments must grow right now.

THE RACE AGAINST INFLATION

How fast your investments must grow depends on how fast inflation is galloping.

Suppose your annual income is $40,000. Let's say inflation is advancing a modest 3 percent a year. Figure 13.2 shows that your income must rise to more than $53,000 in a decade to buy the same things it does now. If inflation steams ahead at 5 percent, you'll need more than an extra $11,000 in only five years just to avoid losing any purchasing power. And what happens if your expenses *rise* rather than merely stay the same?

Your income will have to rise that much—*plus* an amount to compensate for inflation!

Double Trouble: Inflation and Taxes

When inflation is not raging higher at the double-digit speed it had for much of the 1970s (and in 1980 as well), it is easy to forget the trouble it causes.

The numbers may even sound small. But, like tiny termites, their damaging potential should not be underestimated.

Worse, inflation's harm is magnified by taxes. Both deprive you of

Years from Now	Inflation Rate			
	3 Percent	4 Percent	5 Percent	6 Percent
1	97.1 cents	96.2 cents	95.2 cents	94.3 cents
2	94.3	92.5	90.7	89.0
3	91.5	88.9	86.4	84.0
4	88.8	85.5	82.3	79.2
5	86.3	82.2	78.4	74.7
6	83.7	79.0	74.6	70.5
7	81.3	76.0	71.1	66.5
8	78.9	73.1	67.7	62.7
9	76.6	70.3	64.5	59.2
10	74.4	67.6	61.4	55.8
11	72.2	65.0	58.5	52.7
12	70.1	62.5	55.7	49.7
13	68.1	60.1	53.0	46.9
14	66.1	57.7	50.5	44.2
15	64.2	55.5	48.1	41.7
16	62.3	53.4	45.8	39.4
17	60.5	51.3	43.6	37.1
18	58.7	49.4	41.6	35.0
19	57.0	47.5	39.6	33.1
20	55.4	45.6	37.7	31.2
21	53.8	43.9	35.9	29.4
22	52.2	42.2	34.2	27.8
23	50.7	40.6	32.6	26.2
24	49.2	39.0	31.0	24.7
25	47.8	37.5	29.5	23.3
26	46.4	36.1	28.1	22.0
27	45.0	34.7	26.8	20.7
28	43.7	33.3	25.5	19.6
29	42.4	32.1	24.3	18.5
30	41.2	30.8	23.1	17.4

FIGURE 13.1 How the value of $1 declines at various yearly rates of inflation.

Years from	Inflation Rate		
Now	3 Percent	4 Percent	5 Percent
1	$41,200	$41,600	$42,000
2	42,436	43,264	44,100
3	43,709	44,995	46,305
4	45,020	46,794	48,620
5	46,371	48,666	51,051
6	47,762	50,613	53,604
7	49,195	52,637	56,284
8	50,671	54,743	59,098
9	52,191	56,932	62,053
10	53,757	59,210	65,156
11	56,369	61,578	68,414
12	57,030	64,041	71,834
13	58,741	66,603	75,426
14	60,504	69,267	79,197
15	62,319	72,038	83,157
16	64,188	74,919	87,315
17	66,114	77,916	91,681
18	68,097	81,033	96,265
19	70,140	84,274	101,078
20	72,244	87,645	106,132
21	74,412	91,151	111,439
22	76,644	94,797	117,010
23	78,943	98,589	122,861
24	81,312	102,532	129,004
25	83,751	106,633	135,454

FIGURE 13.2 Suppose your annual income is $40,000. Here is how much it must grow to keep pace with inflation and not lose any purchasing power. *Source:* Towers Perrin.

money. Like muggers lurking in a darkened doorway, they can catch you by surprise.

Let's say inflation is 3.5 percent a year. Imagine you're in the 28 percent tax bracket.

Now look what they can do to your investment in a mutual fund that buys stock in blue-chip corporations.

If your stock fund grows 10 percent a year, inflation and taxes melt that decent-sounding return quickly. Everett Allen, who was a retirement planning expert at Towers Perrin, computed your losses:

✔ After deducting taxes, growth is reduced to 7.2 percent.

✔ After deducting both taxes and inflation, growth is reduced to 3.57 percent.

And how long would it take your investment to double in value?

✔ At 10 percent annual growth: 7.53 years, according to Allen.

✔ After deducting taxes alone (reducing the growth to 7.2 percent): 10 years.

✔ After deducting taxes and inflation (3.57 percent growth): 19.7 years.

Think you can hide from this danger by putting your money into "safe" investments?

Take a look. What could be safer than certificates of deposit? People buy them precisely for the sake of safety. And they do provide safety in two ways: (1) The interest they pay is predictable. You know what you're getting. (2) Your principal (your deposit) won't decrease.

But do they protect you from inflation? You be the judge.

If your CD grows 5.75 percent a year:

✔ After deducting taxes, growth declines to 4.14 percent, Allen said.

✔ After deducting taxes and inflation, growth slows to 0.62 percent. A glacial crawl.

And how long would it take your investment to double in value? Better get comfortable. It's a long wait.

Even at a 5.75 percent return it would take 12.4 years, according to Allen's calculation.

At 4.14 percent growth, it would take 17.1 years.

It would take a mind-boggling 112.4 years to double at the rate of return after both taxes and inflation.

Yup. *One hundred twelve years*—plus almost five months, to be precise. That's bad.

COPING WITH INFLATION

Certificates of deposit (CDs) are supposed to be the ultimate in safety.

Then how could something that's supposed to be so safe be so bad?

The answer is that there are two kinds of "safe": short-term and long-term.

CDs and other interest-paying investments provide short-term safety. They are safe in the sense that they pay a predictable rate of interest. And they protect your initial deposit (or principal, as it's called in investment terms).

However, they wilt in the heat of long-term competition against inflation. In exchange for short-term safety, they sacrifice the potential for sizable growth over the long haul.

That means while inflation is nibbling away at your money's buying power, those *fixed-income investments* are not growing enough to make up the difference.

Fixed-Income Investment   An investment that pays a fixed rate of interest. Examples of this type of investment are government and corporate bonds, certificates of deposit (CDs), Treasury bills, and stocks that pay a fixed dividend.

If you put $100 into investments that provide short-term reliability, after five or ten years you most likely still have your $100. Even better, you'll probably also have a modest amount of accumulated interest. At best, you'll be only slightly ahead of your original $100 in terms of what you can buy. At worst, you'll be lucky if inflation (plus taxes) haven't actually reduced the buying power of that money.

The predictability of fixed-income investments is seductive. But their slow growth compared to inflation is dangerous.

Since 1926 the return over and above inflation on short-term government bonds (which mature in five years or less, and include Treasury bills, with maturities of a year or less) has averaged a sickly 0.6 percent, according to Jeremy J. Siegel, author of *Stocks for the Long Run*, a definitive history of financial markets.[1] That's a mere fraction above zero growth. Long-term bonds have fared little better, paying a ghostly 2 percent above inflation.[2]

If you invest in either one of those popular investments, you are treading water. Trees grow faster than your money. It would take your long-term bonds 40 years to double in purchasing power.[3] It would take short-term bonds a mind-numbing 120 years.[4]

In contrast, the average stock would double in buying power in 10 years.[5]

If an unexpected medical emergency or family crisis takes a bite out of your nest egg, you likely won't live long enough to see fixed-income investments replace that money. You'll have to tighten your belt and get used to living on less.

"Investors cannot hope to stay ahead of inflation with fixed-income securities," says Siegel, who is a professor of finance at the University of Pennsylvania's Wharton School. "The worst part is, it leaves no margin of safety against inflation."

A Better Course of Action

What's your alternative to fixed-income investments?

Stocks and stock-based mutual funds don't give you short-term safety. Over short periods of time, these growth investments are liable to rise and fall in value. Sometimes, this roller-coaster ride is steep and fast and scary.

---

[1] Jeremy J. Siegel, *Stocks for the Long Run*, 2d ed. (New York: McGraw-Hill, 1998), p. 14.
[2] Ibid.
[3] Ibid.
[4] Ibid.
[5] Ibid.

A $100 investment today may be worth $90 tomorrow. Or $80 a week from now. Obviously, that is not protecting your initial investment (principal) in the short run. But further down the road (whether it is months or years), your $100 will grow into much more. And grow faster than inflation makes one dollar shrink in value.

That's long-term safety.

Frankly, during the worst of economic periods that growth may take longer than you'd like. But throughout modern history, in the end stocks have stayed ahead of inflation.

Despite war, calamity, disease—despite the leisure-suit fad of the 1970s, despite the designated hitter rule in baseball, despite the spread of karaoke—despite anything history can throw at us, growth investments have provided long-term protection against inflation.

"There is no question that, generally speaking, you get higher total return and stand a much better chance of beating inflation with stocks than bonds," says Catherine Friend White, president of the financial planning firm FinArc, in Lexington, Massachusetts.

"The average stock has returned a little over 10 percent a year since 1808. . . . We don't have data for quite that length of time for bonds, but they seem to do about 6.5 percent over the very long haul.

"So if you've got a time horizon of seven years or more, it's a reasonable assumption that you're going to be better off in stocks in your fight against inflation."

And inflation is the biggest threat against anyone who is retired—or plans to be one day.

Adds White, "The speed of inflation is the first thing your investment return must be measured against."

Invest for
the Long Haul

Investing is like long-distance travel. Some people get where they want to go the fast way, by flying.

Others prefer to keep their feet on the ground, so they take a train.

A third group is more concerned about saving money than travel time. They opt for a bus. Sometimes they decide they really can't afford the journey at all, so they don't leave home. They've saved money, all right. But they simply never get anywhere.

When you are forming an investment plan, you have to make similar decisions. You choose investments that best suit your circumstances and time frame.

Generally, investments can be divided into three categories: for aggressive investors, for middle-of-the-road investors, and for cautious investors.

A bundle of aggressive investments is like flying: It will get you where you're going faster.

> "Most people spend more time planning a two-week vacation than their retirement."
>
> —Anonymous

A middle-of-the-road mix is the equivalent of taking the train: It's for anyone willing to travel slower for the sake of not being scared by a bumpy flight.

A cautious mix is the investment version of traveling by bus—or staying home. In the short run you've saved some money. But whether you stick that cash into bond mutual funds, money market funds, or certificates of deposit, the result is the same. Due to inflation, that money's buying power shrinks with each passing day (although each type of investment may shrink at a slightly different speed). Pretty soon the money won't buy a plane or train ticket at all, even if you want to.

Many investment advisers say you should choose an investment mix in one of those three categories no matter what your time frame is. In other words, some advisers say a cautious investment mix may be right for you even if you are many years away from having to take money out of your 401(k) account.

We will explain all of these choices, but we'll also discuss the advantages of using an aggressive strategy with as much of your retirement account as possible—if possible, with all of it—especially when you have a long time frame.

BE AGGRESSIVE UNLESS . . .

An aggressive strategy makes sense when you don't need your money right away. It is a long-term approach to investing.

It is most likely to be right for you if you are young, or if you are many years (or even decades) away from retirement, or if you won't need your money soon.

If you do need a chunk of your money within two or three years, let's say, to make a down payment on a home, pay tuition, or some other major goal, then a moderate or cautious strategy may be better *with that amount of money*. A cautious approach is better if you have no other way to pay for that expense.

With that approach, you can count on having the full amount you need, when you need it. It won't be reduced by an unexpected market tumble.

You should still apply a long-term, aggressive approach to the rest of your account.

RISK AND REWARD

The more uncomfortable you get when the stock market goes through its inevitable roller-coaster ups and downs, the more you should use a less aggressive strategy. That's the advice of many investment gurus.

But one result of a less aggressive strategy typically is that your investments grow less.

If that sounds familiar, it should. It's another way of stating the long-standing investors' credo: no risk, no reward. It echoes one of life's well-known rules: no pain, no gain.

In the case of investments, the pain and risk are inflicted by those gut-wrenching ups and downs of the stock market. The reward for holding on to your investments until the end of these runaway roller-coaster rides is that your investments grow in value. You also collect income along the way in the form of dividends, interest, and (in the case of mutual funds) profits from the sale of stock the funds own.

The flip side: Investments that fluctuate the least reward you the least.

Figure 14.1 illustrates this relationship between risk and reward. As risk rises, so does the prospect of reward. Remember, any single, individual investment may fail to live up to its promise. It may tank. Go bust. Fail. Go out of business. It may simply lag behind others.

But risk and reward dance together faithfully when you look at the performance of entire investment categories.

That describes the never-ending tango between risk and reward over long periods of time. Over those long periods, your primary enemy is inflation. The idea is to choose investments whose growth (plus income payments to you) will exceed the ravages of inflation by as much as possible.

That's different from risk in the short run. In the short run, risk means loss of your principal's value. When you put $1000 into a money market fund, you expect it still to be worth $1000 a day, a week, a month, even a year later. You expect the value of your principal to be protected.

(Although it should still be worth $1000—plus interest—a year later, the buying power of $1000 will be somewhat less due to erosion from inflation. That's long-term risk.)

Viewed through the eyes of someone seeking to protect the value of his or her money in the short run, a scale of riskiness is the reverse of what it is in the long run.

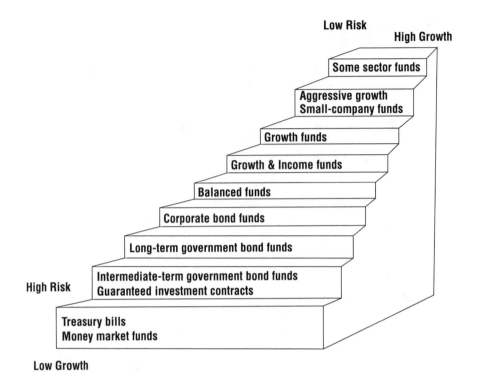

FIGURE 14.1 Long-term risk is caused by an investment's inability to keep ahead of inflation. In the short run, the order of riskiness is reversed. The risk over a short period of time is that your account balance will shrink in size.

THE DIFFERENCE BETWEEN RISK AND FEAR

So, to achieve short-term safety, you end up sacrificing long-term growth.

That's the result of voluntarily investing in funds or other securities that fluctuate less in the near future. They grow less over the long haul.

Good idea? Not if you want a larger nest egg in the future. The purpose of a 401(k) plan is to build your account for the future.

When the market goes down—and it is constantly bobbing up and down—you don't lose anything if you don't actually sell shares in your investments.

And you're generally not supposed to sell shares that are in your 401(k) account. They're supposed to remain in there for the long haul.

So why seek protection from something that can't hurt you?

If you put your money into funds that fluctuate less in the short run, you are buying protection from short-term risk. But that short-term, *potential* risk does not cost you money if you don't sell shares. Meanwhile, by investing in those lower-growth funds, you are in fact sacrificing real monetary gain in the future.

Think about this. Any time the market goes down, your "loss" is only theoretical. The lower prices you read in stock and mutual fund listings in the newspaper only matter if you sell something. If you are investing for the long haul, shares should simply stay in your account. A temporary market decline does you no real harm.

It hurts you no more than reading about, say, a professional boxer getting clobbered. Both are in the newspaper. But neither has actually happened to you.

Sure, those stock and fund prices apply to your investments. But if you don't sell shares, you don't suffer any loss.

A market slide may be scary. But that's not the same as *risky*. Nothing bad really happens, unless you bring it on yourself by selling.

The astounding thing is that some misguided people do precisely that by needlessly selling shares. Usually, it is out of panic. Sometimes, they think they're supposed to. Their faulty reasoning is that it makes no sense to hold onto something whose value has declined.

A few are trying to outsmart the stock market. They figure they'll sell their shares, then buy them back after the market falls even more. That way, they can own the same number of shares for less money, or own more shares for the same amount of money. Either way, they figure, they're ahead of the game.

The trouble is that they are extremely likely to lose money in the process.

Selling as the market declines is not very difficult. But buying back shares before they rise again in value too much is hard to do. Most people buy back too late, after they've lost out on part of the climb in value. The portion they miss out on can never become part of their own investment growth. Worse, they end up paying more than they expect for their old shares.

In trying to outsmart the market, these people outsmart themselves.

"It's a fool's game," Ed Giltenan, a spokesman for the mutual fund company T. Rowe Price, told *Investor's Business Daily* newspaper.[1]

The reason is that the market often rebounds from declines in short, strong bursts that are hard to see coming in advance.

The price is steep for not anticipating those explosive recoveries. *IBD* illustrated how easy it is to miss out, with a study by H. Nejat Seyhun, a University of Michigan professor. Seyhun showed the growth of $1000 invested in a cross section of stocks on the New York, American, and Nasdaq exchanges in 1963. If the money was left in place, by 1993 it would have grown into $24,300.

But an investor who sold off shares during market downturns, then missed out on merely the 10 best days during that decade's 7802 trading days would have only $15,400 by 1993.

Missing just those 10 days would have cost an investor about $9000.

If the investor missed out on the 90 best days—maybe because of being too busy on his or her own job, or unsure about what to do—$1000 would have grown into only $2100.

The investor would have ended up with as much money by investing in slowpoke one-month Treasury bills, *IBD* said Seyhun found.

As we discussed previously, this strategy of trying to outsmart the market is called market timing. Investment professionals can't reliably succeed at it. Don't you expect to.

TIME IS MONEY

Let's return to our comparison of 401(k) investing to travel.

Would it make sense to travel any other way if flying were 100 percent safe? Not if safety and how fast you reach your goal were the only things that matter.

And that's how safe investing can be.

Investing can be as safe as always flying on Air Force One—plus taking super precautions. You're riding a plane that's diligently maintained.

---

[1] P. Katzeff, *IBD*, Sept. 15, 1998, p. B1.

It's got more than one engine, so the aircraft can fly even if one conks out. Of course, there's always a copilot on board in case the pilot falls ill in-flight. Imagine, as a last resort, whenever you board the aircraft, you strap on not one but two parachutes.

Investing in a 401(k) plan has built-in safety precautions, too. First, the vast majority of investment choices are mutual funds. Unlike investing in individual stocks, where much of your money's safety hangs on the fate of only a few companies, a mutual fund spreads your money among many stocks and other securities. That's called *diversification*. It enables you to avoid the danger of putting all of your eggs in one basket.

Second, the more funds your plan offers, the more you can diversify by dividing your money among several funds. And with a large fund menu to choose from, the better your chances of finding several suitably aggressive funds.

So, here's the case for investing aggressively in your 401(k) account:

✔ You can invest in funds, which provide built-in diversification against risk.

✔ You can invest for the long haul, which gives your investments time to rebound from any temporary market setback.

✔ You get where you want to go fastest.

The decision is yours. All three investment approaches—aggressive, moderate, and conservative—will be included in the discussion of how to form an investment plan, so you can make your own decision about your overall strategy.

Even people who want to make an aggressive, long-term game plan may need to use more conservative tactics for any isolated, short-term spending goals they may have.

The comprehensive discussion in the next few chapters will enable you to custom-tailor investment decisions to a variety of circumstances in your life.

Chapter 15

Invest for
Steady Growth

Investing can be scary and discouraging for a lot of reasons.

One of them has to do with the fact that 401(k) investing is largely (if not exclusively) a matter of selecting mutual funds. And there are some 9000 funds to choose from.

How in the world can a nonprofessional investor sort them out? How can the average person on the factory floor or in a corporate office or behind a cash register ever hope to find one or two winners?

The solution stems from a simple fact: You *don't* have to sift through 9000 funds to find one or two winners.

All you've got to do is check out the funds offered by your plan, whether there are three of them or a hundred. And even that is easier than it sounds. The stock market has already done much of the work for you.

Certain types of funds tend to perform better than others over time. As long as you invest for the long haul (whether that's three years or 30), you can rely on those long-term tendencies. Focus on the categories that provide the top results. Then all you have to do is identify the best-performing funds within those categories that are most likely to continue doing well.

Fund categories not only describe what the funds are and how they seek to make money. They're also a useful guide to how well a typical fund in that category will do.

The best funds will tend to do even better. The worst will tend to lag behind. One of your main goals as an investor is to maximize the chances that you are selecting the better-than-average performers.

HOW FUNDS ARE CATEGORIZED

Mutual funds can be divided into as many categories as pastry in a French bakery. The two most basic categories are *stocks* and *bonds*. Most funds invest in one or the other. Some invest in both.

Stock   Buying stock makes you an owner of a company. Each share of stock is a portion of ownership. If a business has distributed 1,000,000 shares and you own 10,000, you own 1 percent of that company.

Bond   A bond is a loan to a business or governmental body. If you buy a bond, you do not receive any ownership in the business or unit of government. You are simply a lender, like a bank. A bond is an IOU from the organization that issues it and accepts your money. In return for your loan, the borrower promises to pay you a specific interest rate at stated intervals, such as monthly, for a specified number of years (called the *term*). After that, the borrower agrees to repay the loan (the *principal*).

Did your eyelids begin to droop just then? Sorry. *Stocks* and *bonds* are Wall Street words. But it's important to be familiar with the dialect of dollars and cents. Otherwise, you'd be like someone from, say, France, trying to understand baseball without knowing what a pitcher and catcher are.

Here's a better way to understand the two basic categories of funds. Stock funds are intended to roll up big gains in their share price. Rising share price makes the fund grow in value. For that reason, you can think of funds that focus on increased value as *growth funds*.

At the other end of the mutual fund spectrum are *income funds*. Bond and money market funds are the most familiar examples for many people. The goal for these funds is to pay income to their shareholders. Interest is the most common type of income.

So, the world of mutual funds can be divided into two broad camps: growth funds and income funds.

Other categories indicate where the companies (or governmental bodies) are located: in the United States, overseas, or anywhere on the globe.

Some categories have to do with the size of the companies a fund invests in: large, medium, and small. Other groupings concern the types of companies: low-priced ones expected to rise in value once they remedy whatever is dragging them down, or healthy companies that are expected to produce above-average earnings.

Then there are the numerous specialty categories: funds that invest in a single commodity like gold or only a single industry like automobile manufacturing or high tech.

On any given day or in any given week, month, or even year, one category will be performing better than all others. Its success may be due to any combination of factors: business conditions, governmental policy, new inventions, interest rates, war, peace, phases of the moon.

But the world is a constantly shifting place. Today's winner soon enough falls back into the pack.

DON'T BE SEDUCED BY NEARSIGHTED "BEST OF" LISTS

Look what happened to 1996's 15 highest-flying mutual funds that invest in U.S. stocks. (See Figure 15.1). A year later only one of them managed to return to the top 15. Nine couldn't even crack the top *1000*. Five finished below the top *2000*! ("Top" begins to seem like an inappropriate description.) Two actually achieved the dubious distinction of falling to the cellar, performing among the 100 lowest-ranked of all 2637 U.S. general stock funds in 1997.

What makes their disappointing encores all the more shocking is that the list of 1996's top dogs intentionally excludes specialty mutual funds and funds that focus on businesses in fast-growing foreign economic hot

Rank in 1996	Fund and Performance	Rank in 1997
1	Van Kampen Growth • 1996: 61.99% • 1997: 27.01%	1,129
2	Firstar MicroCap • 1996: 60.06% • 1997: 13.63%	2,336
3	Warburg Pincus Small Company Value • 1996: 57.00% • 1997: 17.67%	2,137
4	State Street Research Aurora • 1996: 56.88% • 1997: 46.98%	24
5	Phoenix-Engemann Small and Mid-Cap Growth • 1996: 52.37% • 1997: 26.41%	1,211
6	Dreyfus Premier Growth and Income • 1996: 48.93% • 1997: 20.94%	1,879
7	Fremont U.S. Micro-Cap • 1996: 48.70% • 1997: 6.99%	2,526
8	Jundt U.S. Emerging Growth • 1996: 44.32% • 1997: 33.87%	236
9	Pacific Advisors Small Cap • 1996: 43.70% • 1997: 6.95%	2,529
10	Rydex OTC • 1996: 43.46% • 1997: 21.85%	1,814

FIGURE 15.1 Here today, gone tomorrow. Red-hot returns one year are no guarantee of future success. Almost all of the 15 best-performing diversified U.S. stock funds in 1996 cooled off so much in 1997 that they failed to stay in the Top 15. Some plunged to the bottom of the heap in 1997.
Source: Lipper, Inc.

Rank in 1996	Fund and Performance	Rank in 1997
11	Robertson Stephens Partners • 1996: 43.33% • 1997: 18.08%	2,108
12	MFS Strategic Growth • 1996: 42.04% • 1997: 50.40%	12
13	Lindner/Ryback Small-Cap • 1996: 41.15% • 1997: 31.69%	523
14	Morgan Stanley Institutional Fund Aggressive Equity • 1996: 40.90% • 1997: 33.31%	276
15	MAS Mid Cap Value • 1996: 40.77% • 1997: 39.59%	67

Notes: Excludes different share classes of same fund. Some funds may have changed names.

FIGURE 15.1 *(Continued)*

spots. Such funds are notorious for ups and downs steep enough to make a jet pilot airsick. We didn't want to stack the deck with exotic funds like that, which suffer from sharp shifts in their fortunes from year to year.

Instead, we wanted the types of funds you are far and away most likely to invest in: nonspecialized (called diversified) U.S. stock funds.

The lesson: Don't be seduced by "Top 10" lists for this month, this quarter, or even this year.

It's very likely that today's hot dogs will be next year's dogs—period.

When you are shopping for funds likely to excel repeatedly in the future, look for funds that have excelled not just once—but again and again over time.

Consistency Is a Beautiful Thing

Look again at Figure 15.1. Van Kampen Growth earned a number-one ranking in 1996 on the strength of its 61.99 percent return that year. It swooned to No. 1129 in 1997 because its performance sagged.

But its 1997 return of more than 27 percent was, by itself, not bad. In fact, a fund that produces that much year in, year out would be a very good one to invest in.

The real problem is inconsistency. One good year is no guarantee of more good years to follow. And a fund's inability to keep pace with other top-performing funds in a year when the market soared—which is what happened in 1997—is a sign that fund may not be able to sparkle consistently.

So, don't base investment choices on a performance snapshot that shows a fund at its one (and maybe only) shining moment.

Look for a fund that's able to overachieve repeatedly.

LOOK FOR A WINNING CATEGORY

Over long periods of time, each category of funds has established a performance track record.

For example, stock funds do better than bond funds. Mixed stock-and-bond funds do better than bond funds, but not as well as stock funds. Money market funds don't even do as well as bond funds. Basically, they are turbocharged savings accounts—but without insurance protection.

Within the broad categories, various subcategories outperform others. The best track record over the past 20 years is held by funds that invest in the large, blue-chip companies that make up the Standard & Poor's 500 index, the widely followed barometer of the overall stock market, according to Lipper, Inc., a mutual funds research firm.

The next most successful group also leans toward big blue-chip corporations, but in addition includes companies that are smaller than the biggest whales of Wall Street. It is the growth subcategory of funds that invest in companies whose earnings are expected to grow especially fast. (The growth fund subcategory is one in a group of several subcategories that we refer to as the *growth class of funds* as distinguished from those classified as *income funds*. See Chapter 17.)

Figure 15.2 shows how certain subcategories stack up against each other. During the 20 years ending in September 1998, funds imitating the S&P 500 racked up average annual returns of 15.98 percent, according to Lipper. Funds in the growth subcategory were next with 14.75 percent.

Medium-sized corporations (generally businesses that are worth $1

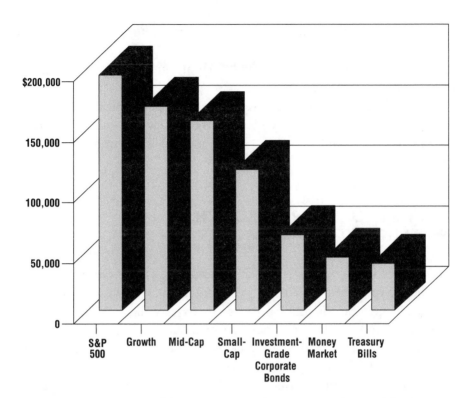

FIGURE 15.2 Growth of $10,000: Various categories of mutual funds produce different yearly returns. This chart shows how much $10,000 would have grown if you had invested it in different types of funds or Treasury bills over the past 20 years.
Source: Lipper, Inc.; CDA/Wiesenberger (Salomon Bros. 1-mo. T-bill index).

billion to $5 billion, known as *mid-cap funds*), were close behind with a 14.29 percent average annual return.

That was better than the 12.91 percent turned in by funds that invest in small, fast-growing companies, which are known on Wall Street as *small-cap funds*.

All of those subcategories turned in better yearly returns than investment-grade corporate bonds, which averaged 9.69 percent returns over that period.

Bringing up the rear were good ol' money market funds (7.62 percent average annual return, Lipper says) and one-month Treasury bills (6.88 percent average annual return, according to the CDA/Wiesenberger research firm).

Figure 15.2 translates these annual rates of return into dollars-and-cents performance. It shows what a $10,000 investment would have grown into over the course of the past 20 years, growing at each category's average annual rate of return.

For example, if you had invested $10,000 in a typical mutual fund mimicking the S&P 500 two decades ago, 20 years later you'd have $193,997. That would reflect the growth in value of the fund's share price, plowing back in any dividends it paid.

AIM FOR LONG-TERM GROWTH, NOT SHORT-TERM FIREWORKS

The price of long-term success is short-term risk. That means the value of the money you invest is liable to go up and down. In the case of a mutual fund, it happens as the fund's price per share (as well as any income from dividends and capital gains) fluctuates over short periods of time. Those periods may be as brief as a day, week, or month. Or they may last as long as many months, a year, or more.

Whatever the time period, one of basic laws of the investment jungle is this: Risk and reward generally go together.

The better a category's performance is over the long haul, the wilder and wider its performance will be as it jumps up and down over short periods. That sort of seesaw performance is called *volatility*.

Volatility Fluctuations in a fund's performance, also called its total return (its share price plus any income from dividends and capital gains).

The good news is that when assessed over long periods, volatility declines. That's because the market is not turbulent all the time. In fact, it is often calm for long stretches. In any case, the market goes up much more and much more often than it goes down. So when viewed across a span of many years, time dilutes the impact of violent but short market gyrations.

If you prefer to avoid short-term volatility altogether, you can invest in securities whose performance does not fluctuate much. That's exactly why some people invest in money market funds, bonds, guaranteed investment contracts (GICs), Treasury bills, and so on.

These instruments' freedom from volatility means your principal is less likely to fall in value. When you put $100 into a money market fund, you can be confident it will still be worth $100 (plus interest) a week, month, or year later.

But that freedom from risk also means absence of reward. As Figure 15.2 illustrated, investments that protect the value of your money in the short term grow the least over the long run.

At the opposite extreme are categories of funds that have grown sensationally over short periods. But they may fall into a coma for long periods as well.

That's what happens with many sector or specialty funds.

Take gold. If you had landed on Wall Street in December 1993 after a long visit to, say, Mars, you'd think that gold was the greatest investment on planet Earth. During the previous 12 months, mutual funds investing in gold-oriented businesses had skyrocketed almost 90 percent, according to Lipper.

A $10,000 investment in gold funds at the start of that year would have been worth nearly double by the next New Year's Eve.

But that was just an temporary blip on the gold radar screen. A chilly economy had sent investors scurrying for the warm glow of the precious yellow metal.

Reality returned right away. In the five years from July 1993 through June 1998, gold bugs suffered staggering losses. A $10,000 investment would have been melted like gold in a smelter to an anemic $5551, losing almost half its value, according to Lipper.

You might as well have spent the money on cotton candy and comic books.

The lesson: Beware of hot-shot fund categories. Categories like sector funds and emerging market funds (funds that invest in companies doing business in lesser-developed nations) can produce dazzling returns.

The trouble is that different sectors will be hot year to year. Ditto for various emerging markets. Financial services and Russia funds can enjoy great results one year, only to fade the following year, when telecommunications companies and Latin American funds are thrust momentarily into the spotlight.

The broad, overall categories appear to be consistently hot only because a succession of their segments run hot and cold. The action shifts from one distinct industry and region to another. Individual funds rise and fall dramatically.

To keep up, you must be willing to devote time to keeping track of your particular sector's fortunes. To avoid being stranded in a suddenly cold fund and sector, you must be able to bail out of a losing fund on short notice. Then you've got to find someplace else to invest your money.

But in your 401(k) plan, you may not be allowed to move your money quickly enough. If your plan allows transfers only weekly, monthly, or quarterly (or even semiannually or annually), you could be forced to watch a fund plummet in value while you are unable to do a thing about it.

THINK LONG-TERM

So, the best funds for your 401(k) account are certainly not the ones that will protect your principal in the short run, while losing buying power over time to inflation. If you put money into a bond fund, a fund holding Treasury securities, or a money market fund, that will safeguard its value for the foreseeable future. But it won't grow. And it will eventually lag behind inflation.

You don't need to worry about short-term fluctuations while your money is inside your account. All or most of your money should be in your account for a long time, long enough to rebound from any temporary setbacks on the stock market.

If you don't need your money for 5, 10, or 15 years, you can generally outwait even the most gut-wrenching of the periodic setbacks that assail Wall Street.

In fact, the market usually rebounds much faster than that.

Look what happened after the Crash of 1987. The stock market plunged a gut-wrenching 508 points (22.6 percent) on October 19. That was the dramatic end to a two-month fade that saw the market sink 36 percent in value.

But, right after October 19 when prices hit the bargain basement, if you had bought a mutual fund mirroring a key market barometer, the Standard & Poor's 500-stock index, you would have ended up with a 5 percent *profit* within two years!

Places to Park Your Money

The only time you should devote money in your 401(k) account to short-term investments is when you know you'll need that specific amount of money soon. One example: You are about to borrow from your account to pay for a family emergency. Another good reason might be if you are retired and know you'll need, say, $10,000 in six months for a down payment on a new home.

Those are situations when you need to make sure you'll have the amount of money that you're counting on. A money market account will preserve your money.

But don't use it for longer periods of time. In investments like a money market account your money merely shrinks in value over longer periods due to inflation.

(One more thing: If you have a good reason for removing money from a growth fund, but can't put it into another growth fund right away, it's okay to park it temporarily in a money market fund.)

KEEP YOUR EYE ON THE RIGHT BALL

If funds that invest in the largest stocks have done so well, why doesn't everyone always invest only in funds that buy nothing but the largest stocks?

In recent years, that is exactly what the most successful mutual funds have done.

But there's no guarantee this will remain the path to riches and glory.

For one thing, even professional fund managers have no way of knowing which individual jumbo-company stocks will be *the* best ones to hold. Even if they did, no two funds could always buy all of their stocks at precisely the same moment, at precisely the same price. Price fluctuations measured in pennies, nickels, and dimes—let alone the ones measured in dollars—would decide the difference between the No. 1 performing fund, No. 2, and so on.

But more importantly, stocks of the very largest companies haven't always dominated the stock market as they have since the mid-1990s.

Medium-sized companies have had their day. So have small companies. Funds that shop for cheap bargains have ruled the roost. So have funds that buy only the most expensive, gold-plated stocks.

The stock market is a never-ending horse race, with various steeds jockeying for position. The lead keeps changing hands.

Any one style or approach may dominate for a month, a year, several years at a time. Then market forces shift to favor some other style or approach.

Regardless of the size of the companies they invest in, the one certainty is that the broad category of diversified U.S. growth stock funds (as opposed to income funds, specialty or sector funds, or foreign stock funds) will continue to excel.

Chapter 16

Plan Ahead: Investment Strategy, Goals, and Time Horizon

"Sometimes your best investments are the ones you don't make."[1]

That's the advice of Donald Trump, no slouch when it comes to deciding how to utilize his financial resources.

Equally important, of course, is deciding which investments to indeed make.

You do that through a process called *asset allocation.* That's a fancy way of saying that you must come to grips with the fact that you've got a limited amount of money (otherwise, you could afford to buy your dream beachfront villa in Tahiti and tell your boss . . . well, whatever you *want* to tell your boss) and you must decide not only which investments to make, but also how to divide your precious dollars among them.

(And you absolutely, positively must invest in more than one thing. That is a bedrock principle of diversification—the need to avoid putting all of your eggs into one basket.)

---

[1]Donald Trump with Tony Schwartz, *Trump: The Art of the Deal* (New York: Warner Books, 1987), p. 226.

TWO SCHOOLS OF STRATEGY: CHOOSE ONE

As a 401(k) plan member, you are standing at a fork in the investment road. In front of you, two paths go in divergent directions. Both will take you to your goals. But each follows its own route. They represent different investment styles.

You've got to choose one or the other.

One fork represents the *buy-and-hold* strategy of investing. This strategy calls for you to invest in the best-performing, most steady growth funds offered by your 401(k) plan. Then you stick with them, even when the market dips. When the market recovers, your growth funds will, too.

But if you switch into "defensive" funds (that is, any fund that provides more short-term stability in exchange for less long-term growth) when the market drops, you'll still be in those defensive funds when the market recovers. You'll lose out on a lucrative part of the market's advance. The longer your money stays in defensive funds, the more of the market's gain you'll forfeit.

Buy-and-hold is a single-minded strategy, which avoids wheeling and dealing.

Nevertheless, as we discussed in the previous chapter, selecting growth funds does not necessarily mean selecting funds that perform the very best over a relatively short period like the past year. Highly aggressive growth funds or flamboyant sector funds may produce dazzling results for a month, three months, six months, or a year. But they may fade into oblivion for long periods after that.

What you want are workhorse growth funds. You want funds that are geared for growth and achieve that for sustained periods, without fluctuating a lot more than the overall stock market.

The other fork represents what is often called the *asset allocation* strategy of investing. (Because of this, buy-and-hold investors often describe their investment selection process as choosing the best "mix" of investments, rather than referring to it as an "asset allocation" process.)

Asset allocation strategists say you should select investments based not only on performance but also on your level of risk tolerance. That is, if you get queasy thinking about your investments when the stock market declines, asset allocators say you should select investments that tend to decline less in a market downturn. You should do that, they say, even though those investments will grow less over time than the bucking bronco variety of funds.

In short, asset allocation strategists say it's okay to sacrifice investment growth for the sake of sleeping better during market turmoil.

Why is that okay? Because if you don't, you probably won't invest at all.

Asset allocators argue that less-productive investments are better than none at all.

In contrast, buy-and-hold strategists tell you to keep your eye on the ball—building your nest egg as large as possible over the long run. Don't worry about market downturns because the market has always rebounded. Always has, always will, they say.

Because of that, buy-and-hold strategists ask why you should settle for funds that will earn you less money over the long run. You shouldn't, is their answer.

Besides, sometimes the supposedly safer types of funds that asset allocators advocate don't live up to their billing. They end up fluctuating wildly, too, in the short run. Sometimes disastrously.

So, buy-and-hold investors urge you to think about long-term results. On the other side of this ideological clash, asset allocators preach that it's okay to pay attention to your nerves—invest in a style that will make you comfortable, even if it means less wealth over time.

There you are. It's your choice.

Eenie, Meenie, Minie, Mo . . .

The debate between the two schools of strategy boils down to this: The asset allocation school preaches a better-safe-than-sorry approach to investing. Asset allocators accuse the buy-and-hold school of advocating a dangerously aggressive strategy.

The buy-and-hold crowd insists that it is the asset allocators who prescribe a risky strategy. Switching from one type of investment to another every time the stock market twitches, the buy-and-holders say, is a recipe for higher taxes (unless done inside a 401(k) account), higher costs, and lower performance. They say their own approach advocates steadiness and aims for the best possible results.

BUY AND HOLD

Buy-and-hold is the simpler of the two strategies. Find the best growth funds available in your plan, put your money in, and stick with them.

However, good reasons to exit from a growth fund can arise from time to time.

If, for example, a new manager takes over the fund and its long-term performance becomes permanently impaired, you've lost one of your original key reasons for investing in that fund. (We'll discuss this situation more in Chapter 20.) But with buy-and-hold investing, you don't switch funds merely because the stock market is going through one of its periodic tantrums.

If you pull your money out of a growth fund and put it into a money market fund or some other form of cash, you risk missing out on the market's rebound. As we've discussed, market recoveries occur unpredictably and fast. Even investment pros can't react quickly enough. If you pull out of your growth fund while you wait for the "right" moment to get back in, you will almost certainly miss most of the recovery. That deprives you of a big part of investment growth. Once the spurt is past, you can never make up for having missed it.

Spending Money

An investment strategy is about two things: (1) making your money grow, and (2) providing money for expenditures.

One threat to having enough money to spend is a decline in the stock market. If you need exactly $10,000 by a certain date (let's say for a home-purchase down payment) but your funds decline to less than $10,000 in value, you won't have sufficient cash for your down payment.

Simple.

The asset-allocation school of strategy solves that dilemma by advising investors to set aside enough money into investments whose value is much less likely to shrink when the market drops. The classic example is a money market fund.

How does the buy-and-hold school cope? After all, in the short run growth funds are liable to become worth less when the stock market falls.

The buy-and-hold investment school offers several choices:

The Squirrel-Away-Those-Nuts Scenario. Start investing early, and put all of your money into growth funds. By using a buy-and-hold strategy over a sufficiently long time, your nest egg grows enough to provide extra money for spending. Need 10 grand for a new-home down payment? Sell enough fund shares to raise the dough. Meanwhile, your remaining fund shares continue to grow.

Pragmatic Compromise Scenario. This borrows from the asset-allocation school. Start by putting your money into growth funds. But several months before your spending goal arrives, sell enough shares to put money into something else (like a money market fund). Raise only enough cash to make up for an unexpected drop in the market before your down payment (or whatever) is due.

How much is enough?

Well, how much can the market fall in a short period? Declines larger than 20 percent are rare, plunges deeper than 25 percent rarer still.

So, if you need $10,000, put $2500 into your money market fund. Then, if a sudden drop in the market reduces your $10,000 worth of growth fund shares to $7500 in value, you'll still have a total of $10,000 for that down payment.

If the market is calm, the economy is cruising, and newspaper headlines are boring, you may wait until, say, eight months before the down payment is due before shifting money out of your growth funds. Perhaps you first shift it into a more conservative fund (like a balanced fund or a bond fund). Then two to four months before the due date, you transfer that money again, this time into a money market fund.

The more the market is moving up and down, the earlier you begin the process and the earlier you make the shift into a money market fund.

More Cautious Scenario. This borrows even more from the asset-allocation school. Put the whole $10,000 into funds that are more stable in the short run, like a bond fund or balanced fund.

This combines conventional asset allocation with a buy-and-hold strategy. But all the rest of your money stays hard at work in growth funds.

ASSET ALLOCATION

Now let's discuss asset allocation. We'll describe this from the perspective of those who choose to use a traditional asset allocation strategy for all of their investments. The discussion also applies to someone who wants to be a buy-and-hold investor, but wants to use the third scenario just mentioned (the combined asset-allocation/buy-and-hold method) to make sure of having enough money available to meet spending goals.

With a traditional asset allocation approach, you decide how to allocate your assets (or divvy up your money) by selecting mutual funds and other investments that are right for you in your personal circumstances. Your mix (your investment choices as well as how you divide your paycheck contribution among them) will be custom-tailored for you.

The asset allocation school says that because everyone is different, there is no single formula everyone should use to select one's investment mixture. Every investor's choices should reflect a unique blend of needs, objectives, and circumstances.

You may want to keep your present home as well as buy a vacation cottage. The older couple who live next door already want to downsize from their empty nest, even though they're 10 years away from retirement. Perhaps you've got your eye on some sleek sailboat. In contrast, your neighbors are looking forward to helping pay their grandchildren's college costs.

Even when others have the same goals you do, no one else has your precise mix of goals, savings, income (with or without a spouse), job, family responsibilities, living expenses, and time frame. You and the fellow next door may both want the same expensive, new set of golf clubs. But you're 15 years younger than he is. He's got twice as many children. He's got grandchildren to pamper. Your spouse works; his doesn't. And his nest egg is one-third smaller than yours.

The cost of those golf clubs—and of everything else in your lives—will impact your respective finances differently.

As a result, how each of you invests should also be quite different. Your respective nest eggs—your investment portfolios—should contain different investments that promise different results and carry different risks.

The right mix depends on three things:

1. Your investment goals.

2. Your investment time horizon.

3. Your tolerance for risk.

That's it.

Those three factors are the key to forming your asset allocation. (In contrast, buy-and-hold growth investors try to overlook risk tolerance in their long-term strategy.)

For traditional asset allocators, though, those three factors are the key to getting what they want: enough money in their nest egg, without too much anxiety along the way.

In forming an investment game plan, asset allocators address those key factors one at a time. They are steps in the asset allocation process.

CHOOSING YOUR INVESTMENT GOALS

For investors in either school, the first step is to decide what your investment goals are.

Your main goal should be to build up your 401(k) account for retirement. Your account's primary purpose should be to support you in retirement.

But everyone's situation is different. Maybe you'll have to start taking income from your account as soon as you retire. Maybe you've got a one-time expenditure coming up, like paying for your daughter's wedding.

Or perhaps your story is precisely the opposite. Perhaps you're looking forward to earning a paycheck and contributing to your account until age 75. And you've been putting aside extra savings in a bank account to cover a special occasion like your daughter's wedding. That's because you wouldn't dream of dipping into your retirement nest egg.

Whatever the case may be, if you have spending goals coming up you need to make sure you'll have the necessary money. Here is where the two schools diverge.

Traditional asset allocators say how you divide your investment money should reflect your tolerance for risk as well as your goals and time frame. Some of your money may be put into growth funds. But enough will be put into investments that fluctuate less over shorter periods of time. That intentionally sacrifices long-term profits for the sake of what they believe would be avoiding the inevitable ulcers and sleepless nights along the way.

Buy-and-hold growth investors put the pedal to the metal. Their investments are more uniform. The bulk of their money goes into growth funds.

They divert only as little as they'll actually need for an upcoming expense into short-term investments that make sure their money doesn't shrink *in the short run*. The rest of their money is kept hard at work, growing, in growth funds or other growth-oriented mutual funds.

What Are Your Goals?

Not sure how much you'll need to set aside? No problem, no matter which strategy's school you join.

Turn back to your Spending Checklist (Figure 11.3) in Chapter 11. Take all of the expenditures you listed there and copy them in Figure 16.1, which is an investment goals work sheet. If you left out any then, now's the time to list them.

Help Yourself . . .

While filling in Figure 16.1, if you realize you left an important spending goal off your retirement budget (Figure 11.4), revise the budget. Then you may also need to revise your calculation of how much retirement income you'll need. Do that by updating the first step (Work Sheet Step 1) of your income work sheet in Chapter 12.

Number each item you list in Figure 16.1 according to your priorities. In the fourth column, rank the most important number 1, the next as number 2, and so on.

Next, in the fifth column, rank them according to time horizon. Jot down the date by which you need to pay for this goal. Then rank the one you need first as number 1 and continue in order (that is, the goal that can wait until last gets ranked with highest number).

Now see how closely your priorities and your time horizon match.

Item/Goal	Cost	Check Mark (for Special, Onetime Goals)	Rank (If Time and Money Were No Object)	Deadline (Date and Rank)	Order of Preference (in the Real World, Where Time and Money Do Matter!)
Big-Ticket Spending Priorities					
1.	$				
2.					
3.					
4.					
5.					
Routine Expenses					
1.	$				
2.					
3.					
4.					
5.					

FIGURE 16.1 Your investment goals.

In the sixth and final column, assigned a final order-of-preference number. This is the order in which you will actually tackle these goals. Some of your goals may have very different ranks in priority and time horizon. For each of those you'll simply have to decide where in your personal pecking order each should stand.

TIME HORIZON

Picking a deadline or timetable for each goal does more than help you establish your order of preference. It also helps determine what types of investments are right for you.

For a buy-and-hold growth investor, that's a simple process. As discussed earlier in this chapter, to raise cash either you sell growth-fund shares or you shift the desired amount of money into a stable, short-term investment. We described three ways to do this.

For a traditional asset allocator, how you divide your money among various investments is more complex and it is a continuous process. Your portfolio is always divided among faster- and slower-growing funds, to reflect how much stock-market gyration you can stomach without getting seasick.

The closer a traditional asset allocator gets to a spending deadline, the more money he or she may shift out of high-performing but volatile funds into lower-octane but more stable funds.

For a traditional asset allocator, the important questions are: How much money should I contribute to funds that invest in stocks? In bonds? And how much to funds that invest in volatile stocks? How much to less volatile stocks?

If you're a traditional asset allocator, the goals that are furthest in the future can be paid for with the most volatile stock funds. That's because they've got the most time to recover from short-term market downturns. Meanwhile, your money will grow.

In contrast, you can pay for upcoming goals by selling stock funds now—before an unexpected market decline reduces their value—and parking the money in a money market fund until the spending deadline arrives. Or you can sell shares of a stock fund, move the money into a bond fund, and meet your spending deadline with income from the bond fund.

We'll discuss the differences between stock and bond funds in more detail in Chapter 17.

What Is a Growth Stock Fund, Anyway?

A ll roads lead to Rome.

And, if you take the route mapped out by the previous three chapters, you'll see that all roads in Part Three of this book lead you to the same investment approach:

✔ Invest for the long term.
✔ Invest for growth.

The best way to do that is with diversified growth stock mutual funds.

Ah, but not so fast, you say. *How about explaining what a growth fund is?*

GROWTH IS JOB NO. 1

Begin by reminding yourself of your goal: long-term growth. Eliminate from consideration all funds that aim for some other target. And many do.

Remember, there are numerous categories of funds. The goal (also known as the objective) of a fund determines its category. But they all fall into one of two broad classifications: growth funds or income funds.

Growth funds focus on raising the value of their shares.

Income funds focus on paying income.

As a group, growth funds are more rewarding. They create greater returns or profit over the full marathon distance. Over shorter, sprint distances their performance will rise and fall more than income funds. That's why income funds are better at protecting the value of your initial investment (your principal) during short intervals. The trade-off is that they don't grow as much over substantial periods of time.

With an income fund, your money may be safer for a day, week, month, or even a year. But it is at greater risk over the long haul, because it loses buying power to inflation.

The Name Game: "Growth," "Value," and "Income" Funds

Wall Street lingo can be confusing, especially when it uses the same word to describe related—but different—things.

Take the word "growth." It means different things at various times. In the broad sense, it describes the goal of non-income funds. The goal of growth funds is raising the value of their shares. They are geared for people who are more interested in seeing their investments rise in value than in receiving steady income.

But another way the term is used is to describe the types of stocks a fund invests in. Basically, there are two types: regular growth-oriented funds and value-oriented growth funds.

Regular growth funds shop for vigorous companies whose earnings are growing at above-average rates. Stock like that may be relatively expensive.

Value growth funds invest in the stock of relatively inexpensive companies whose value is expected to rise under the right conditions.

The main thing to remember is this: both "value" and "growth" mutual funds can belong to the growth class of mutual funds, where growth in the broader sense refers to funds that try to become worth more over time.

Value-oriented growth funds often do so by investing in beaten-down stocks. Growth-oriented funds do so by investing in robust companies with growing sales and profits. Those rising earnings pump up the price of the companies' stock. That, in turn, pushes up the share price of funds investing in that stock.

More about Value versus Growth

Value funds invest in companies whose stock is priced below what the fund manager thinks it is worth. These include stocks dumped by investors because of some bad news affecting the company, its industry, or the overall economy. A value fund manager who thinks that company will rebound from the news may buy its stock while it is priced at a bargain.

A growth fund invests in companies whose earnings are growing rapidly.

Don't be confused by the fact that both value- and growth-oriented funds may belong to the growth class of funds.

In contrast, income funds are the hedonists of the fund world. They live for today. They buy stocks and bonds that pay out money instead of plowing their own profits back into themselves for future growth. In turn, the funds relay those payments to their own shareholders.

Growth funds are the beavers of the fund realm. They build toward a better tomorrow. They reinvest as much as possible of their own earnings back into themselves.

Dividends and Capital Gains

Whether funds are growth or income, they can receive income from their underlying stocks. That income is in the form of dividends paid by the stock. It can also consist of profits on the occasional sale of stock. Wall Street calls profits like that *capital gains*.

Income mutual funds have more income to pass along to their own shareholders because they commonly own more dividend-paying stock. They may also own bonds that pay interest. That interest is paid to the fund's shareholders in the form of dividends.

Funds of any kind are required to relay almost all of their income to their shareholders.

What We *Mean by Growth Fund*

When we talk about growth funds, we mean only funds that devote all of their efforts to growth. When we refer to growth funds, we're talking about funds that:

- ✔ Invest in U.S. businesses.
- ✔ Aim for growth rather than income, and whose return is primarily from growth.
- ✔ Buy stocks in a variety of industries rather than a single industry.

This last characteristic is called diversification. Sector funds are concentrated rather than diversified. Sector funds are growth funds in terms of their goals. But their narrow focus on stocks in a single industry makes them vulnerable to long dry spells. Individual sectors can suffer more hard times than boom times.

That point is doubly important. Not only does diversification reduce the volatility of general stock funds; it makes investing easier for you.

It gives a fund manager the freedom to invest in the best growth industries instead of being restricted to one industry. The manager can invest in several at once. And the manager can get in and out of industries in response to each one's current fortunes. In other words, the burden to be a Wall Street wizard is on the fund manager instead of on you.

With sector funds, *you've* got to be the investment pro, picking the right industries to invest in, deciding the best moments to shift your money from sector to sector. It forces you to play a high-stakes chess match against the best players in the world. The odds are stacked against you.

Another group of funds seek both growth and income. Naturally, it doesn't matter how a fund rewards you—rising share price, or periodic income payments, or both. All that counts is that a fund does its job. And among such dual-personality funds, the ones that do the job best are those that aim more for growth than for income.

As a very rough rule of thumb, mixed funds whose income comes more from stock dividends outperform funds that depend on bond interest payments. So, *growth and income* and *equity income* funds have out-produced *balanced* funds in the past 20 years.

So, here's what each type of growth fund does. (We've included sector funds in this roundup but, remember, they're the bucking broncos of the growth-fund group. If you're a professional rodeo cowboy, you may know how to ride one and hop off without breaking your neck. But the average city slicker will find that riding one is way too dangerous.)

You'll see these terms and descriptions in a lot of the literature your plan gives you. This will help you understand the similarities and differences among the categories of growth funds.

TYPES OF GROWTH FUNDS

Capital Appreciation Funds

These funds pull out all stops in an effort to make your money grow or appreciate in value. As a result, they're also known as *aggressive growth funds*. They seek that appreciation by investing in the fastest-growing companies. Some businesses like that are young, so they may not be very stable or durable. Capital appreciation funds may also use exotic investing methods such as *options*. Further, such funds reserve the right to shift tactics. Moreover, they may buy and sell stocks frequently, which is costly and can create taxable trading profits. Those costs and extra tax burden get passed on to shareholders. But inside your tax-sheltered 401(k) plan, you are immune from those taxes!

In the end, as a category these funds produce enviable gains. But individual funds can be expensive and erratic, jumping up and down in performance.

Growth Funds

These are less aggressive than capital appreciation funds, so they're less volatile and risky in the short run. They invest in more mature companies whose earnings are expected to grow faster than average. Rising earnings drive the value of the stock owned by the fund up, so the fund's own price per share rises. Growth funds often invest mainly in big corporations.

S&P 500 Funds

These funds try to match the performance of the Standard & Poor's 500 index, which is a widely followed barometer of the overall stock market's biggest companies. They are increasingly popular for several reasons. Few actively managed funds succeed at beating the S&P 500 index, so a fund that mirrors the index's performance is doing better than most. Also, an index fund usually has lower expenses than actively managed funds. That's because an index fund doesn't have to engage in costly strategizing, research, and trading. All it's doing is imitating whatever its index does—which usually involves few changes each year. That's why they are described as passively managed funds. Most of their stock is from larger companies. But they also invest in medium-sized and small stocks.

Small-Company Stock Funds

These are generally more volatile and aggressive than large-company growth funds and S&P 500 index funds. That's because they invest in small companies, which can grow faster than big companies. But they are more vulnerable to competition. With fewer shares trading on stock markets, it's easier for heavy buying and selling to push small-company stock up or down in price. The fund's price yo-yos in the same direction.

(By the way, when a fund is referred to as a small-cap fund, nobody is talking about its hat size. The "cap" refers to market capitalization. That measures a company's size by multiplying the price of its stock by the number of shares it has issued.)

Sector Funds

These funds invest in the stock of companies in one industry. Sector funds are also known as specialty funds. As a category, sector funds produce glamorous results. But individual subcategories may go through hot and cold periods. Their performances may fluctuate wildly. That makes the individual subcategories and funds in them very volatile and risky in the short run.

Growth and Income Funds

These invest in companies with steady earnings as well as dividends. That way, they provide shareholders with income, but the fund's own share price enjoys more appreciation than it would with a plain-vanilla income fund.

Index Funds

S&P 500 funds are one type of index fund. Index funds imitate a variety of indexes, from the S&P 500 to the small companies represented by the Russell 2000; the Lehman Brothers Aggregate Bond Index; and the Morgan Stanley Eurasia, Australia, and Far East (EAFE) Index. There are as many types of index funds as there were animals aboard Noah's ark.

An index fund generally owns most of the same stocks and bonds its index does, and in the same proportions. Because the makeup of most indexes changes infrequently, index funds don't incur trading costs often. That also keeps taxes on profitable selling of securities to a minimum. Moreover, there is little need to pay for brainy strategists and analysts since the fund isn't trying to figure out anything. It is simply playing monkey see, monkey do with its index.

So, index funds can be low in cost and low on taxes.

Best of all, S&P 500 funds have outperformed more than 70 percent of all actively managed funds in recent years, thanks in part to their built-in lower expenses and taxes.

If you invest in a fund tied to a big-company barometer like the S&P 500, you can never do much worse than that cross-section of the market itself. (It will trail the actual index's return by the amount of its own expenses.) That's safety!

So, S&P 500 index funds have grown popular due to their safety and low expenses. But you should beware of a few things about them:

- An index fund tied to a cross-section of the market can't lag behind the cross-section by much; but it also can't beat that cross-section.

- Don't be a sucker for index funds that add bells and whistles. Those add-ons can be an excuse for extra fees. And they can cause the fund to veer from its index, detracting from performance.

- You don't need extra protection from taxes on a fund's profitable sale of its own stocks and bonds. Your funds are inside a 401(k) plan, where you're excused from having to pay such taxes.

Equity Income Funds

These funds are very similar to growth and income funds, but with more emphasis on income-producing stocks.

More Critters in the Zoo

There are more categories of growth funds. For example, there are funds that specialize in medium-sized companies. Others invest in a geographic location. That may be as small as a single nation, or it may be defined as anyplace outside the United States or even as the entire world. And there are indexes for virtually every category.

Some funds invest in other funds. The idea is to spread their eggs among even more baskets, reducing short-term risk. The long-term cost, however, is lower performance.

Unfortunately, a fund's strategy is not always reflected in its name. Read a fund's prospectus, including the part that describes investment objectives, to see what a fund's goals, tactics, and range of investments are.

TYPES OF INCOME FUNDS

Income Funds

These invest in stocks that pay dividends, which are relayed to their own shareholders. The income they pay makes them reassuring, but their share price doesn't grow much.

Balanced Funds

These funds invest in both stocks and bonds. They are the kissing cousins of equity income and growth and income funds. But their income comes from bonds as well as dividend-paying stocks. Some balanced funds use a barbell approach. They invest in growth stocks for rapid appreciation of value. They also invest in short-term bonds, which provide both income and a cushion against the growth stocks' short-term tendency to bounce up and down in price.

More of the Players

Asset-Allocation Funds. These take balanced funds one step further. They invest in cash (the third major asset category) as well as stocks and bonds. They may put money into other investments, too, such as real estate. The idea is to create a type of mutual fund with built-in shock absorbers against short-term fluctuations in the stock markets.

When the stock market declines, reducing the value of stocks and stock funds, money you have in cash does not lose value. Bonds may actually increase in value. So, over any relatively brief stock market downturn, cash (which includes money market funds and stable-but-tradable securities like short-term Treasury bills) and bonds prevent this kind of fund from losing too much value.

Life-Cycle Funds. These also divide your money among different investment categories. Often, funds like this are offered in groups of three, each one a different mix of stocks, bonds, and cash. The one with the largest portion of stock will fluctuate most in the short run, making it the riskiest in the near term—but the one likely to grow the most over time. The one with the least stock will be touted as the most stable day to day. But that's the one that's likely to produce the smallest nest egg over the long run.

FIXED-INCOME FUNDS

Meet another beast in the zoo.

Fixed-income funds are another name for bond funds. Their name refers to the fixed rate of interest or other income they pay to shareholders. This makes them popular as a source of current income for living expenses. But they grow much less than stock funds, and growth stock funds in particular.

That makes them a dangerous place to put your money for long periods of time. You may like getting steady income from them, but your money will lose value with time due to inflation.

One big potential mistake to avoid is this: Even though bond funds provide income, they are not as safe in the short run as money market funds. That's because the price of shares in a bond fund can and does fluctuate.

If you're looking for someplace to park money that you'll need for an upcoming spending goal, put it into a money market fund instead.

Types of Fixed-Income Funds

Bond funds have almost as many stripes as stock funds. They are categorized by the type of bond borrower: a corporation or a government body. That has a lot to do with whether the bonds are taxable or not.

Some are categorized by how long it takes the bonds they own to reach maturity. That's because rising interest rates will typically drive down prices for bonds and bond funds with the longest maturities more than those with shorter maturities. When interest rates fall, funds with shorter maturities rise less.

Here's why bonds work that way: It's more difficult for a borrower to persuade a lender to tie up money in a loan for a long period of time. That's because the longer money is tied up, the greater the risk that inflation could flare up and erode its purchasing power. To overcome the lender's fear, a borrower has to offer a higher interest rate. But, after you make your loan, if interest rates rise, your lower-rate bonds lose part of their relative benefit. They may lose their benefit completely, and you may be stuck with that bond for a long time.

Look at it this way. If you buy a bond paying 7 percent interest, but a month later borrowers start to pay 8 percent, the resale value of your bond goes down. Who wants a bond paying less than other bonds?

Fortunately, like the market for used cars, there is a resale market for bonds.

And the way that market adjusts for the lower relative interest paid by a bond is to adjust the purchase price of a bond up or down. After all, that's what the interest rate is measured against.

Maturity. A fund that invests in bonds that mature in 10 years or more (generally, up to 30 years) is called a long-term bond fund. A fund that invests in bonds that mature in five to ten years is an intermediate-term bond fund. A fund that invests in bonds that mature in one to five years is a short-intermediate bond fund. And a fund that invests in bonds that mature in three years or less is a short-term bond fund.

Taxable. Bonds issued by corporations are taxable.

The rate of interest paid by a taxable bond fund reflects how reliable the borrower is. A company considered a poor credit risk has to pay more interest than a creditworthy corporation.

Higher interest rates may be tempting. But remember: the higher the rate, the more risky your investment may be.

Investment Grade. This term describes bonds whose credit rating is strong. Two rating services, Moody's and Standard & Poor's, rate these more reliable borrowers as Aaa, Aa, A, Baa, or AAA, AA, A, and BBB. Lower ratings indicate that the borrower is less reliable. The corporation issuing the bonds is considered more vulnerable to falling on hard times and defaulting on its bonds. You should think long and hard about putting your money into a bond fund that invests in lower-rated bonds.

Junk Bond Funds. Generally, these are funds holding bonds rated Ba or BB or lower. Don't be seduced by the name they usually use: *high-yield bond funds.* They pay a high interest rate (or yield) to make up for their shaky trustworthiness in repaying loans. Companies that issue junk bonds can default, and that can leave you and your fund holding the proverbial bag. That seldom happens. But fear that it can forces companies that issue them to pay higher interest.

Tax-Free Bond Funds. These funds invest in bonds issued by states, cities, and towns. A fund that says (perhaps in its name) it invests in municipal bonds actually buys bonds issued by any level of state or local government. Interest paid by these funds is generally exempt from federal taxes but not state taxes. Income from a fund that invests in bonds from a single state is generally tax-exempt for residents of that state; it is probably exempt from federal taxes, too.

But, just as there's no such thing as a free lunch, don't expect all payouts from a bond fund to be tax-free.

Profits from the sale of bonds in the fund (called capital gains) paid to shareholders may be taxable. (Of course, capital-gains payouts by a fund in your 401(k) are immune from taxes.)

U.S. Treasury Funds. These are funds that invest only in such IOUs as Treasury bills (which usually mature within a year), Treasury notes (a year to 10 years), and Treasury bonds (10 years or longer). Treasuries pay interest that is federally taxable but state tax-free.

U.S. Government Funds. These invest in Treasuries as well as IOUs issued by other federal agencies and in mortgage-backed securities guaranteed by a government agency. Bonds owned by these funds usually pay slightly higher interest than Treasuries do because repayment of the bond's principal is not directly promised by the Treasury itself.

THE *NEW* NAME GAME

In this chapter, you've learned how to tell one type of mutual fund from another.

Soon, you may have to learn a few more names. Two research firms whose data is used by many 401(k) plans to track the performance of mutual funds are updating their classification systems.

Neither your 401(k) plan nor your funds will be required to use the changes. But if they do, you may start to receive literature with slightly new terminology.

Back to the Drawing Board

The new classifications won't require any mental heavy lifting. They're not dramatically different from what you've already learned in this chapter. And they'll still help you find what you want: diversified growth funds to invest in.

The new systems will pigeonhole funds according to two yardsticks. The main one will focus on the size of the companies in which a fund invests: large, medium, or small. Some funds will be categorized as *microcaps* because they invest in companies smaller than "small-cap." Others will be labeled *flex-cap* because their money is invested in more than a single-sized company.

The second new yardstick: Classifying funds according to their level of aggressiveness.

The old system described the method used by a fund to make you rich. The new system will emphasize the short-term volatility of the fund's investment approach.

Old categories such as *capital appreciation* and *growth and income* are going to be phased out.

Instead, funds will be typecast into one of five categories: *aggressive, growth, general, value,* and *income.*

Those correspond roughly to the old categories of *capital appreciation, growth, index, value,* and *income.*

There are important differences, though. For one thing, only the most aggressive of the old *capital-appreciation* funds will be in the new *aggressive* category. A fund's aggressiveness will be judged by such things as how few stocks it invests in. Putting your eggs in fewer baskets (by investing in fewer companies' stocks) can lead to higher returns over the long haul. But it can lead to wilder fluctuations in performance in the short run.

Don't panic, though. Your goal remains the same: Finding diversified U.S. growth stock funds that consistently turn in above-average performance.

In the new system, you'll focus your search on the *aggressive, growth, general,* and *value* categories. Also, feel free to shop among S&P 500 index funds or index funds that invest in a cross-section of the entire stock market, known as *total market index funds.*

Better yet, all of the following familiar, current categories will remain unchanged:

✔ S&P 500 index funds.

✔ Fixed-income funds.

✔ Sector funds (such as technology and financial services).

✔ World, global, and international funds.

✔ Balanced funds.

✔ Income stock funds.

The next chapter will explain more about which ones to pay attention to—and which ones to ignore.

18

How to Pick a Growth Stock Fund

A esop, the ancient storyteller, had it right. In the race between the tortoise and the hare, bet on the tortoise.

Life is a marathon, and so in the end steady progress beats the flashy sprinter.

The same is true in investing. Hotshots look good in advertisements. They are exciting to read about. But many don't take your money far for long.

Sexy sector funds, exotic foreign funds, glamorous gold funds—all have their moments in the investment spotlight. Some have more than one moment. Some make repeat appearances. But none delivers the goods consistently year in, year out.

For that matter, *no* fund hits the bull's-eye every year.

But if you want to see your nest egg persistently increase in value, stick to growth funds.

GROWTH FUND HEAVY HITTERS

We described the various types of growth funds in Chapter 17. What they all have in common is their quest for rising price per share over time. Their price is what grows. If you own something—anything—whose price rises from year to year, it's more valuable to you. Naturally, that applies to mutual funds, too.

You'll get the most benefit out of funds that not only rise, but keep on rising.

That's why sector funds and funds that invest in foreign businesses are dicey propositions. Yes, they have great years from time to time. But all industries go cold periodically. Ditto for foreign countries. The industries in one nation can boom one year, then go bust the next. Profits swing from industry to industry, from nation to nation.

As categories, sector funds and international funds often look attractive on the surface.

But that's due to accounting sleight of hand. You know the old saying: *There are lies, damned lies . . . and statistics.* Well, statistics explain the sometimes superior performance of sector and international funds.

Statistically, those categories rack up good returns overall. But that's only because select subcategories perform well. Year by year, the action frequently switches from one industry to another and from one geographic region to another. One year it's health care sector funds; the next it may be real estate sector funds.

It is simply impractical for a nonprofessional investor to keep switching money from one type of sector fund or one national fund to another, year after year, let alone in each business quarter. You've already got enough responsibilities. It's hard enough for investment professionals to succeed at this game of investment hopscotch. For someone with a job far from Wall Street, let alone with a family, friends, and quite possibly community, religious, or other obligations, it is way too heavy a burden.

Then there are funds that invest in small and medium-sized businesses. Over the decades those categories have done well. But in recent years they've been dramatically overshadowed by funds that invest in large, blue-chip corporations.

That leaves capital appreciation funds, growth funds, and—in recent years at least—index funds investing in large, blue-chip corporations as the heart of the growth-fund batting order. In addition, most investment professionals refuse to kiss off small-cap and mid-cap funds despite their recent lean years.

Figure 18.1 illustrates that profitability pecking order over the past 20 years. Notice how growth-type funds show higher average annual rates of return than other fund categories.

One Size Does Not Fit All

Funds that invest in small, medium, and large businesses are called small-cap, mid-cap, and large-cap funds. "Cap" refers to capitalization, or the market value of a company. It's determined by multiplying the price of a company's stock by the number of shares.

Large-cap companies are often defined as having a market value greater than $5 billion. Mid-cap usually means a company worth $1 billion to $5 billion. Small-cap generally describes a company smaller than $1 billion. There's even a term for describing corporations smaller than $300 million: micro-cap.

Many funds invest in more than one size group.

Hybrid growth-and-income categories generally come next.

Bond funds are clustered around the bottom of the performance list.

Some sector funds, like those that invest in financial services companies (brokerages, banks, and so on) have done superbly, especially during the strong market of the late 1990s.

But sector funds that invest in businesses like gold-mining stocks only rarely have enjoyed the Midas touch. Their spectacular individual-year gains are too few and far between to make up for ongoing volatility. This subcategory finishes near the bottom of the heap.

The advantage bestowed by growth stock funds is even more dramatic when average annual return is translated into the dollars and cents earned by investors. Some growth-oriented categories, like capital appreciation, leapfrog past some income-oriented categories, whose bottom line benefits are eroded by the sales commissions (called *loads*) they impose on investors. Those fees have the effect of reducing their categories' average annual performance.

Figure 18.2 shows how much a $10,000 investment in each category grew over the past 20 years. Even if you had put your money into a category that averaged less than one percentage point better than another, that fractional difference may have produced nearly $20,000 extra for you!

Just as growth funds boasted the best average annual returns, they also did the best job of making people's investments grow. In fact, their

Type of Fund	Growth Fund?	Average Annual Total Return
S&P 500 index	✓	15.98%
Financial services (sector)	✓	15.63
Growth	✓	14.75
Growth and Income	✓	14.32
Mid-cap	✓	14.29
Equity income	✓	13.58
Income		13.35
Balanced		12.95
Small-cap	✓	12.91
International	✓	12.39
Capital appreciation	✓	12.15
High-yield bond		10.37
General bond		10.00
Corporate bonds A-rated		9.69
Intermediate U.S. government bond		9.15
Intermediate corporate bond		9.10
Short-term U.S. Treasuries		8.67
Money market funds		7.62
Treasury bills[1]		6.88
Gold-oriented (sector)	✓	3.79

[1]CDA/Wiesenberger (Salomon Bros. 1-month T-bill index).

FIGURE 18.1 Growth-oriented stock funds dominate this list of fund categories (and Treasury bills) with the best average annual returns in the 20 years ending September 30, 1998. (Stock funds listed invest in type of businesses described. Intermediate bond funds invest in bonds that generally mature in five to ten years. High-yield bond funds invest in bonds issued by companies with lower creditworthiness. As a result, they must pay high interest to attract investors. Short-term U.S. Treasuries funds invest the bulk of their money in Treasury bills and notes with maturities of less than three years.)

Source: Lipper, Inc.

Type of Fund	Growth Fund?	What $10,000 Turned Into after 20 Years
S&P 500 index	✓	$193,997
Financial services (sector)	✓	177,833
Growth	✓	167,721
Mid-cap	✓	155,922
Growth and Income	✓	146,538
Capital appreciation	✓	139,052
Equity income	✓	137,287
Income		120,735
Small-cap	✓	116,183
Balanced		112,746
International	✓	106,770
High-yield bond		70,001
General bond		64,049
Corporate bonds A-rated		62,060
Intermediate corporate bond		55,345
Intermediate U.S. government bond		54,975
Short-term U.S. Treasuries[1]		52,770
Money market funds		43,444
Treasury bills[2]		37,855
Gold-oriented (sector)	✓	27,470

[1]Stock funds listed invest in type of businesses described. Intermediate bond funds invest in bonds that generally mature in five to ten years. High-yield bond funds invest in bonds issued by companies with lower creditworthiness. As a result, they must pay high interest to attract investors. Short-term U.S. Treasuries funds invest the bulk of their money in Treasury bills and notes with maturities of less than three years.

[2]CDA/Wiesenberger (Salomon Bros. 1-month T-bill index).

FIGURE 18.2 The advantage of growth-oriented stock funds is even more dramatic when average annual return is translated into dollars and cents. This table shows the growth of $10,000 invested during the 20 years ending September 30, 1998.
Source: Lipper, Inc.

benefit was magnified because relatively less of people's initial investment was siphoned off to pay salaries for fund managers, purchase paper for office copiers, and carpet executive suites.

Load Funds often charge sales commissions, which are called loads. They are typically a percentage of the money you invest or withdraw. A load can amount to as much as 8.5 percent of that money. A *front load* is charged against the amount you invest at the outset. A *back load* is assessed on the amount you withdraw. Some funds allow you a discount for keeping your money in place longer. A fund that does not charge a load is called a *no-load*. Some fund companies discount their loads or waive them altogether for 401(K) plans.

That efficiency helped funds that invest in medium-sized companies (mid-cap stocks) jump up a notch. Capital appreciation funds soared much higher in the dollars-and-cents ranking.

All the more reason to zero in on the growth stock funds in your 401(k) plan.

CUTTING TO THE CHASE

The $64,000 question is, how can *you* pick individual growth funds that will live up to the lofty standards set by their category?

Keep Your Eye on the Prize

Start by reminding yourself what your top priority is: growth. By retirement, you want your pot of gold to be as large as possible. In retirement you want to be able to enjoy as much yearly income as possible, for as long as you need to. Having *more* than enough isn't a bad idea, either. After you pass along to that great stock exchange in the sky, being able to leave a little behind for the kids, for dear old alma mater, or for your favorite pet shelter is nice.

Shop for Consistency

What you're looking for are funds that deliver not only growth but consistent growth. That means you should stick with what are known as diversified stock growth funds.

Diversified means nonsector funds. Sector funds invest in only one industry. They are concentrated rather than diversified. Funds in sectors such as technology and health care have enjoyed long winning streaks. Their stock holdings in just a few industry subgroups, though, make them vulnerable to violent performance fluctuations from time to time. Sooner or later they go through long dry spells. Worse, some sectors spend more time acting like Skid Row than Rodeo Drive.

Sector funds are chancier than diversified growth funds. And they yo-yo up and down much more. Some do enjoy spectacular growth spurts. But their gains are not consistent.

Don't settle for flashes in the pan—except for any mad money you're willing to risk. Even then, you must be willing to spend more time and effort watching them, and you must be willing to pull out on short notice when their latest boom goes bust. Then you've got the bother of deciding where to put your money: into either another sector fund, a diversified growth fund, or a money market fund.

You might as well start with the best growth fund on your plan's menu. Within your 401(k) plan you may not have many sector funds to choose from. You might as well select a fund that will give you growth, without making you chase after it.

Look for Winners

When you have more than enough funds to choose from, the central question is, how do you make your final selections?

The answer is that you should look for the best performers. Performance is measured by total return—the increase in value of a fund's share price, plus any interest, dividends, or other income the fund pays.

To find out what a fund's return is, you only need to look as far as your daily newspaper or in the fund prospectus. Large newspapers print tables listing total return for thousands of funds. Most list each fund's return since the beginning of the year. Some newspapers list return for other time periods as well. (See Chapter 19.)

You can understand this total return number better if you know what goes into it. Again, many newspapers print each of these components.

The biggest chunk of return is from a rise or decline in the price per share.

Share price is called *net asset value* (NAV). It indicates how much a fund's investments (stock, bonds, and other holdings) and cash are worth.

Each fund sets its NAV daily. A fund adds up its assets, subtracts expenses, and divides that total by the number of shares investors hold.

The reason that NAV alone does not tell each fund's complete story is that NAV does not reflect the value of dividends and interest paid to shareholders. In fact, a fund's NAV falls whenever a dividend is paid. That's because dividend payments are taken out of a fund's hide.

The cash used to pay you is no longer part of the fund's total assets.

What you need to know is the whole ball of wax: the combined increase in share price plus the value of *distributions.*

Distributions   Funds are required to pay out each year almost all of their interest, dividends, and profits from the sale of stocks and bonds (capital gains) they had invested in. Together, those payments of interest, dividends, and capital gains are called distributions.

You get that information in the total return number.

The total return tells you the size of a fund's total benefit to each shareholder. It's calculated as a percentage figure. A total return of 10 percent, for example, means the fund's value per share plus its distributions gained 10 percent. It is typically reported as a yearly percentage figure.

A 10-percent total return is the equivalent of a fund paying 10 percent interest, without any rise or fall in its share price.

In reality, it us usually a combination of rising value and distributions, with most of the gain for stock growth funds coming from escalating share price.

> **Cumulative Return and Average Annual Return**   Total return can also be calculated for periods longer than one year. Then, it is called *cumulative return.*
>
> When you divide cumulative return by the number of years involved, you get the *average annual return* for that period.

LOOK FOR ENDURANCE

You're looking for funds that will grow a lot in the future. One clue is how much a fund has grown in the past. But for how long in the past? The past month? Six months? Year?

As we've discussed, in your search for funds that are winners you must look well beyond the Top 10 list for this month, this quarter, or even just this year. Yes, you want a fund that has performed well. But you want a fund that shows potential for making you a lot of money in the future as well.

Don't be misled by funds that got lucky once. Don't be seduced by funds that happened to be in the right place at the right time—for the first and last time in their existence. Beware of funds whose own investments happened to soar, but for reasons the fund manager didn't foresee and can't duplicate.

Start by looking for funds that are doing well now.

Put aside the ones that are not diversified U.S. stock growth funds. That means culling out funds that happen to be top performers at the moment but are riskier in the long run, like sector funds and international funds.

Of the current highfliers remaining, check their past history. Past performance is not a guarantee of future success. But it's one of the few indicators of future performance you've got. If a fund has consistently shown the ability to grow a lot in years past, then it may be able to continue doing that if its strategy hasn't changed and its leadership is intact.

The flip side of that is true as well.

Don't look only at a fund's historical record. Check its current performance, too. That's the easiest way to spot any signal that the fund has lost its golden touch.

How far into the past should you look?

Two of the most useful time frames are three and five years.

What Three Years Tell You

Start by checking a fund's record over the past three years. That shows you how well a fund manager is faring against his or her best current competition. It also focuses on performance during recent market conditions.

As a result, 36 months are enough time to start to weed out the one-trick ponies of the fund world—funds that do well briefly, but can't sustain it.

The most valuable thing you can learn from examining a fund's three-year performance is whether it's got any problems—right now. A three-year period isn't long enough to mask present shortcomings with strong results from the more distant past. And if a fund is wrestling with difficulties, it may not recover. You may want to invest your money in another fund.

But don't rush to judgment. After putting your money into a fund with a good, steady, long-term performance, you shouldn't abandon it if the fund suffers a bad year. (We'll discuss the right time to bail out of a fund in Chapter 20.)

Look Back Five Years

In contrast, a five-year period shows you how well a fund has done under a variety of circumstances. It shows how well a fund has performed through thick and thin.

If a fund has succeeded whether the stock market is up or down, whether the economy is hot or cold, and no matter what a host of other variables are doing, then its investment approach is more likely to thrive in the future, when conditions will be just as variable and just as unpredictable.

If a fund has a good five-year history but is slipping now, that's a potential red flag. Does it have a new manager? Has its investment style changed? Is the economy simply punishing the industries on which it has made heavy bets?

If the problem is ongoing and likely to continue (like a new manager

Fund	Past Three Years		Past Five Years	
	Average Annual Return	Rank	Average Annual Return	Rank
Legg Mason Value Trust	31.49%	3	26.38%	1
Sequoia	31.15	4	24.99	2
White Oak Growth Stock	20.85	205	24.80	3
Vanguard Index Growth	28.57	7	24.08	4
Rydex Nova	28.69	6	23.84	5
Fidelity Dividend Growth	27.51	10	23.74	6
Enterprise Growth	25.99	21	23.31	7
Wilshire Target Funds Large Company Growth	26.42	15	22.87	8
Reynolds Blue Chip Growth	26.52	16	22.82	9
Accessor Growth	25.21	28	22.67	10
Janus Twenty	30.73	5	22.39	11
Nationwide III	28.72	7	22.37	12
Alliance Premier Growth	25.13	30	22.32	13
Vanguard World U.S. Growth	24.64	50	22.15	14
Dreyfus Appreciation	25.05	34	22.05	15
PIMCO Stocksplus	24.32	73	21.75	16
One Group Large Company Growth	25.91	22	21.72	17
PBHG Advisor Enhanced Equity	26.01	20	21.69	18
Torray Fund	22.43	137	21.64	19
Van Kampen Exchange	22.96	129	21.63	20
Capital Exchange	21.74	168	21.61	21
DG Investors Equity	25.10	31	21.56	22
Morgan Stanley Institutional Equity Growth	21.97	159	21.55	23
First Funds Growth and Income	24.57	60	21.16	24
State Street Research Exchange	24.83	44	21.09	25
Number of growth funds during this period		1,901		1,165

Note: Excludes different share classes of same fund.

FIGURE 18.3 Funds with endurance. All of the 25 best-performing diversified growth stock funds during the past five years were among the top 15 percent over the past three years as well. You should check recent, shorter time periods to see if these long-distance runners are showing signs of growing winded. *Source:* Lipper, Inc.

or change in style), that may be a good reason to avoid investing in that fund. If the problem is easily correctable or temporary and brief, the fund may still be a good long-term investment. But proceed with both eyes open.

Figure 18.3 lists diversified growth stock funds with the highest average annual returns over the past five years. Notice how almost all of them were also among the top 10 percent (ranked 190 or better) during the past three years. In fact, every single one was in the top 15 percent (ranked 285 or better) during the past three years.

But by looking back farther than three years, you lasso funds that may not show up in the shorter, three-year ranking because of one bad year—which may actually be due merely to a few bad months.

Measuring a fund over five years has another advantage: It weeds out the flukes.

Funds capable of performing well longer are what you really want, anyway.

Some funds make large bets on narrow segments of the economy, and come up winners—for brief periods, at least. Even if they are not sector funds in a formal sense, they behave like a sector fund—whether it is intentional or accidental. Military conflict or political turmoil can panic stock markets. Gold, oil, or other valuable commodities often shoot up in price. That drives up the stock of companies in those industries. Investors flock into funds holding such stocks, driving up their prices.

Their returns are inflated, making such funds look good over periods ranging from one to three years. Their numbers are real. But their future prospects are fuzzy.

Return figures for five years or more aren't inflated nearly as much by such fleeting appearances in the limelight.

That's why it's important to check return figures for longer periods.

How to Do Your
Investment Research

"**R**ead all about it . . . !"

For most people, the most convenient source of information about mutual fund performance is their daily newspaper. Most large daily papers print tables showing many funds' current NAV and total return so far for the year.

You can also find this information at a number of Internet Web sites. Funds themselves often post data at their own Web sites.

In addition to their daily snapshot of how funds did the previous day, many large newspapers publish a cornucopia of valuable information about funds: analyses of individual funds, fund families, fund managers, and the overall mutual fund industry; news affecting 401(k) investors; and performance data for thousands of funds over various time periods.

Meanwhile, your local library may stockpile reports from financial scouting services that analyze and handicap mutual funds.

Over in cyberspace, an increasing number of 401(k) plans operate Web sites, where plan members can obtain information about their own accounts, about the investment options offered by their plan (including performance data on individual funds), and about investing. Some describe how mutual funds have performed in the past, and based on that give hypothetical forecasts of how your portfolio would grow using various combinations of funds in the future.

These forecasting models generally reflect the asset allocation approach to investment planning. They advise you to cope with any squeamishness you feel when the stock market rock-'n'-rolls by selecting funds that tend instead to slow dance.

That may make you feel more comfortable during the market's periodic imitations of a Mexican jumping bean. But those funds will cost you money in the long run. The very characteristics that prevent them from fluctuating more in the short run also prevent them from growing more in the long run.

A better way to cope with the ups and downs of the market is to hold onto your shares. By not selling, you don't suffer any loss. You don't have any reason to feel squeamish. And you can go back to thinking long-term.

Asset allocation means sacrificing a larger nest egg.

Buy-and-hold means taking the long view to build a larger nest egg.

HOW TO CHECK OUT A FUND

Information about funds comes in all shapes, sizes, and flavors. No two newspapers go about this in exactly the same way. No two Internet sources are alike. No two specialized financial reports scope the investment dope identically.

Use one or more sources that suit your personal tastes and needs.

Knowing *what* information to seek is the key.

For example, *Investor's Business Daily* (for which the author of *Getting Started in 401(k) Investing* writes) devotes one section daily to mutual funds. Every Monday *IBD* runs a chart listing the top 25 growth funds for the previous three months, based on investment return, and a chart listing the top 25 growth funds for the prior 36 months. These help make Monday an especially good day to start your search for a growth fund to invest in.

Here's how they can assist you:

The three-month chart shows, first of all, which growth funds are currently delivering the biggest bang for investors' dollars.

Second, by looking at performance over the past 36 months, the three-year chart screens out any flash-in-the-pan funds. During serious military and political crises, for example, prices of commodities like gold and oil may skyrocket. Sector funds investing in those become the darlings of Wall Street. But when whatever passes for normalcy in our crazy world returns, those sector funds sag back into the pack—or fade badly.

Used together, the 36-month and three-month charts show not only who's hot but who's got stamina and endurance.

There's more.

Only funds with at least $100 million in assets are eligible for listing. That restricts these charts to funds that have performed well enough to earn the confidence of a lot of investors. Those investors include professional money managers for wealthy institutions (such as universities and corporations) and individuals. These pros are part of Wall Street's "smart money." They certainly are not right all of the time. But, ironically, even when they are wrong, their sheer weight in numbers and dollars means they can buoy the price of a mutual fund.

The charts are also limited to those funds that have earned a three-year performance ranking of "B" or better from *IBD*. Every day, in these special charts as well as its inside tables listing thousands of funds, the paper publishes its rankings of funds, based on performance. Funds in the top 5 percent of the industry earn an A+ ranking. Those in the top 10 percent are ranked A. The top 15 percent get an A– ranking. The top 20 percent are ranked B+. And so on.

So, the ranking gives you insight into how an individual fund performs against all other funds. This makes it easier to spot those with strong track records.

The inside tables provide another tool to help you choose a fund. Every fund's five-year, after-tax total return is listed. This performance figure is valuable for three reasons:

1. It extends the time horizon of the three-year chart. This widens your search, giving you a second chance to spot a very good growth fund that may have briefly stumbled enough to be knocked out of the top-25 chart over the most recent three years. But if the fund has performed exceptionally well and consistently over a longer period, you'll be able to spot it thanks to its five-year return.

2. The five-year time horizon highlights the strongest and most consistent performers over the long haul. The 36-month period is short enough to let in funds that did unusually well only recently. The five-year return column shows which funds are capable of sustaining top performance over the marathon distance.

3. The five-year, after-tax performance clarifies your bottom-line return. This tells you how well each fund did over the past five years after estimated taxes were paid. Since earnings inside your 401(k) account are free from taxes until you start withdrawals, your five-year return on this fund (if you owned it) was better than the listed return figure.

If you have investments outside your 401(k) account (or if you're approaching retirement and plan to take money out of your account for investing in funds—which will make their earnings taxable), this column in the inside tables shows how much money you would have taken home after settling up with Uncle Sam. It assumes an average ordinary income tax rate of 35 percent on dividends and 28 percent on long-term capital gains. Because you probably would be in a lower tax bracket, your actual take-home return was likely to be higher.

Spotlight on Individual Funds

Also in the Monday mutual funds section are a second set of charts, showing more details about some of the best five-year performers. Only funds with a 36-month ranking of A– or higher are eligible.

Each of these charts focuses on a single fund. Inside every fund's chart are five sets of bar graphs, which illustrate how each fund has done so far that year in comparison to the S&P 500, and how it did in each of the four previous years versus the broad market benchmark. Each fund's chart gives its 36-month ranking and other details, such as how far the fund tumbled in its two worst declines during the past five years.

The 10 stocks that make up most of each fund's portfolio are listed, along with data indicating the strength of each of those stocks. Each fund's chart also shows what stocks the fund has been buying and selling. You can decide for yourself whether each fund is fishing in the right pond.

Likewise, you can compare the investments made by these top-ranked funds and look for similarities in how skilled fund managers think. If you invest in individual stocks—either inside a very flexible 401(k) plan or outside on your own—there's a lot you can learn from the pros.

Also listed in each fund's chart: how long the current manager has been on the job. Often, the best-performing funds' managers have long tenure.

If a fund has a new manager, you should ask yourself whether that fund's family has an investment strategy that works for a lot of its funds. Look at the tables inside the mutual fund section. Check other funds owned by that company. A new manager in an overall strong fund family may not be cause for concern. But a new manager in a family whose other funds don't perform well—watch out.

Back in the special charts with bar graphs, examine the fund's performance during the period the new manager has been at the helm. Has performance slipped? Especially, has it slipped relative to the S&P 500? If so, you've spotted a red flag that bears further examination.

Check Other Time Periods

On other days, *IBD* charts the 25 best-performing growth funds over shorter periods, such as 6 months, 12 months, and 24 months. These charts can help you fine-tune your search for investments.

For one thing, these shorter-period charts can help answer your questions about a fund with a new manager. Despite having been a winner in the past, can you spot evidence of the fund's return slipping now that a new pilot is at the controls?

Another useful gauge: Every other Wednesday the paper carries charts that list the 25 funds that have done best since the stock market peaked in 1990 and the 25 that have done best since the low point of the market in 1990. (The market suffered a bad downturn that year, after Iraq invaded Kuwait.)

These charts are reminders that the stock market has always rebounded from difficulties. It also provides a way to see the most successful funds over a longer time span than five years.

As your search homes in on certain long-term growth funds, get their prospectus, annual report, and semiannual report. The prospectus will describe a fund's investment style. The annual and semiannual reports will show you what each fund invests in.

Aim for funds that buy stock in strong companies, with solid earnings growth rates. Those are the funds you can hold onto for the long haul.

EXPENSES

Never put the cart before the horse. Some funds boast about being "tax-efficient." Some brag about their low expenses.

So what? The only thing that matters is how much money you keep at the end of the day.

A low-tax or low-cost fund is not much good if its total return is less than a more expensive fund's.

By all means, check out fund expenses and taxes. But base your selections on after-tax and after-cost total return, and a fund's future prospects.

When all other things are equal, go for the lower-tax, lower-cost fund.

What Costs Should You Beware Of?

Unless you have an exceptionally generous plan, you're going to get socked for two kinds of fees and expenses. The only questions are how much of each you'll have to pay and whether your share of these costs is rising.

Basically, plans charge administrative costs and investment management fees.

Administrative costs cover the fees charged by people and organizations like the trustees and record keeper. (See Chapter 7 for a description of who's who in your plan.) These are the folks who take care of all the paperwork, who handle your money, and who make sure your plan is obeying the myriad rules and regulations that govern 401(k) plans.

In addition to those costs, plan members pay managers of the investments in their plan. These fees vary from manager to manager. Various types of investments have different costs, too. Even the same types of investments impose different fees. Two mutual funds with the same investment objectives and style but run by competing fund families, for example, can charge fees that are not the same.

Investment management fees are spelled out in the prospectus for each mutual fund. Prospectuses are deadly dull reading. They're written by lawyers for other lawyers. (Fortunately, the government recently gave funds the green light to provide you with easier-to-read versions of prospectuses written in plain English. They're still as exciting as watching a wall clock tick. But they are easier to understand. And they do contain important information, such as how much your fund is charging you for trusting your money with them.)

In the front of the prospectus you'll find the *expense ratio*. This tells you how much the fund's annual operating expenses are. It's presented as a percentage of the fund's total assets. The lower this ratio, the less you're paying.

You'll also find an illustration in the prospectus section on fees and expenses, showing how much the expenses eat away from your return on a hypothetical $1000 investment earning 5 percent a year for one, five, and ten years.

These expenses hit you in your wallet or pocketbook. Every percentage point you pay in fees reduced your fund's return by the same amount. Only a minority of companies pick up these fees for their plan members.

An examination of fees and expenses by the U.S. Department of Labor (DOL) cited a study that had found expense ratios for growth funds ranging from 0.2 percent to 6.49 percent. The average was 1.42 percent. You should be asking yourself (not to mention your plan administrator) whether a fund is worthwhile if its expense ratio is higher than 1.5 percent.

Bear in mind that stock funds generally have higher expense ratios than bond funds. Index funds tend to have lower expenses than actively managed funds.

Real Money, Real Pain

The Department of Labor report illustrated the negative jolt of fees and expenses. Suppose a worker has $25,000 in a 401(k) account. Imagine his or her investments are earning an average return of 7 percent annually for 35 years. With yearly fees and expenses of 0.5 percent, the nest egg will grow to $227,000 over 35 years.

But if fees and expenses total 1.5 percent, the account will blossom to only $163,000.

Merely adding one percentage point in fees and expenses chops off 28 percent from the account balance. For that plan member, the issue of whether those fees and expenses are worthwhile is literally a $64,000 question.

But don't shoot yourself in the financial foot. If a fund is dramatically outperforming all others available to you, paying its expenses may be worthwhile. If a fund's yearly return exceeds the return from other options by more than the expense ratio, then you should stick with the better-performing fund.

(Plan members also shoulder individualized fees for taking advantage of optional services like loans. These pay-as-you-go fees are either part of administrative costs or a third category of costs.)

Investment management fees are commonly larger than administrative fees. They usually account for 75 percent to 90 percent of a plan's expenses, according to the DOL study. Generally, administrative costs and investment management fees are automatically deducted from your account.

Fees and expenses themselves aren't necessarily a problem.

The DOL study identified two issues that are real problems. First, many plans are shifting administrative costs onto plan members. And second, often plans do not disclose or explain their fees and expenses clearly. For example, banks and insurance companies are not yet required to describe their charges as clearly as mutual funds are in their prospectuses.

As a result, plan members often have little or no idea how much they are paying.

Without question, people and organizations serving your plan are entitled to compensation. But if you have questions about the fees and expenses levied by your plan and various investment choices, you should ask your plan administrator or benefits office for help in understanding them.

Chapter

Taking Care of Your Account

Okay. You've bought shares in your first mutual fund in your 401(k) plan.

Now what?

Well, your plan requires continuing maintenance, like a car or a plant or a pet. Here are the things to watch out for.

HOW MANY FUNDS IS ENOUGH?

After buying your first fund shares, you may start to wonder whether one fund is enough. The answer depends on several circumstances.

First, how many funds or other investment options are in your plan? How many choices do you have? If your plan only offers three choices, and one of them is a money market fund while the second one is a bond fund, your decision is easy.

The third one is probably some sort of stock fund or the closest thing to that on your plan's menu. It may be a modest performer if your company opted for an investment that fluctuates very little in the short run.

So whether this third choice is a diversified growth stock fund or a fund with built-in shock absorbers (such as a balanced fund, lifestyle fund, growth and income fund, equity income fund, or asset allocation fund), it should provide a better long-term return than a money market or bond fund. Take it.

Then start lobbying your company and plan administrator for more, better investment choices in the future.

Even if you have more choices, your decision isn't necessarily really tough.

Suppose you've got four growth funds to choose from. If they've all got similar performance records and similar prospects for the future, you could start to stick your money into two or three of them.

One advantage is that you are diversifying, cutting down your investment risk. If a torpedo hits one of the funds, all of your money won't be jeopardized. Let's say the genius manager who has steered the leading fund to a decade of glorious returns retires. The fund's performance starts to wobble under the successor's management. You've got to decide whether to bail out of that fund (see next section). Meanwhile, your money is divided among other funds where it is safe.

Another advantage is that you'll probably start to closely watch all of the funds you've put money into. It's human nature. You'll begin to notice small differences in performance. You may see small differences in how they invest your money. This ongoing tutorial will help prepare you to make future fund selections.

A third advantage is that a wider selection may make your choices easier and less time-consuming. If you've narrowed your decision to several look-alike funds, choose more than one. After all, the most important thing is to put your money to work as soon as possible. Rather than obsess and wonder which single fund to select, select two or three.

You can always keep track of their performance after that and consolidate your money into fewer funds, sticking with the ones that turn out to be best.

On the other hand, one potential disadvantage to splitting your money is cost. You may have to pay additional fees to your plan. Likewise, if each fund in your plan charges an entry fee or sales commission you will have to pay those.

You'll have to weigh fees and expenses against the potential benefits. If the costs are modest, it may well be worthwhile.

If all of the growth funds are not similar, it's still all right to choose more than one as long as you select the one, two, or three whose records and prospects most closely resemble each other.

WHEN TO SELL A FUND

Let's say you commit yourself to a long-term investment strategy. You're poised to select growth stock funds that promise to reward you with the largest, steadiest cumulative return between now and retirement. At the same time, you're the first to admit you're no Rambo. You're no braver than the next guy or gal when the stock market has one of its periodic conniption fits.

You know an asset allocation approach would give you a smoother ride. But an asset allocation approach would require you to voluntarily give up some of the potential long-term growth of your nest egg. Sure, growth stock funds twitch every time Wall Street hiccups. But in the end a buy-and-hold strategy will reward your patience.

So you've decided to go for maximum steady growth.

That doesn't mean you'll never have to bail out of a mutual fund. Even with a long-term strategy, from time to time you may have to get out of a fund and replace it with another.

The *wrong* time to sell is when your fund is merely playing Simon Says, nose-diving along with its competitors.

Perhaps a tinhorn dictator has invaded his neighboring, oil-rich sheikdom. Or the Federal Reserve has jacked up interest rates even though the economy has slowed to a crawl.

Your first decision, then, is to figure out whether your fund is merely reacting to far-reaching conditions affecting all other funds as well. If so, sit tight. Your fund hasn't lost its touch. Chances are it will bounce back when the headlines stop screaming or the economy starts humming again.

Meanwhile, there may not be anything better to put your money into.

Even if there is something performing better at the moment (some sort of fund that zigs when everyone else zags), if you shift your money into it you almost certainly will fail to get back into your good old growth stock fund in time to benefit from the market's inevitable rebound. By the time you do get back in, you'll have lost out on much of the market's recovery.

Meanwhile, the life-preserver of a fund that you latched onto for safety? It will zig downward just as the rest of the market finally zags skyward.

Telling Right from Wrong

The correct time to sell is when your fund stops doing the things that sold you on it in the first place. When a top-ranked fund becomes merely rank, it's time to head for the exits.

One thing that will reverse a fund's fortunes is called *style drift*. Style drift is what happens when a fund abandons its own game plan and starts to use a different investment strategy from the one it staked out in its prospectus. A fund is free to seek its own fame and fortune in practically any way its brain trust of managers and researchers sees fit. But it is required to warn all potential investors how it plans to do that. And it is supposed to be true to its word.

Each fund's description of its intended investment approach is general. It is not a blueprint, locking the fund into specific stocks, bonds, and other investments. It merely describes in general whether the fund will use a meat-and-potatoes recipe of stocks and bonds. Or whether its tastes will be more exotic, favoring specialized investment tools like options and futures contracts. Will it stick to home cookin', buying only U.S. stocks? Or will it prefer a menu spiced with foreign securities? Does it have a hankering for "chunky" morsels—large-company stocks? Or will it nibble on small or medium-sized businesses? And what will it drool after—undervalued stocks, or pricey stocks that promise big future earnings?

For example, suppose you had invested in a fund that promised to buy the stocks of large U.S. corporations. Your decision had been based on the fact that big, blue-chip businesses were the dynamos of the American economy during the late 1990s. They racked up ever-growing earnings. Their stock prices soared. Funds that owned them prospered.

Then without warning your fund began to pare back on big corporations, replacing them with stocks of small technology companies it was sure would grow like weeds in a daisy field. But they didn't take off after all. And your fund's return began to slide.

That would be a case of style drift. And that would be a time to consider getting rid of that fund.

Style drift can also occur when a new manager takes the helm of a fund. The newcomer may prefer a different approach, or simply may not be as good at executing the former skipper's game plan.

Whatever the cause of performance erosion relative to growth benchmarks, how long should you wait before pulling the plug?

After all, even great managers can suffer a bad year from time to time. Withdrawing prematurely can cause wasted stress and inconvenience. It could also mean losing out on future stellar returns from a manager who hasn't in fact forgotten how to make money.

A rule of thumb is to exercise patience for one year with any fund that has demonstrated consistent superiority. But if weak performance relative to other growth leaders and growth-fund benchmarks continues after that, strap on your parachute. If your former wonder fund is still heading for a crash landing after 18 to 24 months, hit the silk!

Be especially wary if a fund's deterioration is very steep. A research group at the Charles Schwab brokerage firm found that when a fund slumps into the bottom 25 percent of its peer group in terms of performance, investors improve their long-term returns by declaring, "Later, dudes."

Your Needs Change

Another reason to get rid of a fund has nothing to do with the fund itself. It's when your own investment profile changes.

Suppose for years your long-range game plan has called for you to buy a fishing boat once your reach retirement. Nothing fancy, mind you. Just a simple 20-foot outboard, no deck, no cabin. You're more than willing to buy a used craft. You'll need $13,000.

Now after, say, 40 years on the job you're 12 months away from accepting your gold watch and punching out for the last time.

All along you've been investing in long-term growth funds. But what now?

Option #1 (Also Known as the "Having Your Cake and Eating It, Too" Scenario). You don't have to make any special arrangements.

Of course, this scenario is possible only if you started early enough, if you invested in growth stock funds, and if year by year you contributed enough, so now your nest egg is big enough to withstand a 30 percent plunge in the stock market the week before you're supposed to pay for your new boat. Even if the market were to collapse like that—highly unlikely, but possible—and your account suddenly loses 30 percent of its worth, you'll still have enough money in it to buy the boat . . . and generate sufficient income to pay for living expenses during your first year of retirement, as planned and budgeted.

Option #2 (Also Known as the "You've Got More Options Than You Think" Scenario). It's time to shift $13,000 into something less risky in the near future. You're looking for a fund that will not fluctuate much, no matter what happens in the market. Reasonable candidates: a growth and income, equity income, or balanced fund. All seek growth while churning out income. The balanced fund, which gets its income from bonds, will be the most stable in the short run.

For even greater stability, consider a bond or other fixed-income fund. Three to six months ahead of casting off, you might shift your money into a money market fund.

When you start your countdown 12 months or so away from retirement, if the market forecast for the next year is for anything less than smooth sailing—or if the financial waters are already choppy—lean toward your more conservative options when you first shift $13,000 out of a growth fund; then move into the money market fund earlier.

The sole occasion when you should consider allocating money to something other than a long-term growth stock fund is when your own investment profile changes. You are no longer a purely long-term investor when you need a specific amount of money at a date that is fast approaching.

That date makes you a short-term investor with the money you plan to spend. Whether it is for a boat, a down payment on a house, college tuition for a grandchild, or a new car—all have specific price tags. You can't afford to have the earmarked funds lose value. You can't accomplish what you want with less than the planned amount of dollars.

That's when you need to set aside the money in a fund that won't fluctuate down in value just at the moment of fiscal truth.

But the rest of your money should be kept hard at work in long-term growth funds, building for the more distant future.

The Fund Grows Too Large

Often, after a mutual fund lands atop one of those Top 10 listings in a major magazine, the fund is deluged by money from investors.

The fund loves it, right?

Not always.

In fact, some funds respond by slamming their door shut in the face of wanna-be investors.

The reason a fund would do that is because of a nagging fear that a mutual fund can grow too big for its own (and shareholders') good. Once those new dollars arrive, they become part of the fund's assets. Fund size is measured in terms of its assets, whether those consist of stock in which the fund has invested or cash sitting in the fund's bank account. All of it has a dollar value: That's the fund's assets size.

So much new money can arrive that fund managers can't put it to work fast enough in the type of investments the managers know best.

The problem, say some money managers, is that a "bloated" fund can't find enough shares of the right stocks at a low enough price to remain a winner. A fund that becomes too big, they say, drives up the price of stocks it wants to buy by virtue of needing so much.

These skeptics say that a fund that's too big can no more navigate discreetly through the stock market than, say, an elephant can tiptoe quietly through the tropical wilds without being noticed.

Defenders of big funds dismiss that argument. The stock market is huge, they counter. And investment professionals buy and sell stocks in small enough portions to avoid tipping their hands.

Some funds do take the drastic step of closing their doors to new investors—but they usually let existing shareholders or people in 401(k) plans continue to invest.

One major reason these funds pull up the drawbridge is that their newly arrived cash is earning next to nothing, sitting in the bank or money market. That lowers the fund's overall performance statistics.

Sometimes managers cope with a flood of fresh cash by changing their investment style. Unable to find enough of the investments they know best, they start to invest in companies that are bigger or smaller than what the fund specializes in. Similarly, a fund that likes to shop for bargain-basement stocks may detour into buying high-priced S&P 500 index stocks.

This is a cause for concern. What a fund's expertise is may not matter. Only its success matters. But veering from its strength could be a first step toward a lower performance.

Size itself may not be a problem for a fund. But as a fund's assets grow, watch its returns and watch what it is investing in. If returns start to lag while the rest of the market perks along, or if a fund starts to change its investment approach, you're looking at red flags.

Proceed with caution.

Merger

If your fund merges with another fund that has a mediocre or worse long-term record, watch out.

The key question is whether the unified fund that results will successfully use the weaker fund's money.

The answer will depend on two issues:

1. Who will manage the merged fund? Will it be the manager of the stronger of the two original funds?

2. Will the merger provide cash that the manager of the survivor fund can use to take advantage of promising investment opportunities?

When your fund management bombards you with propaganda about why you should give this little experiment a chance to work, see if they address those issues.

If they don't—or if this looks like a marriage between two forgettable funds—consider putting your money to work in a different fund.

BEWARE OF SCAMS

Every so often federal investigators make headlines with a splashy prosecution of a scam artist. The scamster may turn out to be president or treasurer of a small business, diverting worker contributions into the officer's own pocket or leaving company matching funds in the company's own bank account, instead of worker 401(k) accounts.

Fortunately, abuse of 401(k) plans is rare.

But when it does occur, it is most likely to take place in small companies that are ailing financially. That's particularly true when company officials run the plan or handle its investments.

The culprit figures that if the money is borrowed—just temporarily, of course—to pay company suppliers, who'd notice? Besides, wouldn't all the employees be better off if the boss does something to help the company and thereby protects their jobs?

Unfortunately, if the company continues to bleed red ink there's never enough spare cash to pay back to the plan.

Sometimes problems arise due to lack of resources or innocent errors. Money is missing because of a bookkeeping error or delayed paperwork, not because of felonious mischief.

While problems of any kind are uncommon, it's best to know the warning signs in advance.

Some things to watch out for, according to the Department of Labor:

✔ Your account statement is frequently late or never reaches you.

✔ Your account balance is unexplainably wrong.

✔ Your account balance or individual investments drop by more than can be explained by what happened on the stock market.

✔ Matching contributions from your company don't appear on your statement, or the amounts are too small.

If any of those red flags crop up, before you call Eliot Ness do a little homework.

First, compare account balance figures on your pay stub with your account statement.

Also, dial into your plan's touch-tone telephone hot line or check your account's status on-line by computer.

Remember, you can't take these precautionary steps if you don't keep your account statements and plan literature.

And if your plan record keeper and/or plan administrator are not executives or employees of your company, ask them for an explanation.

There are other warning signs to watch for:

✔ Former employees having difficulty getting their payouts, access to their accounts, or information. Delayed payments or incorrect amounts are also a potential problem.

✔ Investments you have not chosen appearing on your statement.

✔ Musical chairs among investment or plan managers.

✔ Unusual or unexplained transactions or expenses, like a loan to company officers or plan trustees.

Ask the plan administrator or the plan contact person in your benefits office for an explanation before jumping to conclusions and taking rash action.

Likewise, don't misinterpret normal administrative delays as illegal abuse. Most companies, for example, have up to 15 business days after the end of each month to put your own contributions into your account. That means a lag of about 45 days is perfectly normal.

A company can take even longer depositing its matching contribution into your account. It can take as long as the plan's regulations allow, and it is the company that writes those rules. The majority of corporations deposit their matching contributions only once annually.

If you think there's a problem, check your plan's rules. You'll find them in the summary plan description. If you still think funds are being handled incorrectly, ask the plan administrator or benefits office what's up. Describe the situation. Present documentation you have. And politely and in a businesslike fashion ask for an explanation.

Remember, chances are there's a perfectly reasonable one.

But if you still can't get a satisfactory answer, contact your local office of the Department of Labor's Pension and Welfare Benefits Administration. Look for its telephone number in the blue pages of your phone book. Or call the PWBA at 202-219-8776.

ANNUAL CHECKUP

Once a year you should pull in for a pit stop. Pop the hood, pull the dipstick, check the spark plugs. Give your account a thorough once-over.

Take a look at your funds and see how they are doing.

Question #1: Are they doing okay?

Question #2: Are they doing what you expect?

Question #3: Are they doing okay compared to other funds?

Asset allocation strategists put an additional spin on this annual checkup ritual. They advise investors to compare their funds to others in the same category. Further, they advocate juggling your investments to restore the proportions you originally intended in your account.

Let's say you wanted 70 percent of your money to be in S&P 500 index funds, 15 percent of your money in small-company stock funds, and the remaining 15 percent to be in bond funds. But suppose the economy has been wonderful the past year, and your S&P 500 funds grew much more than the other two. Now 78 percent of your money is in S&P 500 funds, 18 percent is in small-company stock funds, and only 4 percent is in bond funds.

Asset allocators would say it is time to restore the 70-15-15 ratio called for by your game plan.

One way to do that is not by pulling money out of any funds, but by changing future allocations of your weekly contributions. Over time, that would restore the intended balance.

Of course, that approach is best only if you are using an asset allocation strategy. As we've discussed, an asset allocation strategy requires you to sacrifice long-term investment performance for the sake of funds that won't—or at least aren't *supposed* to—bob up and down as much in the short run.

In contrast, if you use a long-term buy-and-hold strategy part of your job is to remind yourself that short-term turbulence can't hurt if you are not selling shares. And you're not, if you are keeping them invested for the long haul. As a result, you don't need to sacrifice long-term growth for less volatile investments. Keep all of the money you don't need for an upcoming expense in diversified growth stock funds.

But you still need to perform an annual checkup. Here's why.

You need to see if your diversified growth stock funds are still performing the way you expected them to when you first bought shares. Compare them to the other growth funds on your plan's investment menu. Are they still among the leaders?

Compare them to other leading growth funds industry-wide over the past year, three years, and five years. Are yours still among the leaders there, too?

A tune-up for your car involves more than putting air in the tires and washing the windshield. It means lifting the hood to check the engine. You should look inside your funds, too. Are the managers who ran each of them when you first bought shares still on board? If a manager has left one, has that affected the fund?

Check each fund's investments and investment style. Has anything changed significantly, or is the fund still doing what it does best? Is the fund investing in the same industries in the same portions as before? In large companies? Medium-sized? Small?

Is the fund still investing in expensive, S&P 500 growth stocks? Or in undervalued mavericks?

A fund doesn't have to keep investing in the same industries year after year. In fact, you should not expect one to. That's precisely what you're paying a manager to do: Shop around and find the very best industries. Skill at that is part of what makes a superstar rather than a run-of-the-mill manager.

But comparing a fund's industry sectors to its sectors a year ago is simply a good way to start to get a handle on a fund. It is a starting point in understanding a fund.

Finally, check a fund's expenses. Total return, after taxes and after expenses, is your main concern. It doesn't matter how heavy a fund's expenses and taxes are if its net total return is still better than its competitors'. But if performance is slipping and expenses and taxes are rising, that can cut down a fund's bottom-line performance. (Although taxes aren't an issue inside your 401(k) account.)

Besides, in a weak economy when the market is doing worse than before, expenses (and taxes) may have relatively more impact on the bottom line. For example, if your fund's expense ratio is 1.5 percent, that's not so important if the fund's return is 30 percent. But if your fund's return slips to 10 percent and its expenses inch upward to, say, 1.7 percent, your net return is a lot less. Again, compare it to your other options.

To find all this data, start with these sources: your fund's prospectus, annual report, and semiannual report, and your account statement (the printed version, the touch-tone phone version, or the version on your plan's Web site).

Consider switching future contributions to another fund that's doing better only if your current fund's performance is falling, and falling more than the market overall and other funds available to you in your plan.

Consider taking action if its relative disappointment has persisted at least one year. Stop considering—and pull the trigger—if its relative underperformance lasts 18 to 24 months.

You may want to pull old money as well if underperformance is severe and the fund shows no sign of being able to reverse the free fall: new manager, merger with another fund, unrepentant style drift.

Chapter 21

Sources of Information

Now that you know what information to look for, you need to know where you can find it.

Basically, you have three choices: newspapers and magazines, specialty research publications, and the Internet.

Each of those can help you accomplish various tasks.

Your first task is to identify the growth stock funds offered by your plan.

Your second job is to decide which of the available funds are the most consistent long-term top performers.

Your third step is to narrow your choices by identifying which long-term winners are best positioned for continued success: which ones have the management team that got them so far still intact, which have not changed their winning investment style, and which use an investment approach that doesn't depend on quirks or temperamental cycles.

All that's required by the first step—identifying the growth stock funds offered by your plan—is a look at each fund's prospectus or how the fund is identified by other plan literature or in news publications.

The second step—deciding which of the available funds are the most consistent long-term top performers—requires examining the vital signs of your options. Those vital signs tell you the current status of mutual funds. They also give you your first look at how a fund has done in the past, with clues about a fund's prospects for future performance.

This is some of the most basic information about a fund: price per share, which is also called net asset value (NAV); previous day's rise or fall in price; and percentage change in NAV. Percentage change in NAV since the day before as well as since the start of the year are commonly provided.

NEWSPAPERS AND WEB SITES

Daily newspapers and Internet Web sites are your most widely and most often available sources of this essential data—the temperature, pulse, and blood pressure of mutual funds.

Availability *now* is one of their strengths. It is part of what distinguishes them from other types of information sources. In the real world—in *your* life—when you're ready to begin searching for the best available investments, you want to get started today, at the precise moment that's most convenient for you.

Checking the vital signs of mutual funds is just a starting point. You should not focus on daily changes with an eye to buying and selling shares as prices tick up or down. Steady, methodical accumulation of shares should be your goal.

The most useful daily newspapers and Web sites provide additional information about how funds have done over longer periods of time. You need that because repeated good performance in the past is one of the key signs of a fund's prospects for good, *long-term*, future performance. A flash in the pan is useless. The fact that a fund finds itself king of the hill for a month, for a quarter, or even for one year doesn't tell you whether a fund got there by accident or by hard work, whether it is doing something that works all the time or only during once-in-a-blue-moon situations.

You need to know whether a fund has what it takes to sustain a high return year in, year out.

You'll find that longer-term performance information in listings that describe each fund's return for various time periods, in charts and tables that focus on the most durable winners, and in stories that point out winners and losers and explain what's behind the numbers.

Information is the food of investment life. The fresher the better.

In daily newspapers, you are looking at information that reflects the previous day's stock market results. Longer-term information typically is also keyed to the previous day's results. Some long-term data is as current as the last day of the previous month. The top of any table, chart, or listing will tell you what the as-of date is.

When studying information on a Web site, always check the as-of date of data. Is the data current as of today? Yesterday? Last week?

You need to know whether you're looking at information that is as timely as possible. You need to know whether you're looking at information that reflects, say, that jump or fall in the market yesterday or the week before.

One word of caution concerning Web sites: Watch where you step. As with any source of information, print or electronic, credibility is the Holy Grail. Some Web sites are produced by news or financial services organizations with a tradition of reliability. Others are produced by organizations with a vested interest in selling you something.

In addition, in the spirit of free and open democracy some Web sites permit the public to post messages or "articles." Some may be contributed by people with a financial interest in steering you toward a particular investment.

Always ask yourself what you know about a source of information, and how you know you can trust it. There's not necessarily anything wrong with a Web site having a point of view. Just be sure you understand what it is.

MAGAZINES

Many useful magazines are published weekly, biweekly, or monthly.

In their pages you can find listings of performance over time periods that are at least as long as the magazine's publication cycle. In other words, a monthly magazine might list performance data covering the previous month, since the magazine's prior issue. (Obviously, the as-of date will match or precede the date of publication, depending on how swiftly the magazine obtains and prepares data right before deadline.)

Magazines (like newspapers and Web sites) also publish longer-term data.

Because they can't compete with newspapers and Web sites as sources for daily updates, magazines try to provide in-depth analysis of investment trends and of winning and losing funds over various time periods. (Newspapers and Web sites fight back by providing their own detailed analyses.)

Another thing you can look for in magazines is information identifying potentially rising mutual-fund stars, which may be worthy of your investment dollars in the future.

In any case, consider doing this: After using newspapers and Web sites to narrow down your choices on the basis of current and past performance, look for stories in magazines about your top prospects. It's not that you can't find stories like that in newspapers, too. In fact, you can. And should.

But magazines can provide a second opinion. Look for information that contradicts or confirms what you've already learned. (When a contradiction pops up, it's up to you to weigh the two sources and decide which seems more credible. Maybe you'll decide to do more research.)

Since you've already begun to narrow down your choices, you're looking for information that makes one option more or less attractive than it already is.

A key thing to look for is evidence that explains why you can count on a fund to continue its past success. Likewise, watch out for clues as to why a fund may not be able to continue its past success. Perhaps a long-time manager has departed. Or a fund is showing signs of wandering from its tried-and-true investment style. Or it is using an investment approach that depends on quirks or temperamental business cycles. Or the fund is finding success hard to take—perhaps its performance is slipping because it has grown too large.

Of course, newspapers and Web sites can also provide analytical reports and periscopes on the future.

It's up to you to choose one or more sources of information that you trust and that suit your tastes and needs.

SPECIALTY RESEARCH SOURCES

Specialty research publications can provide at least some of all the information you can find in newspapers, on Web sites, and in magazines. Their drawbacks are their expense, the inconvenience of having to go to a public library (unless you do in fact want to pay the hefty price tag for your own subscription), and—ironically—the great amount of detail many provide.

They are a source of basic information. They are also a source of in-depth analysis.

Many are available as printed publications and on-line at various Internet Web sites. Some are also available on CD-ROM for perusal on a personal computer equipped with a CD drive.

The printed versions in libraries are typically in loose-leaf binders.

Understand Rating Methods

Some research sources rate or rank mutual funds. *Investor's Business Daily*, for example, compares all of its listed funds against each other. Its 36-month rankings reveal how a fund stacks up against all others listed. The idea is to help you choose the best long-term performers.

In contrast, Morningstar, Inc.'s ratings are based on what's called *risk-adjusted performance*. That means a fund may be rated higher in part because of lower risk.

That system may be more useful to someone who wants to avoid funds whose return may fluctuate a lot in the short run. (That's what investors using an asset allocation strategy do.) So, a person who wants to invest in funds most likely to provide the highest long-term return—regardless of occasional volatility—would find Morningstar's data and analysis more relevant than its ratings.

Also, some research sources rate funds only against others in their own category. This system may also be less useful for someone who wants to select the best-possible investments overall.

SELECTED INFORMATION SOURCES

Newspapers

Investor's Business Daily, 800-831-2525.
Wall Street Journal, 800-568-7625.

Web Sites

www.bloomberg.com   Site includes a calculator that will help you figure out how large your 401(k) plan

	account will be in a specified number of years. You can plug in assorted assumptions, such as how much you contribute, the size of your company's matching contribution, and the rate of return on your investments.
www.fidelity.com	Information and planning tools from the world's largest mutual fund company.
www.investors.com	Information from *Investor's Business Daily*.
www.morningstar.net	Information and analysis from the research firm Morningstar, Inc.
www.schwab.com	Information about Schwab's own funds and others it sells.
www.vanguard.com	Information and planning tools from the second-largest mutual fund family.
http://wsj.com	Information from the *Wall Street Journal*.

Magazines

Forbes, 212-620-2200.

Fortune, 800-621-8000.

Kiplinger's Personal Finance Magazine, 202-887-6400.

Money, 212-522-1212.

Modern Maturity, 800-424-3410.

Specialty Research Sources

Morningstar Mutual Funds: A loose-leaf binder, with a page for each of 1600-plus funds. Current and past performance data and analysis on each fund.

Value Line Mutual Fund Survey: Individual fund reports similar to Morningstar's.

Standard & Poor's/Lipper Mutual Fund Profiles: Half-page profiles of mutual funds.

CDA/Wiesenberger Mutual Funds Updates: Monthly updated directory, with past performance of and data on more than 9000 funds.

Plan or Fund Documents

Prospectus.

Annual report.

Semiannual report.

Summary plan description.

Social Security Benefits

EARNING YOUR ELIGIBILITY

Social Security benefits are a reminder that Adam and Eve were expelled from the Garden of Eden. To be eligible for benefits, you must work and pay Social Security taxes. (However, if you are a dependent or a survivor of an eligible worker, you can also get benefits.)

Your eligibility is measured in terms of the "credits" you earn as a taxpaying worker. In 1998 you receive one credit for each $700 in earnings from wages and salary, up to a maximum of four credits a year. (To keep pace with the rising cost of living, the amount of money needed to earn one credit is increased periodically.)

People born in 1929 or later need 40 credits (10 years of work) to become eligible to receive credit. People born earlier need fewer. If you were born in 1928, you need only 39 credits. If you were born in 1927, only 38; and so on.

Once you cross that threshold of eligibility, any extra credits you earn do not increase the size of your monthly check. However, the higher your *income*, the higher your benefits. Also, although you can't increase the size of your benefit check by working more years, you *can* increase the money you receive by delaying the start of receiving benefits.

CALCULATING YOUR BENEFITS

Basically, your benefits are based on your earnings averaged over your working lifetime.

If you were born after 1928 (and are retiring any time after 1990), the system calculates your average earnings over your 35 highest income years. Fewer years are used for anyone born in 1928 or earlier. The Social Security Administration adjusts your earnings for inflation, then determines your average adjusted monthly earnings over those 35 (or fewer) years. Finally, your average adjusted earnings are multiplied by a formula that's spelled out by law.

Generally, that formula calculates an amount of money that replaces about 42 percent of your earnings. The percentage is lower for higher-income people and higher for lower-income people.

EARLY RETIREMENT: IT HAS A BUILT-IN PENALTY

Early retirement sounds like a great idea. You are allowed to start receiving benefits as early as age 62.

But watch out! The system actually penalizes you for early retirement. Your benefits are reduced by five-ninths of one percent for each month before your full or regular retirement age. Worse, the reduction is permanent.

For people born in 1937 or earlier full retirement age is 65. But because people live longer (and to avoid bankrupting the system), the full retirement age is being pushed back in gradual steps. As Figure A.1 illustrates, for people born in 1938 full retirement age is 65 years and two months; for people born in 1939, it is 65 and four months. Each year later you were born pushes back your eligibility for full retirement. It will be 67 years of age for people born in 1960 and later.

How the Penalty Impacts You

Here is how the five-ninths of one percent (i.e., 0.556 percent) per month penalty reduces your benefits:

If your full retirement age is 65 and you sign up to receive Social Se-

If You Were Born in . . .	. . . Then You Can Start to Receive Full Benefits at This Age:
1937 or earlier	65
1938	65 and 2 months
1939	65 and 4 months
1940	65 and 6 months
1941	65 and 8 months
1942	65 and 10 months
1943–1954	66
1955	66 and 2 months
1956	66 and 4 months
1957	66 and 6 months
1958	66 and 8 months
1959	66 and 10 months
1960 or later	67

FIGURE A.1 Age when you become eligible to receive full Social Security benefits.
Source: Social Security Administration.

curity when you're 64, you will receive about 93.33 percent of your full benefit. That's because 0.556 percent multiplied by 12 months, or 6.67 percent, is subtracted from 100 percent.

Here's what happens in dollar terms:

Single Person. Let's say you recently turned 65 and your annual pay during the past 35 years averaged $50,000. As Figure A.2 shows, you would be eligible for full monthly benefits of $1269. But if you had signed up for Social Security 12 months before turning 65, your benefits would be about 6.67 percent ($85) less, or only $1184.

Month after month, that's a lot of money to lose—especially if you're like most people and Social Security is providing around 42 percent of your retirement income!

Your Age in 1998	Your Family	Your Earnings in 1997				
		$20,000	$30,000	$40,000	$50,000	$61,200 or More
65	You	$784	$1,043	$1,197	$1,269	$1,342
65	You and your spouse	$1,176	$1,564	$1,795	$1,903	$2,013

FIGURE A.2 Examples of Social Security benefits. Approximate monthly benefits if you retire at full retirement age and had steady lifetime earnings similar to your 1997 earnings.
Source: Social Security Administration.

Married, Sole Wage Earner. Same basic scenario concerning age and preretirement income. Predictably, if you were married and the only breadwinner in the couple (and you and your spouse were the same age), the Social Security Administration would penalize both of you. Worse, the rules require your spouse to be hit proportionately harder. (That's only one of many rules buried in the fine print that turns off so many people once they hit their Golden Years.)

Your wage earner's share of the basic $1903 is $1269 (see the $50,000-income column in Figure A.2), and *that* would be reduced by about 6.67 percent to $1184 (the federal agency rounds numbers down). Your spouse's share of the $1903 is $634, which would be reduced by another, *tougher* formula, 25/36 of a percent (0.694 percent) per month of early retirement, or in this example 0.694 percent times 12, which equals 8.33 percent.

That spousal $634 minus 8.33 percent results in $581.

Together, your benefits would amount to $1765. That's shown in the second row of Figure A.3.

Two Wage Earners. Likewise, if you and your spouse both worked, qualifying each of you for your own, higher retirement benefits, both could still suffer penalties for early retirement.

You Retire at Age	Your Benefit		Your Spouse's Benefit		Total
65	100%	$1,269	100%	$634	$1,903
64	93.33	1,184	91.66	581	1,765
63	86.66	1,099	83.33	528	1,627
62	80	1,015	75	475	1,490

FIGURE A.3 Early retirement penalty. If you and your spouse are the same age, you were sole breadwinner with an average annual income of $50,000, and your full retirement age is 65, here are your approximate benefits if you retire at various ages.
Source: Social Security Administration.

EXTRA CREDITS FOR DELAYING RETIREMENT

So much for the bad news. The good news is that by delaying retirement you can boost your benefits.

That happens for two reasons:

First, your benefits are calculated according to your 35 highest paid years. If you are paid more in your extra year or so of work than you were in what had been the lowest-paid years, the difference may be enough to push you onto a higher Social Security benefits plateau.

Second, delayed retirement earns you a special credit.

This credit is a percentage that is added to your benefit. It varies, depending on your age, as shown in Figure A.4. If, for instance, you were born in 1940 and will turn 65 in the year 2005, the credit is 7 percent for each year (or 0.583 percent per month) that you delay retirement beyond that birthday.

If you had average earnings of $40,000, which would make you eligible to receive $1197 a month starting at 65, delaying it a year would bump your benefits up to $1280.

(If you were born in 1950, your yearly postponement credit is set to be 8 percent. Figure out any credit boost based on that.)

If You Were Born in . . .	. . . Then for Each Year You Delay Retirement Your Benefits Will Rise
1917–1924	3%
1925–1926	3.5
1927–1928	4
1929–1930	4.5
1931–1932	5
1933–1934	5.5
1935–1936	6
1937–1938	6.5
1939–1940	7
1941–1942	7.5
1943 or later	8

FIGURE A.4 Social Security credits for delaying your retirement.
Source: Social Security Administration.

Unfortunately, delayed retirement credits go only to the living former wage earner in a joint-benefits couple. Your spouse does not receive a boost until you, ahem, die. Then your spouse gets yours.

Index